College Teaching at
Its Best

OTHER BOOKS BY CHRIS PALMER

Shooting in the Wild: An Insider's Account of Making Movies in the Animal Kingdom (Sierra Club Books, 2010)

Confessions of a Wildlife Filmmaker: The Challenges of Staying Honest in an Industry Where Ratings Are King (Bluefield Publishing, 2015)

Now What, Grad?: Your Path to Success After College (Rowman & Littlefield, 2015)

Raise Your Kids to Succeed: What Every Parent Should Know (Rowman & Littlefield, 2017)

Now What, Grad?: Your Path to Success After College, 2nd Edition (Rowman & Littlefield, 2018)

Design Your Life for Success (Rowman & Littlefield, forthcoming)

Death and Dying (Rowman & Littlefield, forthcoming)

* * * * *

All proceeds from the sale of this book will go to fund scholarships for students at American University School of Communication.

College Teaching at Its Best

Inspiring Students to Be Enthusiastic, Lifelong Learners

Chris Palmer

ROWMAN & LITTLEFIELD
Lanham • Boulder • New York • London

Published by Rowman & Littlefield
An imprint of The Rowman & Littlefield Publishing Group, Inc.
4501 Forbes Boulevard, Suite 200, Lanham, Maryland 20706
www.rowman.com

6 Tinworth Street, London SE11 5AL, United Kingdom

British Library Cataloguing in Publication Information Available

Library of Congress Cataloging-in-Publication Data
Names: Palmer, Chris, 1947- author.
Title: College teaching at its best : inspiring university students to be enthusiastic, lifelong learners / Chris Palmer.
Description: Lanham : Rowman & Littlefield, [2019] | Includes bibliographical references and index.
Identifiers: LCCN 2018056828 (print) | LCCN 2018061552 (ebook) | ISBN 9781475832815 (electronic) | ISBN 9781475832792 (cloth : alk. paper) | ISBN 9781475832808 (pbk. : alk. paper)
Subjects: LCSH: College teaching. | Teacher effectiveness. | Effective teaching.
Classification: LCC LB2331 (ebook) | LCC LB2331 .P344 2019 (print) | DDC 378.1/25—dc23
LC record available at https://lccn.loc.gov/2018056828

♾™ The paper used in this publication meets the minimum requirements of American National Standard for Information Sciences—Permanence of Paper for Printed Library Materials, ANSI/NISO Z39.48–1992.

Printed in the United States of America

Contents

Preface

ACHIEVING EXCELLENCE AS A TEACHER

This book is a practical guide for professors who are interested in being more effective teachers. I researched, planned, wrote it, and implemented its principles as a teacher, and share it now as a retired professor.

It is organized into thirteen chapters that encompass all the things a professor must do to prepare to teach; to stimulate learning and love of learning; to understand and engage all students; and to help them find direction, purpose, and mission in their lives.

Here is an overview of what the book covers.

- *Chapter 1: Realize the Importance of Professors*
  Recognize the importance of instructors, and how the best teachers focus on inspiring lifelong learning, both in themselves and in their students.

- *Chapter 2: Manifest Good Values*
  Understand that good teaching is rooted in good values, not the mastery of content alone. To become a better teacher, you must become a better person. Caring, empathy, and compassion are important.

- *Chapter 3: Create an Effective Syllabus*
  Use the syllabus as a basic road map for the course. This chapter discusses how to create an effective syllabus.

- *Chapter 4: Establish a Philosophy of Grading*
  Every professor should have a grading philosophy. Learn how to evaluate students more effectively.

- *Chapter 5: Harness the Power of Caring*
  Look at the issue of caring, why it matters, and how to show you care in the first few classes of a course. The highest value of a teacher may often lie in the mentorship she can provide to her students.

- *Chapter 6: Convey Your Passion*
  Incorporate into your teaching the importance of demonstrating passion and enthusiasm. Discover how to convey passion to students, and how to motivate your students to want to learn and participate.

- *Chapter 7: Promote Active Learning*
  Evaluate the role of the class lecture. Is the traditional lecture an outdated pedagogical tool? Consider the pros and cons of lectures versus active learning approaches, and see how to make lectures more effective.

- *Chapter 8: Support and Encourage Quiet Students*
  Recognize the moral responsibility professors have to help the less talkative members of their class. Quiet students can sometimes seem like unmotivated students, but that is almost always not the case.

- *Chapter 9: Make Large, Lecture-Based Classes Feel Smaller*
  Overcome the challenges of fostering learning in large classes, where it is almost impossible for the instructor to get to know all the students. Often the environment is not conducive to discussions. But there are ways to get students to feel connected and have a sense of belonging in large classes.

- *Chapter 10: Add Variety to Your Class*
  Keep students alert and energized by adding variety to your classes. Games, role-playing, humor, guest speakers, field trips, videos, and other devices decrease passivity and increase learning.

- *Chapter 11: Finish the Semester Strong*
  Maintain enthusiasm and compassion all semester. Fifteen weeks is a long time, and both students and professors can get stressed, exhausted, and cranky. This chapter offers ways to keep fatigue and negative thoughts at bay.

- *Chapter 12: Be Responsive to Students*
  Focus on the importance of being responsive to students outside of class. Learn how to handle email and office hours, how to provide feedback on work, and how to consider the whole student as you evaluate performance and foster success.

- *Chapter 13: Other Professors and Students Give Their Views on How to Excel at College Teaching*
See the observations and stories of other professors and students about what works for them in the classroom. These thoughtful observations illustrate the creativity, care, and enthusiasm that so many of my colleagues exhibit day in and day out.

* * * * *

I have also included four appendices:

- *Appendix I* is the handout I created for the workshops I give regularly on teaching effectively.

- *Appendix II*, written by Professor John Richardson, is about finding a great mentor.

- *Appendix III* is for any readers curious about my classes. Professor Tom Kaufman wrote this appendix describing a class I taught. He calls his essay "Teaching as Performance Art."

- *Appendix IV* is an essay I wrote on rethinking tenure. It discusses the pros and cons of tenure and its impact on teaching.

I hope you find this book to be a useful guide as you chart your course through the challenges and rewards of college teaching.

Acknowledgments

In chapter 13, entitled "Other Professors and Students Give Their Views on How to Excel at College Teaching," you will find more than 50 short essays contributed by professors and students about what works for them in the classroom.

These stories illustrate the creativity, care, and enthusiasm that so many professors and students exhibit day in and day out. I warmly thank the authors, whose names (listed alphabetically) are as follows:

Professor Dennis Aig, Professor Earl Babbie, Professor Naomi Baron, Crystal Berg, Robert Boyd, Professor Elizabeth Cohn, Anna Cummins, Professor Laura DeNardis, Aditi Desai, Sirjaut Kaur Dhariwal, Professor Daniel Dreisbach, Professor Barry Erdeljon, Stephanie Flack, President and Professor Les Garner, Professor Bill Gentile, Professor Jenson Goh Chong Leng, Professor Joseph Graf, Professor Martha Gulati, Sarah Gulick, Elizabeth Herzfeldt-Kamprath, Professor Gregory A. Hunt, Professor Leena Jayaswal, Professor Kiho Kim, Gaby Krevat, Shannon Lawrence, Ashley Luke, David Mullins, Professor Gemma Puglisi, Professor John Richardson, Professor Gianna Savoie, Professor Sam Sheline, Professor Rick Stack, Professor Christopher Sten, Professor Maggie Burnette Stogner, Professor Scott Talan, Grant Thompson, Amelia Tyson, Professor Angela Van Doorn, Kent Wagner, Professor Paul Wapner, Phil Warburg, Professor John Watson, and Nick Zachar.

I am indebted to the many pedagogical experts and scholars who have inspired my thinking on post-secondary teaching. In particular, I want to laud the original scholarship and pioneering work of (in alphabetical order) Dr. Patrick Allitt, Dr. Ken Bain, Dr. Stephen Brookfield, Dr. Daniel Chambliss, Dr. Carol Dweck, Dr. James Lang, Dr. Wilbert McKeachie, Dr. Parker Palmer, Dr. Christopher Takacs, and Dr. Maryellen Weimer. I'm deeply grateful to each of these luminaries, and I salute them for their dedication, expertise, and nuanced thinking. Their wisdom is reflected on every page of this book, and I cite them frequently.

This book would not have been possible without the invaluable support given to me by:

- My wife Gail and my daughters Kim, Tina, and Jenny, who reviewed the manuscript, as well as supported my move into teaching fourteen years ago.

- My friends Robert Boyd, Aras Coskuntuncel, Sam Sheline, Kent Wagner, and Bob Wipler, who went beyond the call of duty to help me.

- Dr. John Richardson, former head of the Center for Teaching, Research, and Learning at American University, who reviewed the whole book carefully and contributed a provocative essay on mentoring in Appendix II.

- My research assistants, including Crystal Berg, Sirjaut Kaur Dhariwal, Elizabeth Herzfeldt-Kamprath, Gaby Krevat, Ashley Luke, and Amelia Tyson, who gave me useful feedback and research help.

- Colleagues and friends at AU's School of Communication, especially professors Bill Gentile, Rick Stack, and Maggie Burnette Stogner, who went out of their way to help me and give me constructive feedback.

- Colleagues at AU's Center for Teaching, Research, and Learning, especially Dr. Naomi Baron and Marilyn Goldwater, professors who encouraged and supported me.

- Other professors at AU, especially Dr. Andrea Brenner, Dr. Elizabeth Cohn, and Dr. Lacey Wootton, who gave me great ideas, as did professors Mike English, Dr. Kiho Kim, Dr. John Watson, and Russell Williams II.

- Wendy A. Jordan, who did a superb job editing the whole manuscript.

- Professor Thomas Kaufman, who wrote a description of one of my classes, which I've included in Appendix III.

Special thanks also to my friend and colleague Anna Olsson at AU's Center for Teaching, Research, and Learning because for many years she invited me to present my ideas to fellow professors at summer workshops and at the annual Ann Ferren teaching conference. Those workshops and presentations helped me to develop the ideas for this book. (The handout for my workshop on effective teaching can be found in Appendix I.)

Above all, I want to thank the hundreds of students I taught at AU who helped me learn to be a teacher. Without them, this book would not exist.

Finally, I'm grateful to the whole team at Rowman & Littlefield, but most especially to Tom Koerner, for believing in this book and publishing it.

All proceeds from this book will go to fund scholarships for students at American University, where I taught for fourteen years after my thirty-plus-year career in conservation and filmmaking at the National Audubon Society and the National Wildlife Federation.

Introduction

Professor as Learner

Good teachers introduce new thoughts. Great teachers introduce new ways of thinking.

Good teachers care about their subjects. Great teachers care about their students.

Good teachers teach us what they know. Great teachers teach us how to learn.

—Adam Grant, PhD, professor of organizational psychology at the Wharton School of the University of Pennsylvania and bestselling author

Although I had no prior experience teaching, I became a professor on the full-time faculty at the School of Communication at American University (AU) in 2004 at the age of 56. Perhaps surprisingly, I was not unusual; most faculty start their teaching careers with virtually no training. Academic career coach Jennifer Polk estimates that less than 20 percent of aspiring college teachers are effectively taught how to teach.[1] For myself I can say that I had no real philosophy other than a vaguely articulated conviction that I wanted my students to do well.

As soon as I was offered the job, I asked my three grown daughters for their thoughts on what made an effective professor. Kimberly, then a recent Amherst graduate, said, "A good teacher is well-prepared and has graded and commented on all the homework. She doesn't give in when whiny students ask for favors." Christina, then at Dartmouth, said, "She maintains good order in the classroom, encourages participation from the students, and takes care to make sure shy students get a chance to talk." Jenny, who attended Princeton, said, "I hate it when teachers start or end class late—it signals they do not respect our time."

I began to get an inkling of what an effective teacher might look like.

Next I met with experienced professors, both at American University and at other institutions, asking them to share their best teaching strategies, techniques, and classroom practices. I gleaned lots of great ideas. For example, my AU colleague, Professor Rodger Streitmatter, offered this advice:

• Be clear what you want your students to learn, and what your learning objectives are;

• Engage with every student and treat all of them as individuals;

• Remember that telling is not teaching, and that to be professionally outstanding in an area does not automatically make you an effective teacher in that area.

Another professor said he insists that every one of his students meet with him one-on-one in the first two weeks of the semester so that he can get to know them better. And another said that she went out of her way to give substantive feedback on papers and tests.

Although all this advice helped me, I still made many rookie mistakes. I was repetitive, talked too much, and gave grades that were too high. I embarrassed students by brazenly pointing out their mistakes in front of the rest of the class. Sometimes I failed to allow a class discussion to blossom, while other times I let discussions run rampant to the point that I lost control of the class altogether.

I allowed verbose students to talk too much and did not properly listen to what students were saying. I rushed through material. I thought it was important to convey all the information I had, not realizing that "getting through" all my notes had little to do with whether my students were learning. Occasionally my students described the homework I gave them as "busy work" and criticized me for wasting their time.

I would sometimes say, "Any questions?" to a roomful of blank faces. Usually, my students' silence meant I hadn't explained the issue well and they were afraid to look dumb. I assumed their lack of response indicated understanding. I would get on such a roll with my own ideas that I would explain things poorly and forget to provide the proper context for those ideas.

I would be too slow to return students' papers or would dash off glib, superficial comments in my hurry to get through them. Sometimes I was given a class that I didn't want—or even know how—to teach. I was worried that I would say something stupid and end up feeling embarrassed and self-conscious—or, even worse, that students would write cutting or scornful remarks about me on such sites as RateMyProfessors.com.

Most of all, I hated when students obsessed over grades. "Professor, why did I only get a B– on this paper?" Incessant questioning along these lines verged on harassment. I was sorely tempted to rid myself of the problem by agreeing to raise the grade, which would have been yet another egregious, rookie error.

Over time, my mistakes taught me that I was an expert on content but had little idea how to convey that content effectively to students.

I was astonished to find no expectation that I would grow and develop as a teacher. But I was so scared of failing that I created that expectation myself; I did extensive research on teaching in an attempt to make myself a better professor. And I continued to ask my colleagues for advice.

I learned from my students too. Every two or three weeks, I asked them for candid feedback, assuring them it would be anonymous. One day a student wrote, "You are not pushing us hard enough. I want to get as much out of this class as possible. Please teach us everything you can. I want to learn more." This feedback hit me hard. Some part of me had already known that I wasn't pushing my students hard enough, but that student's comment meant I could no longer ignore my inner voice. My students didn't want to be passive listeners. They wanted to transform their lives. They wanted real knowledge and the tools to use it.

It slowly dawned on me that the most important question to ask myself as a professor was not "What are my students learning?" but rather "What are my students becoming?" I realized that my real job was not just to help my students with their grades but to help them with their lives.

I pressed on with my research and skill-building, determined to learn all I could about effective teaching. I learned a great deal, and what I learned is reflected in this book.

Early on in my teaching career I realized it would be helpful if I tried to articulate my goals. I resolved to be an inspirational teacher, to help my students develop to their full potential and to love learning, to always be available to my students, and to be someone who continually encourages, supports, and challenges them.

I resolved to provide my students with a life-changing experience. I wanted to be renowned for getting my students actively engaged in their own learning. Above all, I wanted them to be comfortable failing and to reward them for failing, because it is only through failing and persisting again and again that we all learn.

I wrote this book because I believe passionately that teaching is a skill that can be learned and developed rather than a gift you either have or don't have. Teaching is teachable. Good teachers result from study, practice, mentoring, and apprenticeship. This book aims to foster that process.

During my college teaching career, I have noticed that research and scholarship get shared openly with peers, but teaching skills and strategies are disseminated much more privately. Professors—and their students—would benefit if teachers made tips for good teaching less private. Good teaching ideas need to be more easily shared.

Professor Patrick Allitt has pointed out that professors write many books but very few of them are about teaching, even though teaching is one of their major responsibilities.[2] Teaching does not receive the same respect, attention, and deference that scholarship and the discovery of knowledge do.[3]

Teachers should do much more than teach the nuts and bolts of their subject. They need to inspire their students to want to learn. This won't happen if the students are bored or restless.

To develop a vibrant, productive, and memorable class, professors must continually work on inspiring students to become enthusiastic and motivated learners. Such students are engaged, active participants in their own learning.

I strive to follow three main principles when teaching[4]:

First, the professor must care deeply about the class and be fully invested in the students' learning.

To show my investment, I show up early for class, respond quickly to emails and phone calls, and try to give substantive feedback on students' work. I learn my students' names early on. I intentionally convey my passion and enthusiasm through my words and my body language.

I work hard to avoid being that clichéd professor who drones on and on, as bored by the material as the class is. I tell my students that I expect to learn as much from them as they from me, and I ask for their input on how to improve the class. In everything, I try to remind them that we are there to make massive progress on their intellectual and professional development.

Second, the professor must understand the importance of encouraging complete student engagement and empowering students to take ownership of the class.

At the beginning of the semester I lay out the purpose of the class, what the expected outcomes are, and how grades will be calculated. As the semester goes along, I ask for feedback every two or three weeks via anonymous questionnaires and adjust the class according to the needs of the students. I have learned that even when students are doing fine with the material, they appreciate the opportunity to weigh in and have their opinion heard on how the class is going.

I have found that some seemingly pedantic aspects of teaching make a significant difference in the quality of student involvement. Many professors believe it is the students' responsibility and choice, as adults, to attend class or do the homework. However, we must remember that students have many different valid obligations fighting for their time. If attendance is not mandatory, sometimes students will make the choice to skip. If readings are never referred to, sometimes students will not get around to opening the book. We cannot expect students to do more than the amount of work they need to keep up. If I want my class to be truly rewarding, I must set high standards for attendance and study habits.

And third, the professor must understand the importance of encouraging students to work together and learn from each other.

In school I made so many of my lifelong friends and developed so many relationships important to my career that I wanted to give my students every opportunity to do the same.

Employing ice-breaking exercises, asking students to refer to each other by name, and having frequent class discussions creates an environment in which students feel comfortable working with each other. They learn the essential skills of networking and collaboration while also engaging with the class material.

Of course, even when applying these three principles, challenges remain. But keeping the principles in mind helps me strive toward my goal of being an effective professor. I have become much more comfortable running a class and encouraging student involvement. It is a pleasure to teach when the students are engaged and interested and when they speak up, ask questions, and make arguments.

As I gained more experience as a teacher, I began to give workshops on teaching to fellow professors at the invitation of American University's Center for Teaching, Research, and Learning. You can find the handout I used in Appendix I. Here are some of my favorite tips, gathered from my own experiences as a professor and from peers, students, and pedagogical experts:

1. *Syllabus*. Make the learning outcomes as specific and clear as possible and relate these to the assignments and to your grading metrics. Spell out expected student behavior, including professionalism (meet deadlines, show up on time, participate in class, etc.).

2. *First Classes*. Make a serious and obvious effort to learn your students' names. After you introduce yourself, ask your students to introduce them-selves. Ask your students to address each other by name, rather than "he" or "she." Have them fill out a questionnaire about themselves, including goals, interests, passions, and expectations for the course. Discuss the students' answers when you meet with them one-on-one. And have the first of those one-on-one meetings with all students within the first two weeks of the semester. Some of the best teaching is done outside the classroom.

3. *Classroom Atmosphere.* Convey your passion and enthusiasm for the subject and your willingness to provide individual help. Foster a sense of belonging and respect. Encourage high performance and promote active engagement. For a small class, give the students a sense of community by sitting in a circle. Create a safe, nurturing environment in which students feel free to experiment and fail.

4. *Classroom Specifics.* Show up early for class, take attendance, and end class on time. Start class by asking a student to summarize the main points from the last class, and end by summarizing what was accomplished. Write the plan for the class on the board. Have students stand up and stretch, and occasionally play brief games. When possible, enhance the student experience by taking relevant, well-timed field trips as a class.

5. *Classroom Interactions.* Make the class as interactive as possible to transform the students from passive observers to active players. Constantly call on individual students by name to answer questions without first asking for volunteers. This keeps the whole class alert. Encourage the shy students to speak; don't allow long-winded or loud students to dominate the conversation. Listen to students actively during discussion.

6. *Beyond the Classroom.* Manage your office hours to support students. Encourage students to drop by even if they don't have specific questions. Have a sign-up sheet on your door (or do it digitally) so students don't have to wait. In addition to encouraging communication in your office, be responsive to emails and calls from students, and give students meaningful and meaty comments on homework assignments. Reach out to students who miss a class.

This book expands and elaborates on those ideas and contains many more for inspiring students to be enthusiastic and motivated in the classroom. The preface explains how the book is organized.

I hope you find the book useful as you strive to become a more effective teacher. Put the information to work and not only will you help your students get the most value from your classes, but you'll also make your role as teacher richly rewarding.

Chapter 1

Realize the Importance of Professors

The finest teaching touches in a student a spring neither teacher nor student could possibly have preconceived.

—Anne Truitt, sculptor

If you ask average college-bound young adults why they chose a certain college, they typically have a lot to say about the school's reputation. They won't have much to say about its exacting, rigorous, and caring professors. Yet it is the professors at a school who are the key to offering students a life-changing and radically enriching experience.

Of course, I'm not the first to recognize the importance of instructors. The president of Wesleyan University, Michael Ross, wrote in the *New York Times* in 2013 that when young people starting their college careers ask him what they should look for when they get to campus, he tells them to find out who the great teachers are. It doesn't matter much what the subject is, he says. Find a real teacher, and you may open yourself to "transformation, to discovering who you might become."[1]

As Ross recognizes, teaching matters because it can improve students' lives. It is a noble and honorable calling with high stakes. Effective teachers have the power to help students to radically rethink who they want to become and to generate new life possibilities. They can make a massive and sustained difference to the intellectual, emotional, and moral development of their students—how they think, feel, and act—and help them make major progress in their learning. The best teachers look out for the whole student, not just their intellectual side, and not just as it pertains to the subject or discipline taught.

Of course, there is no single best method of teaching, because every student is unique. A class of thirty students is more properly seen as thirty classes with one student in each. Yet there are some common practices that the most effective teachers share.

GREAT TEACHERS INSPIRE DEEP
PERSONAL DEVELOPMENT

They do much more than foster their students' intellectual development. They do more than help them achieve excellent exam results and find a suitable job. Those achievements, while important, should not represent the pinnacle of a college career.

The best teachers instill in their students a longing for something deeper than high grades and professional success. They instill a sense of meaning and identity that transcends those achievements. They help their students prepare not only for making a living, but also for building a life. Academic and cognitive excellence on the part of students must be matched with giving them a sense of responsibility and sound values, so they can find purpose and fulfillment, take on worthy challenges, and know how to work hard to achieve a goal despite setbacks.

This means that, in addition to providing instruction in their specialty subject area, teachers should teach ethics, communications, leadership, and teamwork (in diverse teams).[2] They must branch into these areas, which may be outside their sphere of expertise, to develop their students' potential to the maximum.

Teachers succeed not when their students get high grades, but when their students graduate and go on to make meaningful contributions to their communities and to society. The best teachers help their students focus on their life goals and on lifelong learning, in addition to their exams. They help them learn not only *how* to do things, but also *why* they should do them.

Educator Dr. Ken Bain from the University of Georgia gives a good example[3] in his book *What the Best College Professors Do*. He describes how neuroscientist and Vanderbilt University professor Jeanette Norden helps her medical students acquire skills not only in clinical reasoning but also in personal development. She understands that her students will need those personal skills to work effectively with patients and to handle the strong emotions that inevitably come when dealing with disease and dying. She teaches her students to see patients not simply as manifestations of disease, but as human beings suffering pain, deprivation, and fear.

However narrowly specialized, a good teacher finds creative ways to make the topic she's teaching relevant to the concrete challenges and real-life concerns her students face. In Bain's book, Norden gives the example of how an astronomy professor could use John Barrow's famous statement that "every nucleus of carbon in our bodies originated in the stars" to generate a discussion about how students feel about themselves as part of the cosmos.[4] Students want to know *why* what they are studying matters.

Teachers across all disciplines can similarly guide their students to see the broader context for their learning. They can help students confront questions about justice, inclusivity, ethics, and compassion, and help them explore what it means to be human.

GREAT TEACHERS HELP STUDENTS BE PRODUCTIVE MEMBERS OF SOCIETY

Teaching is important because learning is important, and learning is important because it helps people think for themselves. This thought lays the foundation for a healthily functioning democratic society.

Dr. Drew Faust, former president of Harvard University, persuasively argued that college pays off financially in terms of earnings, employment, and even health.[5] But she also points out that college provides benefits that are more difficult to measure, including a chance for students to engage in real-world problems, to follow their curiosity, to understand themselves better, to meet people different from themselves, to find their passion, to examine information carefully, to nurture critical thinking, and to hone a desire for lifelong learning.

All this can happen with much more alacrity if students have effective teachers. The "return on investment" can be so much more than simply the number derived from employability. Accumulating credits and obtaining a degree are just the starting points toward achieving a worthier life, more civil engagement, and a better society.

A person doesn't really grow up and mature until he realizes that the best way to live is to devote his life to helping other people. Students should strive to graduate from college with the ability to set meaningful goals that are bigger than themselves and that involve helping others. In addition, they must live with integrity, so that their goals can be pursued conscientiously and with enthusiasm. Teachers are pivotal to that process of transformation.[6]

Many educators, including Dr. James Brookfield of the University of St. Thomas in Minneapolis, Minnesota,[7] believe that a main reason to teach—and one reason that teaching is so important—is to give students the ability to be critical thinkers. With that ability, students can, among other things, probe for unarticulated assumptions behind a line of reasoning, and develop self-awareness about their own thinking habits and processes.

Ultimately, teachers are important because, as *The Chicago Handbook for Teachers* explains, they help keep "alive the true basis of democracy: the ability of people to know enough and understand enough about the great issues of their time to help guide their society into its future."[8] As Thomas Jefferson said, "An educated citizenry is a vital requisite for our survival as a free people."

GREAT TEACHERS SHOW STRATEGIC ENTHUSIASM

The best teachers show enthusiasm in teaching and mentoring students. If you extract only one piece of wisdom from this book, it should be that teachers' enthusiasm—or conversely, teachers' apathy—always rubs off onto their students.

Historian Dr. Patrick Allitt from Emory University makes the same point. He writes, "My whole teaching life has convinced me that nothing works better as a classroom technique or gets a better response than simple enthusiasm."[9]

Enthusiasm is essential, but it also must be mindful and strategic. When students are struggling, the best teachers stay enthusiastic but also ask themselves how they can improve their teaching. When students start complaining or flagging, it is tempting for a professor to blame the students for lack of hard work, preparation, or intelligence. But the best teachers don't do that. They take responsibility for the accomplishment of learning in the class and work to improve their teaching. They remain optimistic that students can learn, and reflect that optimism in their demeanor.

GREAT TEACHERS INSPIRE LEARNING, WHICH IS MORE IMPORTANT THAN TEACHING

They realize that *students learning* is more important than *teachers teaching.* Teaching matters only if it helps students learn. Teaching without learning is like a comedian who's not funny.

Teaching is not telling. Telling students content without giving them a chance to process it or create meaning from it does not result in learning. Lecturing, therefore, is not necessarily teaching, and sometimes results in no learning at all. Teaching is not about transmitting information from the brain of the professor to a roomful of students, hoping that some of the content will be absorbed into the students' brains. A professor talking in front of a class isn't teaching if the students are not learning.

Effective teaching is about striving to create an atmosphere in the class where all students can reach their full potential as learners and as human beings. It is about focusing on student learning, encouraging it, and leading forth the capabilities that lie dormant or nascent in the student. After all, *educate* means to "lead forth."

Successful teaching may require more listening than talking, as the professor struggles to understand each student as an individual, and how she learns best. By listening, professors can start to know their students' goals and aspirations, as well as what they don't understand and are grappling with.

GREAT TEACHERS UNDERSTAND THAT THERE ARE DIFFERENT LEVELS OF LEARNING

The best teachers believe students can grow their capabilities, their intelligence, and their talents by hard work and effort. They are fascinated by the process of learning and how people can learn effectively. They encourage their students to think about their own thinking—sometimes called "metacognition"—and foster an environment where deep learning is the goal.

They also understand that there are different levels of learning. Ken Bain, cited earlier, distinguishes three such levels[10]:

- *Surface learning* is the most superficial type of learning, and often occurs when students fear failure and believe that their abilities can't be improved by hard work. If challenged in class, surface learners fear that they will fail. They don't dig deeply into the material because they lack self-confidence and assume no amount of effort will bring them success. As a result, they often simply memorize whatever they can, reproduce it for the tests, and get away with the minimum of understanding. Some surface learners make A's by memorizing content without really understanding the underlying issues or appreciating their importance. But this type of learning is shallow and easily forgotten as soon as the final test is over.

- *Strategic learners* love to compete, excel in exams, and do better than their classmates. They may not care about mastering the material so much as doing just enough to beat everyone else. They are extrinsically motivated by the desire to "win." They tend to learn for the exam and then quickly forget what they've worked so hard to memorize.

- *Deep learning* happens when students love to master the subject, fully understand it, wrestle with the complexities, and challenge the underlying assumptions. Deep learners are intrinsically motivated. Learning causes discomfort because it involves change, and change is jarring, but deep learners come to welcome this, because they know it will lead to imperishable and lifelong learning. Deep learning isn't ephemeral. It stays with the students and doesn't evaporate a few days after the exam.

I believe most students are capable of deep learning, and it is the teacher's job to create a culture of learning where the students *want* to learn deeply.

That's not to say that memorization, a hallmark of surface learning, doesn't have its place. As both Dr. Patrick Allitt[11] and author Peter Brown[12] have explained, without memorization and rote learning, a student has nothing to think about. Still the fact remains that if memorization and rote learning are the only things that happen, the learning (such as it is) will surely disappear after the exam. In deep learning, students examine and perhaps challenge underlying assumptions and the learning takes place in their bones, even as they memorize facts and content.

The real test of how much students have learned is not in the final exams, but in how they think and behave in real-life situations after the exams are over. The best teachers help students shift their focus from exam scores to metacognition, mastery of the underlying ideas, critical thinking, and personal development.

Teachers have a long-term influence on their students that goes far beyond learning a topic. The best teachers help their students both do well in tests *and* learn deeply, while fostering their sense of agency and power to make a difference in the world.

GREAT TEACHERS INSPIRE DEEP, LIFELONG LEARNING

By inspiring students to be deep, lifelong learners, teachers play an important role in helping students find and hold decently paid and fulfilling jobs. According to *New York Times* columnist Tom Friedman, such jobs increasingly will require employees to be lifelong learners. He writes, "The notion that we can go to college for four years and then spend that knowledge for the next 30 is over. If you want to be a lifelong employee anywhere today, you have to be a lifelong learner."[13]

This means teachers need to produce students who enjoy learning and are motivated to continue learning day in and day out. The precise career is less important than having a nimble growth mindset that constantly yearns to learn and improve. The best teachers serve as sparks that ignite the intrinsic drive in students to develop the habits of deep learning.

GREAT TEACHERS UNDERSTAND THE POWER
OF A GROWTH MINDSET AND GRIT

Even when teachers create a culture of deep learning, students only work hard to learn if they have the grit, determination, and fortitude not to give up when beset with setbacks and frustrations.

Some fundamental insights into learning come from the research of Stanford psychologist and Professor Carol Dweck, who created the notion of "mindset" and wrote the book *Mindset: The New Psychology of Success*.[14] She draws an important distinction between a "fixed" mindset and a "growth" mindset.

- A "fixed" mindset, explains Dweck, assumes that basic qualities, such as intelligence and talent, are innate attributes and can't be changed. Students with a fixed mindset tend to stop trying if they don't do well at something because they believe nothing will fundamentally change. They avoid challenges, fearing that they will look inadequate if they fail to live up to the challenges. They claim with great confidence that they're no good at math, or writing, or art, or engineering, or whatever. These beliefs prompt them not to try in those areas and to give up as soon as the work becomes challenging, thus providing more evidence for their lack of ability.

- In contrast, says Dweck, a "growth" mindset assumes that basic qualities such as intelligence and talent are malleable and can be improved and developed through hard work, smart strategies, and coaching. Students with a growth mindset are more willing to take risks and wrestle with challenging tasks in a persistent and tenacious way. Such students are not discouraged by mistakes they make, but look on them as learning opportunities. They are inspired, not intimidated, by smart people and try to emulate them. They know that the more they challenge themselves, the smarter they will become. They value learning more than looking smart. They know that they can strengthen and grow their intelligence by working hard.

Dweck's research shows that it is possible to encourage students to have a growth mindset if professors act in certain ways.

- First, professors can encourage a growth mindset by refraining from praising ability, talent, or intelligence. Doing so promotes a fixed mindset and gives students the message that they have a quality that is fixed instead of one that can grow through diligent effort. It is far better to praise the effort students make, and their strategies or choices. Praising their process and diligence will motivate them to persevere.

- Second, professors should respond in a positive way to failure. Explain to students that failure is how a person learns and improves. When students take on exciting and daunting challenges, they won't succeed every time: Making a mistake is an opportunity to grow, and setbacks are an integral part of the learning process. They are to be not feared, but welcomed. The brain is growing new connections and getting smarter. Failure is a tool for improvement.

- Third, as students grapple with difficulties in class, professors should do more than coax them to keep trying. Rather, they should help them break a challenge down to smaller components and think through the best strategies and resources for moving forward.

The brain is like a muscle; the more it is used, the stronger it gets. As educator Salman Khan of Khan Academy says, "The brain grows by getting questions wrong, not right."[15] By learning new things, embracing challenges, and being tenacious, a person exercises his brain and makes it more powerful. Intelligence is not fixed, but malleable. It can grow and become stronger through hard work.

Dr. Angela Duckworth, a professor of psychology at the University of Pennsylvania, presents insights that resonate with Carol Dweck's research findings. In her book *Grit: The Power of Passion and Perseverance*, Duckworth shows that grit can be fostered and encouraged in students.[16] She argues that success has more to do with grit—passion, perseverance, drive, endurance, and fortitude—than with intelligence.

Students with grit are willing to practice and are determined to work hard. They believe in themselves, have a sense of purpose, and are not deterred by obstacles.

Stressing the importance of learning is a vital task for professors, as is encouraging students to have grit and determination by fostering a growth mindset and a positive attitude about failing. The key is to praise the effort students make, not their innate talent. Students will overcome challenges if they believe that they can and if they have passion, persistence, and purpose.

Dweck makes clear that professors who lower their standards to boost students' self-esteem (and perhaps, misguidedly, the professor's student ratings) are making a blunder, just like overpraising students' intelligence.[17] She writes, "Lowering standards just leads to poorly educated students who feel entitled to easy work and lavish praise."[18]

On the other hand, raising standards in a class without giving students the capability of achieving them also causes students to fail. Dweck argues that professors who believe in a growth mindset can set high standards *and* have students who reach them by unleashing their minds.

The best teachers match high standards with a deep caring about each of their students, because they know that such caring has a significant influence on whether their students engage with the class material and are motivated to learn. This caring by professors helps to create an atmosphere of trust and nurturing in the class, and a commitment to learning.

The best teachers believe, in line with Dweck's research findings, that students' intellectual ability depends on their effort, diligence, and grit. Effortful learning changes the brain, building fresh connections (both neural and conceptual) and increasing cognitive capacity. Hard work and persistence can make students smarter. Success comes, as educator and English professor Dr. James Lang puts it, "not just from ability, but also from planning, strategizing, and working."[19]

GREAT TEACHERS BRING STUDENTS THROUGH THE LOWS AND HIGHS OF INTENSE LEARNING

If learning is so important, why is it so challenging? The answer, as Stephen Brookfield points out,[20] is that learning means the student must change, and change is always uncomfortable. Exploring and grasping new concepts, revising assumptions, acquiring new skills, discarding suboptimal mental models, creating new mental models, confronting complexity, exploring challenging viewpoints, are all changes that can be painful and even scary. Learning means making mistakes, getting feedback, and making further mistakes. This is not an easy process, especially if the topic is of little inherent interest.

Educational expert Dr. Maryellen Weimer—who has reflected thoughtfully for many years on teaching and learning—is intrigued by the teacher-as-midwife metaphor.[21] A good teacher and a good midwife have a lot in common. Both birth and learning are often painful, messy, slow, uncomfortable, hard, and stressful. Learning—and childbearing—are much easier with the support of someone who is nurturing and empathetic. But the midwife, Weimer points out, is not there to give birth for the mother, nor is the professor there to learn for the student. The journey to "understanding must be undertaken by the learner."

Both baby and learning bring, one hopes, intense happiness. Weimer concludes that "we teach to help others experience the joyous wonder of learning." Professors are like midwives. They challenge students to bring out the best in them, and care deeply about their students and want them to succeed. This is what students are seeking—to be challenged and to be nurtured. They don't want to be entertained frivolously or demeaned with an easy grade.

In sum, professors should strive to treat their students as real, complex people who deserve respect, who want to learn, who yearn to work with caring professors, who want to excel and get high grades that reflect a deep mastery of the subject matter, and who want to learn from their professors about what makes a fulfilling life.

* * * * *

REALIZING THE IMPORTANCE OF TEACHING

I don't want to end this chapter on the importance of *teachers* without acknowledging the reality that, at most colleges and universities, focusing on out-of-the-box *teaching* is not a top priority. That adds challenge to professors who are determined to excel as teachers.

Most universities and colleges tend to emphasize *what* is taught over *how* it is taught. When it comes to promotion and advancement up the academic ladder, publications and specialized knowledge matter most. These are things that burnish the reputation of institutions of higher learning; that's understandable. I would argue that a community of alumni grateful for excellent professors lends shine to a school's reputation as well.

Professors receive little, if any, instruction in the art and science of teaching. There is usually little substantive discussion in faculty meetings about teaching and how to teach more effectively. Strategic planning, course content, technology, tuition costs, retention, recruitment—not student learning—consume most of the focus. This book hopes to shift some of the focus back to teaching.

Sadly, many professors have low expectations for improving their teaching skills. They tend to think that teaching is a talent you either have or don't have. But just as students can learn and grow in a nurturing environment, so too can teachers learn and grow. Teaching absolutely is something you can become much better at if you are determined and make the effort. I know, because I did it myself. This book will help you do it too.

Chapter 2

Manifest Good Values

A man is the sum of his actions, of what he has done, or what he can do, nothing else.

—Mahatma Gandhi, peace activist

Good teaching is rooted in good values, not mastery of content alone. But this emphasis on values is often missing in books on teaching.

One writer and teacher who does focus on values is Parker J. Palmer (no relation). According to Palmer, good teaching is not about technique, but rather "the identity and integrity of the teacher."[1] While good teachers use a variety of teaching techniques and methods, Palmer says they share one trait: a strong sense of personal identity infuses their work. That is, they don't put any distance between themselves and the subject they are teaching.[2] They care about the subject and convey that caring to students.

Talking only about tips and techniques for teaching fails to get to the heart of a good teacher's experience. Palmer advises that we need to spend more time discussing *who we are* as teachers and what values and principles govern, or should govern, our teaching lives.[3]

He writes, "We teach who we are."[4] The quality of our teaching fundamentally derives from who we are as people. The better we know ourselves, and the more in tune we are with our ideals, then the bigger our capacity for getting to know and understand our students in all their complexity.

To become a better teacher, you must become a better person. This is not a rigid or hard rule. It is possible to imagine a nasty character who finds a way to be an effective teacher, but generally speaking the best teachers are people of strength, honor, and character.

Often the best teachers *do* know their subject inside out, but they also discover and learn alongside their students, says Professor Naomi Baron, an expert on language, learning, and technology at American University.[5] They know some subtopics better than others. It helps if they are well-read and knowledgeable, but mastery of the content in all its domains is not critical. Values *are* critical.

Teaching is all about helping students learn. It isn't about showing dazzling command of content. It isn't entertaining students and making them laugh. It isn't being charismatic and likeable. Although these things might help, they are not the essence of highly effective teaching. The underlying values that drive a professor's attitude and behavior are much more important.

About twenty years ago, author and cultural critic Neil Postman cautioned in *The End of Education* that education was being replaced by "schooling," in which learning is pursued only for its utility. He warned that education was in danger of simply becoming a means to an end—gaining employment—rather than being a generative process that shapes an ideal society we want to create and live in.[6]

One of the chief tasks of a professor is to instill a sense of meaning, a longing for something higher and deeper. Without meaning, life can seem purposeless.

Ultimately, professors must help their students excel in school so that they can create a life for themselves that has purpose and meaning, and that makes the world a better place. Of course, professors need to teach their students how to become critical thinkers, how to acquire information, how to learn course content, and how to launch their careers, but the best professors strive to add a moral and character dimension to their responsibilities as teachers.[7]

What are these foundational values that are so important to effective teaching? They include caring, compassion, fairness, empathy, enthusiasm, diligence, honesty, authenticity, credibility, responsiveness, humility, professionalism, and self-discipline. These core values make or break a teacher. With them a teacher can truly enrich students' lives; without them a teacher cannot rise beyond mediocrity.

Sadly, teachers may flout these values, perhaps out of self-interest or lack of engagement. For example, they might:

1. Change expectations halfway through the semester, thus confusing students;

2. Make arbitrary class rules without rationale or explanation;

3. Act in an entitled way that doesn't treat students with respect;

4. Collect anonymous feedback from students, then quietly delete critical comments or refuse to address legitimate complaints;

5. Play favorites;

6. Act in a haughty and self-important way;

7. Disrespect the diversity of students;

8. Make sexist or racist comments;

9. Show a lack of compassion for those with disabilities or handicaps;

10. Discourage students from having confidence in themselves;

11. Demonstrate a lack of faith in the ability of students to understand the content;

12. Employ sarcasm and ridicule to gain control;

13. Criticize the student rather than critiquing her work;

14. Use humor inappropriately;

15. Come to class late and expect students to wait;

16. Come to class unprepared and disorganized;

17. Disparage students;

18. Act unapproachable;

19. Allow a handful of extraverts to dominate the class and, in effect, shut out the quieter students, thus making the class less inclusive;

20. Fail to apply class rules and policies consistently;

21. Not let students take charge of their own learning and education, at least to some extent (obviously there are many instances when a faculty member is appropriately "in charge" and students are free to accept what is on offer or not);

22. Promise to grade work by a certain date but fail to do so;

23. Disrespect a student when he comes to office hours by sneaking glances at a phone or watching to see what messages have come in;

24. Assume, when students have difficulties with the class material, that it is the students' fault for lacking intelligence or not working hard enough, rather than acknowledging potential weaknesses in the professor's teaching;

25. Claim to welcome diverse views and all opinions, then bristle and get irritated when the professor's ideas are challenged and questioned.

Superior knowledge of a subject means little if students feel marginalized and disrespected when they need help understanding or appreciating the material. Students quickly lose faith in their professors, as well as enthusiasm about the class, when they find that the professors are unreliable, unkind, unfair, untrustworthy, or undisciplined. The specific behaviors listed above can quickly cut the connection students feel with a class and its professor.

Dr. Maryellen Weimer writes,

> I think it's easy to forget how strongly our behavior influences what students do, what they say, how they feel, and what they think. Most of us don't like to think of ourselves as role models. We are flawed humans who happen to know a lot about a particular content domain, but teaching puts us in a position of leadership. We shouldn't pretend that it doesn't or downplay the responsibilities that come with leading others to learning.[8]

It is challenging for professors to harness the self-awareness or information to see themselves as they appear to their students. The surest way to obtain this insight is through anonymous and frequent feedback from students. The anonymity is essential, so that students have no fear of giving offense or of retribution and can candidly describe how they are experiencing their learning in the class. I discuss this more in chapter 7.

Without values and effective pedagogy, knowledge of content won't lead to student learning. Let's look at some of the foundational values that undergird effective teaching.

CARING

Teachers need their students to *want* to learn, despite the hard work that learning entails, and to *care* deeply about learning. Students are less likely to care if they perceive their teachers as uncaring. Professors who interact meaningfully with students both in and out of the classroom show students that they care.[9]

According to Emory University professor Mark Bauerlein, for most undergraduates, contact between student and faculty outside the classroom "ranges from negligible to nonexistent."[10] Bauerlein adds, "As a result, most undergraduates never know that stage of development when a learned mind enthralled them and they progressed toward a fuller identity through admiration of and struggle with a role model."

The teachers who get the most out of their students are the teachers who care most about their students. The degree to which students feel professors care about their learning is crucial. I explain more thoroughly in chapter 5 how caring is a vitally important element of effective teaching.

Of course, it is not reasonable to assume that all teachers, in all circumstances, should align themselves with my suggested goals. One can imagine a student in a large lecture hall attending a presentation by a seminal and venerated teacher and the student learning a huge amount even though he has zero interaction with the professor. The professor's passion about his subject and his enthusiasm in sharing it can convey a sense of caring in a large class setting.

My point is that not all faculty members at all institutions need to work in identical ways. I believe that contact between faculty and students is critical, but that doesn't mean it is imperative that *every* faculty member have the same goals.

EMPATHY AND COMPASSION

Empathy is feeling for others, and compassion is showing concern for and trying to reduce the suffering of others. Professors embody these values when they understand and share the feelings of a student. An empathetic teacher is aware that students may be suffering from anxiety, cyberbullying, parental neglect, illness, roommate problems, lack of self-confidence, and many other struggles that they don't necessarily want to talk about, but that may significantly affect their learning outcomes, daily lives, or demeanor in class.

Scholarly professors can easily forget how hard it is for struggling students to understand new concepts and mental models. Dr. James Lang writes that, before coming down hard on a student, professors should "take a couple of minutes to speculate on the possibility that something in the background of that student's life has triggered emotions that are interfering with their motivation or their learning."[11] It is important to exhibit compassion without getting too involved or violating the student's privacy.

HARD WORK AND PERSISTENCE

Dr. Ken Bain argues persuasively that teachers are made, not born.[12] Good teachers are created by relentless hard work, persistence, continual learning, conscientious practice, a dedication to continual improvement, and a realization that teaching involves a set of skills that you can improve if you work at them.

The best teachers go out of their way to find mentors and coaches. They believe in constant, never-ending improvement. They are not perfect but never give up trying to improve. As Bain puts it, they "confront their own weaknesses and failures."[13] They are learners, like their students, and proud of it. He adds, "Excellent teachers develop their abilities through constant self-evaluation, reflection, and the willingness to change."[14]

An important component of hard work is the willingness to take risks, make mistakes, and learn from them. Dr. Stephen Brookfield writes, "Risk is endemic to skillful teaching. Good teachers take risks in the full knowledge that these will not always work. Of course, the more you take risks, the more you open yourself up to making a mistake. But you also get better at recognizing when risks are justified and likely to pay off."[15]

Taking risks, making mistakes, and learning from them is a key characteristic of the best teachers, not only for its own sake, but also for the role modeling it provides students.

HONESTY AND TRUST

Students want reassurance that their professors are deeply and unalterably committed to helping them learn and succeed, and that everything a professor does—including assigning homework, grading, holding office hours, and guiding class projects—is focused on fostering their learning. This is what they are paying egregiously high college fees for.

Professors show this commitment by dealing with students in an honest, dependable way, without, for example, suddenly changing grading rubrics, surprising students with unexpected assignments, or altering expectations prior to a final exam.

Developing trust between teacher and students is important. Students must know, deep down, that their professor has their interests at heart and that there is no hidden agenda, no duplicity, no manipulation, no pretense, no phoniness. Learning becomes easier and more enjoyable when students know they are dealing with a professor they can trust to be straightforward, trustworthy, and reliable.

I don't want to imply that all teachers must follow my ideas to the last detail. Dr. Naomi Baron points out that some professors can provide value to students even if they don't focus on "connecting" with them in and out of the classroom. The professors might have admirable goals and be excellent teachers even though connecting with students may not be their top priority. They might focus on inspiring their students to become hugely knowledgeable, or to get smart enough to argue against the professor. Some teachers can make superb role models by revealing how their minds work.

ENTHUSIASM

For students to learn, they must pay attention. One of the best ways to capture a student's attention is through the professor's enthusiasm. Humans are social animals. Students respond to the emotion that they feel in an instructor's energy and passion.

Dr. James Lang writes, "The emotions that we demonstrate to students, especially our positive emotions connected to the subject matter we are teaching, can create a strong positive boost to student motivation."[16] Lang also points out that when a professor's enthusiasm is driven in large part by a self-transcendent purpose (helping others), then students who feel that greater purposefulness will be more highly motivated to learn.[17]

Professors need to help students "recognize the power of their learning to make a difference to the world: in doing so we are both helping direct their attention and giving them the motivation to persist through learning challenges,"[18] says Lang. Regular reminders of the bigger picture—how their learning is going to enable them to make a tangible difference in the world—will help students stay focused.

In a writing class, for instance, professors could periodically remind students that compelling writing has inspired new republics, stopped despots, and inspired civil rights. Students learn better, and feel more enthusiasm themselves, when they pick up on the enthusiasm of their teachers and understand *why* what they are learning is important.

* * * * *

A final foundational value that faculty often overlook is self-care. I think of this activity as a value because neglecting it can undermine a professor's other values. Professors must take care of themselves before they can take care of students. If a teacher becomes mentally or emotionally exhausted, for example, she will be handicapped in her ability to help students learn.[19]

Self-development and renewal is the vital process of enhancing one's capacity to be an effective and fulfilled teacher. It includes a regimen of fitness, healthy diet, adequate sleep, and connection with others. It requires growing intellectually and emotionally.

Self-care is not selfish. It is in the students' best interest for their professors to take good care of themselves. Just like a parent who must secure her own oxygen mask on an airplane before assisting her child, professors must take care of themselves before serving their students. Being overly self-sacrificing will backfire if a teacher becomes an exhausted victim of burnout. Great teaching requires vast amounts of emotional energy. The best teachers attend to their health so that they can be fully energized by their teaching, not exhausted by it.

Dr. Maryellen Weimer writes,

> The realities of academic life can be frustrating, demoralizing, and stressful, but what we need is an attitude that accepts these realities and at the same time understands that with education, there is a greater truth and a larger set of reasons that merit our continuing commitment. If we don't take time to refresh, recharge, and recommit, the value of what we're doing is no longer a driving force. We mustn't settle for less when students need our best.[20]

The best teachers take their professional development seriously and constantly strive to improve.

The behavior and values of professors shape what students learn and how they feel about the learning experience. To give students a consummate learning experience means that the way-of-being of a teacher needs to be rooted in values that bring out the best in students.

Professors who have allegiance to the values outlined in this chapter will more likely exhibit attitudes, behaviors, and practices that lead them to treat their students respectfully without hauteur, and to have confidence in their students' ability to learn and take charge of their own learning.

Adherence to these foundational values, when combined with expertise in content and pedagogy, can produce great teachers who care about students and have their best interests at heart, who are attuned and responsive to student needs, who encourage active learning (as opposed to passivity), who build a sense of community and belonging in the group, who are warm and approachable, who set high expectations for their students, who deliver to students life-transforming experiences, who convey the strong impression in class that they'd rather be nowhere else, who connect what they are teaching with the real world and to the concerns of the students, who bring passion and enthusiasm into class, and who produce good people, not just good test takers.

I want to make the point again that not all faculty are the same and that a professor can be very valuable even when bypassing some of the advice in this book. I feel strongly that the recommendations in the book are sound and that they can help most teachers to become stronger educators. But I recognize that one size need not fit all.

Chapter 3

Create an Effective Syllabus

Nothing great was ever achieved without enthusiasm.

—Ralph Waldo Emerson, poet, philosopher, essayist

The syllabus provides a basic roadmap for the course, as well as vital information: the expectations of the professor, a description of assignments and due dates, the grading system, and the class schedule. An effective syllabus is one that students find clear, understandable, well-organized, informative, challenging, and inspiring.

The syllabus is useful to you as the professor, too, because it helps you think through how best to organize the course content. The first step is to list all the specific dates on which the class will meet, accounting for holidays and other interruptions and breaks. The next task is to schedule classes, lectures, field trips, labs, reading assignments, workshops, seminars, exams, and so on.

In planning class projects, give some thought to what will help students learn but not overwhelm them. For example, try not to schedule a really large reading assignment around the same time as the midterm exam.

The top of the first page should state:

• the name of the institution;

• the semester and year;

• the name of the course and its number;

• when the class meets;

- the class location;

- the name of the professor teaching the course;

- the professor's office location and room number;

- the professor's office hours; and

- the professor's contact information.

Also on the first page, I like to add the following paragraph:

> I encourage you to meet with me regularly, so I can do everything I can to help you get the most out of this course. I want to have at least one meeting with you individually within two weeks of the first class and I want to meet with you individually multiple times over the course of the semester.

Requiring one-on-one meetings like this will not be to every instructor's taste (although I recommend it), and of course it may be impossible with especially large classes. I discuss the idea of one-on-one meetings with students more fully in chapter 5.

The syllabus should then provide the basic information about the course:

- the overall content the course will cover and the central questions/skills that will be addressed (more on this below);

- course goals and student learning outcomes (more on this below);

- how the course is organized;

- the format of the classes—whether they are lecture-based, discussion-based, or a mixture;

- the assignments (readings, labs, exams, discussions, research papers, etc.);

- when each assignment is due and when the exams are scheduled;

- how each assignment is weighted in calculating the grade;

- the grading policy (more on this below);

- whether attendance will be taken;

- whether participation in class is part of the grade and, if so, what percentage of the grade it will form;

- the penalties for tardiness in handing in papers and projects;

- the instructor's policy on the use of technology in class;

- a list of the books students need to buy or borrow;

- the professional behavior expected from students (more on this below);

- the policy on students who arrive late or fail to show up for class, and the penalties for missing class; and

- information the institution requires, such as a statement about diversity and inclusion, and academic integrity and support resources available to students on campus.

It is helpful to be as explicit as possible in the syllabus about goals, requirements, and expectations for the course. Some of the above topics don't need any elaboration, but I've expanded on five of them here.

THE OVERALL CONTENT

Your description of the content of the course should reflect your enthusiasm for teaching the content. It is important to incorporate why taking the class will help students change the world for the better. James Lang calls this self-transcendent motivation (helping other people), in contrast with self-oriented motivation, which is how a student herself benefits (e.g., acquiring a skill or gaining an advantage in finding a job).[1]

While students should certainly be focused on forging successful and fulfilling careers, it is important that they reflect on their potential to have a positive influence on society.

In the syllabus, include inspiring language that drives at the larger purpose of the course. In the description, emphasize the promise to teach students skills that will enable them to improve the world and leave a legacy, not just earn a living.

Go beyond simply outlining the subject matter that the course covers. How will the learning that students experience in the class open new possibilities for helping society to be a better, more humane, and more socially just place?[2] In short, why take the course? The syllabus is a key place to justify the importance of the learning that will take place.

COURSE GOALS AND STUDENT LEARNING OUTCOMES

Statements of course goals are overviews that create context for the course and its purpose and illustrate what you most value about *gaining proficiency* in the course subject. Useful verbs include *understand, appreciate, value, explore, become familiar with,* and so on. For example, gaining understanding works as a big-picture goal, rather than a student learning outcome, which as described below should be more specific.

Student learning outcomes relate directly and explicitly to the self-transcendent purpose of the course. They should be as specific and clear as possible. According to educational expert Marilyn Goldhammer, student learning outcomes are *measurable* statements that define what professors expect students to learn.[3] Learning outcomes can help faculty determine how students will demonstrate knowledge of course content, competency, and skills. They convey the teacher's expectations and create a framework for course content. Continuing the example of understanding, to convert *understand* into a measurable student learning outcome, ask yourself what students would need to do, say, or write to demonstrate their understanding of the subject matter.

Goldhammer says it is helpful to craft learning outcomes by starting with a phrase such as "By the end of this course, students will be able to . . . ," followed by a list of several outcomes. This phrasing can help you to state your outcomes in measurable terms. She recommends using conceptual frameworks such as those outlined in Benjamin Bloom's *Taxonomy of Educational Objectives* to find terms applicable for framing student learning outcomes.[4] Terms that might be used include *describe, identify, demonstrate, analyze, synthesize, compare and contrast,* and *critically examine.*

The more clearly the professor articulates the student learning outcomes, the easier it is to tie them to assessment measurements, such as tests, quizzes, research papers, reflections, presentations, internships, group projects, experiments, and performances. The key question is: For each student learning outcome, how will the students demonstrate mastery?

Goldhammer says that the connection between student learning outcomes and demonstrations of mastery (exams, papers, presentations, labs, etc.) creates cohesion for your students. Whatever the teacher identifies as a student learning outcome needs to be assessed. If something has been identified as important and has been labeled as an outcome but is not being evaluated, the question becomes, "Why is it an outcome, a competency that students need to demonstrate?"

CLASS FORMAT

Describe the class format in the syllabus. In other words, is it lecture-based, discussion-based, a mixture?

You might also want to add something about the tone of the class. For example: "We will strive for class sessions that are lively, engaging, fun, creative, and informative. Our format will combine discussion, presentations, guest speakers, case studies, in-class screenings, and analysis."

HOW GRADES ARE ASSESSED

Take steps to convey very high expectations of the students. Don't put them off or come across as overly demanding or strident, but take the opportunity to express the fact that the class is challenging in a good way.

Contrary to what some people think, students do not generally, in my experience, feel entitled to get a good grade for little effort. They will take it, of course, but in the process, their esteem for the professor and the institution will be damaged irreparably. See chapter 4 for more about grades.

PROFESSIONAL BEHAVIOR EXPECTED OF STUDENTS

I like to include the following statement in my syllabi:

> Students are expected to come each week prepared to contribute their knowledge and share insights with their colleagues. We will all learn from each other. All reading and writing assignments must be completed before coming to class, and written assignments must be free of spelling and grammatical errors. There will be extensive peer review and interaction.
>
> More than your physical presence is required in class. I am looking for attentiveness, vitality and enthusiasm. Participation in class will raise your grades. The give-and-take of information, ideas, insights and feelings is essential to the success of this class. Thoughtful, informed, balanced and candid speech is most helpful, especially when critiquing each other's work.

Consider going a step further in setting the standard for behavior. For example, use a statement such as this to frame the conduct and attitude appropriate for the class:

Students are expected to act in a professional manner, meeting deadlines, solving problems, cooperating with classmates, and generally contributing in a positive way to the class. Working in the real world often means searching for solutions in a group context. Teamwork, listening, empathy, enthusiasm, emotional maturity, and consideration of other people's concerns are all essential to success. Please bring these qualities and values with you to class. It is as important to hone these interpersonal skills as it is to learn new intellectual content. Students will be evaluated on their professional demeanor in class.

* * * * *

Once the syllabus is drafted, review it carefully. Ask the following questions:

1. Does it convey the excitement you feel for the topics you are teaching? Have you demonstrated your personal enthusiasm and your love of learning?

2. What is the tone like? Is it inviting, accessible, and friendly? Is it appealing? Is it informative? Will it make sense to students who are not familiar with the content and may be seeing it for the first time? Will they be convinced to buy into the course?

3. Is it an accurate representation of the course and of you as the teacher?

4. Have you included subheadings to help students readily locate key information, such as class schedule, grading policy, assignment due dates? Consider using bolded topic headings or tables for content such as class schedules.

5. Are the course schedule and assignment due dates clear? Students need to know the specific assignments for the course, precisely when they are due (time and date), and how to submit them. They also need to know the penalties for work submitted late.

6. Does the syllabus reflect your philosophy of teaching and how you view your students? Do you want them to seek you out during office hours? Do you have office hours at stated times, as well as by appointment, so that students with legitimate conflicts can still meet with you?

7. Does the syllabus help to create a prosocial environment in which students are encouraged to be curious, to ask questions, to make and learn from mistakes, to create new ideas, and to value and foster diversity?

8. Educational expert Dr. Maryellen Weimer asks, "Have you ever thought about creating a syllabus that invites students to a (course) they just might want to attend? What would that syllabus look like?"[5]

The biggest problem with most syllabi is that they fail to generate much enthusiasm or passion from within the student. A syllabus ideally makes it clear that the instructor is determined to create a community of learners who are enthusiastic and who support each other.

One idea from David Gooblar, a columnist at *Chronicle Vitae*, is to put all the contractual material online, if the academic department allows that.[6] This will move standard departmental and university policies and requirements out of the syllabus and enable it to highlight the specific material that helps sell the course to students.

The chief purpose of a syllabus is to convince students to buy into the course and be excited about the growth it will help them find in themselves. However technically brilliant and detailed a syllabus is, if it fails to excite the students who read it, it has failed in its central mission and needs to be revised.

Chapter 4

Establish a Philosophy of Grading

> There came a time when the risk to remain tight in the bud was more painful than the risk it took to blossom.

—Anaïs Nin, author

Every professor should have a grading philosophy. At colleges and universities, giving out grades has in some cases become a calcified ritual, but the process should be regularly challenged and reassessed. Ruminating on grades, thinking through what they mean, and assessing their advantages and disadvantages is a useful exercise.

When considered carefully, grades can occasionally be a useful benchmark for students to use in assessing their competence and growth. However, the larger truth is that grades can be subjective, confusing, unfair, overrated, and, in the end, useless.

Many students think, wrongly, that high grades are proof of success. In fact, they may even assume that the whole point of going to school is to receive A's. They think getting high grades will get them a decent job, which in turn will lead to a comfortable life.

But a comfortable life is not what the best professors want for their students. Rather, they want their students to live a fulfilling, responsible, and meaningful life helping others and contributing to society, perhaps even advancing a great cause.

Getting A's for the sake of getting A's so you can get a comfortable job will wear thin very quickly if it isn't supported by a deeper sense of why it all matters. The key is service to others and reaching one's full potential as a human being.

Besides, getting top grades isn't necessarily going to help a student lead a comfortable life anyway. Many of the skills needed to succeed in life are different from the skills needed to get high grades in college. Stanford Professor Carol Dweck says, "We're training kids to get A's, to get the next high test score, to get into the next school, but we're not training them to be dreamers, to have some goal for their lives that will make them feel fulfilled."[1]

GRADES MEASURE SOMETHING, BUT DOES ANYONE KNOW EXACTLY WHAT?

What precisely do grades mean? We know they relate to learning, but how?

The grading system is set up to reward those students who do well on tests and exams. It doesn't necessarily recognize effort, character, grit, optimism, determination, diligence, collaboration, empathy, or self-control. But in the real world, people with those attributes are more likely to succeed than grade grubbers.

I use the term *grade grubbers* reluctantly because it isn't always fair. Many students are focused solely on good grades for three powerful reasons: that is all they know, they fear the consequences of not getting good grades, and they think good grades are what is expected of them and they want to please.

Sometimes students who are intrinsically smart get good grades without much effort. Other times, students with less innate ability can get high grades from diligence, effort, focus, and determination. Intelligence and capabilities are expandable with hard work.[2] Grades make no distinction between the B student who is bright, superficial, and indolent, and the B student who is diligent, assiduous, but a lousy test-taker.

There is evidence, according to Dr. Ken Bain, that "students can 'perform' on many types of examinations without changing their understanding or the way they subsequently think, act, or feel."[3] Bain argues that while some teachers might be satisfied if students get high grades, the best professors "assume that learning has little meaning unless it produces a sustained and substantial influence on the way people think, act, and feel."[4] Professor Maggie Stogner from American University says, "Now, more than ever, in this hyper-distracted world, students sponge up material for the test, and then promptly forget it."[5]

Grades, then, provide little insight into what students are actually learning.

GRADES CREATE MISLEADING INCENTIVES

Ideally, grades would enhance learning. But the truth is that students tend to focus on grades rather than learning. Grades provide extrinsic motivation—motivation driven by external rewards and punishments, as opposed to motivation driven by an internal passion to learn for the sake of learning. They often weaken student interest in the content.

Dr. Maryellen Weimer quotes researchers as concluding, "Grades can dampen existing intrinsic motivation, give rise to extrinsic motivation, enhance the fear of failure, reduce interest, decrease enjoyment in the class work, increase anxiety, hamper performance on follow-up tasks, stimulate avoidance of challenging tasks, and heighten competitiveness."[6]

Deep learners, as discussed in earlier chapters, tend to be intrinsic motivators. They find within themselves a passion to excel, rather than depending on grades for motivation.[7] Author and lecturer Alfie Kohn writes eloquently on this topic.[8] He says that grades tend to diminish students' interest in whatever they are learning, creating a preference for the easiest possible task, and reducing the quality of students' thinking. Moreover, grades tend to turn learning into drudgery.

As Bain points out, students are "most likely to enjoy their education if they believe they are in charge of the decision to learn."[9] Very few people like being manipulated by extrinsic rewards and punishments such as grades. Students want to know that assignments and tests benefit them professionally, intellectually, and personally, and are not simply devices to arrive at some grade.

One problem with schools is that they incentivize students to be cautious about their education. Students are tempted to avoid classes where they might learn exciting and challenging new material but are not guaranteed an easy A. Columnist David Brooks of the *New York Times* has observed that students "have been inculcated with a lust for prestige and a fear of doing things that may put their status at risk."[10]

This fear hurts students in the real world, where they can't always play it safe. Boldness and audacity often are needed, especially in a society where people regularly change jobs and even careers. These changes happen whether people want them to or not: organizations go bankrupt, people get fired, and contracts fall through. If students get through higher education without experiencing setbacks and failures, then real life can be disconcerting and highly stressful for them.

GRADES DON'T ENCOURAGE THE FAILURES THAT LEAD TO SUCCESS

It may seem counterintuitive, but professors should encourage failure. Fail early, and fail often—this is how students learn. Students must realize that failing does not make them failures. Mistakes are a normal part of life. One of the most important skills a student should have is the ability to take risks and overcome fear of failing in an admittedly scary world.

Failure is an unpleasant, but essential, part of striving and learning. Failing means that students are trying hard, taking risks, and getting out of their comfort zones—all necessary precursors to success. Professors who neglect to teach real-world lessons are doing their students no favors.

Students need to experience disappointments, setbacks, and failures in order to develop the resilience required in the real world. Dr. Leonard Sax writes, "The humility born of failure can build growth and wisdom and an openness to new things in a way that success almost never does."[11] Professors must encourage their students to be bold, try new things, take on challenges, and be persevering risk-takers.

For example, professors should encourage students to challenge authority when appropriate, rather than being obedient and docile. Docility and "being nice" might get students high grades but won't get them very far in life. There's a fine line between being well-behaved and being meek. No one wants to hire the latter. Respectful debate and disagreement are healthy.

If students do take risks academically, their grades might decline, but they will be better prepared to lead successful lives. Professors must teach their students that moral maturity matters far more than grades, and that the deepest meaning in life is to be found, not in high marks or a comfortable job, but in the sense of profound fulfillment gained by working on issues and projects that matter and that help others. The goal, in organizational psychologist Adam Grant's formulation, is to be a "giver" rather than a "taker."[12]

Dr. James Lang makes the point that it is important to promote a growth mindset. He says a simple way to do this is to "allow students the opportunity to practice and take risks, fail and get feedback, and then try again without having their grades suffer for it."[13] Early assignments in the semester should be weighted lightly, so that a few mistakes at the beginning of the course don't have students scrambling to raise their grades for the rest of the semester.

It is important for students to understand the teacher's standards of grading. Build low-stakes assignments, quizzes, or other gradable events into classes early in the semester so that students can judge the professor's reaction to their work. Every semester, some of my students who ultimately get high grades in my class get low marks on these early assignments as they adjust to the expectations and style of the course.

GRADES ARE SUBJECTIVE AND BIASED

Weimer cites research that documents "inconsistency in grading by individual faculty members (two different grades for the same piece of work when it's graded at different times) and across individual graders."[14] She points out that rubrics help, but "gender, ethnicity, and knowing who the student is, all influence the grade." A rubric (or standard) defines in writing what is expected of the student to get a particular grade on an assignment. No rubric, however, is definitive.

This subjectivity of grades is muted in exams with multi-choice questions where the students *select* answers. Grade objectivity diminishes when students take exams in which they *generate* answers.[15] With their high degree of inconsistency and subjectivity, it is not unreasonable to be skeptical of what grades mean. Alfie Kohn writes, "What grades offer is spurious precision, a subjective rating masquerading as an objective assessment."[16]

GRADES ARE CONFUSING

When students are told their grades are based on percentages (for example, 20 percent homework, 20 percent midterm exam, 20 percent quizzes, 40 percent final exam), it is difficult for them to determine their grades as the semester progresses. A clearer approach, according to Dr. Mary Clement, a professor in teacher education at Berry College, is to have a total point grading scale.[17]

Each assignment, project, lab paper, quiz, or exam has a certain number of points. These point values are listed in the syllabus, along with the total points required for the final grade. If the students record their points as the semester evolves, they will know at any one time precisely how many points they have and how many they still need to earn to obtain a certain grade.

Clement says, "I get rave reviews about my 'no-mystery' approach to grading on course evaluations, and I believe that the good reviews are due to the clarity and ease of the total point system."

GRADES MAY NOT PROVIDE AS MUCH USEFUL FEEDBACK AS PROFESSORS THINK

Grades provide feedback ostensibly to help students learn and improve. The grade is usually accompanied by comments and suggestions from the instructor. These comments are more important than the grade, but often students pay attention only to the grade.

Weimer quotes one researcher as saying that "the grade trumps the comment."[18] Students often skim over or even ignore the written feedback. Even if they read it, they may not understand it enough to make improvements in response.

Consequently, students continue to make the same errors. Possible solutions include putting grades at the end of an assignment, so students might read the comments first or, even better, posting grades online later and initially giving out just the comments.

GRADING ON A CURVE IS UNFAIR (AND HOW IT RELATES TO GRADE INFLATION AND STUDENT SELF-ESTEEM)

Grading is often done on a curve (perhaps because of university or departmental policy). This means that, for example, the top 30 percent of students receive A's, the next 40 percent receive B's, and the bottom 30 percent receive C's. In other words, as stated by Wilbert McKeachie in *McKeachie's Teaching Tips: Strategies, Research, and Theory for College and University Teachers*, students are graded relative to their peers' performance rather than based on "the degree to which the student has achieved some standard of performance."[19]

Grading on a curve is done to combat grade inflation (because it limits the number of A's that can be achieved). However, it also creates unfairness in a class with many high-performing students, because some of the best students won't receive the A's they deserve.

Grading on a curve creates competition among students in the class and impedes collaboration and peer-to-peer learning. Dr. Adam Grant, a professor at the Wharton School of the University of Pennsylvania, argues that grade curves "create an atmosphere that's toxic by pitting students against one another. At best, it creates a hypercompetitive culture, and at worst, it sends students the message that the world is a zero-sum game: Your success means my failure."[20] If students do A work, they should receive A's, rather than have their grades deflated.

Having said all that, grade inflation is a real problem. In my opinion, most professors, including myself, grade too leniently. Professors come under a lot of pressure to give students high grades so that they can get into top graduate schools. Students who skimp on the reading, talk glibly in class, write poorly, and don't work hard will often receive A's or B's when they should really receive C's or worse.[21] Inflated grades help a student to develop inauthentic and sham self-confidence,[22] says author Caroline Adams Miller.

The best professors know how to engage and challenge their students and how to elicit, or provoke, their interest. One goal is for teachers to provide students with what Miller calls "authentic self-esteem."[23] A student who receives an easy A on an exam (i.e., a grade based on lowered standards) does not gain authentic self-esteem.

Rather, students enjoy authentic self-esteem when they take on tough challenges outside their comfort zone and move forward. The best teachers excel at challenging their students, introducing them to the exciting discomfort of learning—exciting because they are growing and developing, and discomfort because change is always difficult and brings with it the chance for mistakes.

Students are not customers or consumers when in class. Just because they or their parents are paying large tuition fees, they cannot expect an easy grade for little work, or an automatic A. Such a culture of entitlement is pernicious.

A student is entitled to an A grade only if he has worked hard with the material and mastered it. If students (or their parents) feel they deserve an easy grade, then they clearly don't feel responsible for their own learning; this is the very antithesis of what it means to be an effective learner.

GRADES ARE OVERRATED IN IMPORTANCE

Students are led to believe that grades are highly important. But once a student leaves school, no one asks her what grades she got. Employers only want to know that she attended a reputable school, passed her classes, and was awarded the degree on her resume.

It is true that a high GPA can result in honors, which can make a difference with employers and may also open doors to financial awards while in school. But in real life, for the most part, no one cares about grades. People in the real world focus on knowledge, skills, results, creativity, competence, character, and teamwork.

* * * * *

So grades have problems. Then why not abolish them? The short answer is that some students may not do any work without grades. If there are zero consequences for not learning, then some students will stop working. Also, grades are needed for practical purposes, for admission to grad school, for example, and for financial aid.

Let's remember why we are even talking about grading. It is because grades are linked in some mysterious way to learning, and learning is what professors are trying to achieve. Despite all the ways that grading harms learning, it does benefit learning in one obvious way. When students take quizzes and exams, they take them seriously because they want to get a decent grade, and this encourages them to practice recall and retrieval. According to Peter Brown et al., in *Make It Stick: The Science of Successful Learning*, by practicing recall and retrieval, quizzes and exams help students learn; in fact, it is a far better learning technique than simply re-reading the material.[24] The most important role of a quiz or exam, or of any testing, is not to provide a basis for grading, but to provide a basis for learning.

Brown et al. write, "We know from empirical research that practicing retrieval makes learning stick far better than re-exposure to the original material does. This is the testing effect, also known as the retrieval-practice effect."[25] The retrieval effect means that if you want to retrieve knowledge from your memory, you have to practice retrieving knowledge from your memory.[26]

Tests and exams shouldn't simply be considered a way to measure learning and arrive at grades, but as memory exercises. Lang writes, "Every time we extract a piece of information or an experience from our memory, we are strengthening neural pathways that lead from our long-term memory into our working memory, where we can use our memories to think and take action."[27]

To critics who say that memorization is trifling, and that what really matters is high-order skills, Brown et al. make the point that memorization is highly relevant to complex problem solving. "Pitting the learning of basic knowledge against the development of creative thinking is a false choice. Both need to be cultivated. The stronger one's knowledge about the subject at hand, the more nuanced one's creativity can be in addressing a new problem."[28]

Still, the case against grading remains strong. Rosamund Stone Zander and Benjamin Zander make one of the most persuasive arguments for a radical change in grading in their book *The Art of Possibility*.[29] They say that grades reveal little about a student's mastery of a course's content, and give insight only into how they compare to other students. The Zanders see this comparison as pointless, futile, and damaging. Instead they recommend that professors help each student develop mastery to the greatest possible extent and to be "all they dream of being."[30]

They call this practice "giving an A." They argue that it transports grades from "the world of measurement into the universe of possibility."[31] Following this method, a teacher hands an A to every student at the start of the semester. This puts every student at ease, but it comes with a condition. Every student must write a letter to the professor dated the last day of class explaining in detail what they did to earn the A and the new person they became by taking the class.

In writing such a letter, the students place themselves in the future, looking back. In a bold act of creative imagination, they write the letter as if myriad impressive accomplishments had already been realized. The goal is for students to reveal their true selves and to begin to identify the obstacles they need to overcome to reach their full potential.

"Giving an A" gets students out of the ugly drama and "maelstrom of competition, survival, backbiting, subservience, and status seeking" that accompany the pursuit of grades, say the Zanders. It transports them to a higher level where their generosity, innovation, creativity, willingness to make mistakes, playfulness, and desire to learn and collaborate can be nurtured and encouraged.[32]

Skeptics of "giving an A" will naturally point out that giving a student an unearned A is ridiculous because it ignores the fact that some students have great mastery of the material while others do not. It lumps everyone together. But the Zanders are not suggesting that people ignore accomplishments and competence. Despite the reference to measurement that the A implies, the Zanders are not "giving an A" as a gauge of student performance against some standard. They give the A to "finesse the stranglehold of judgment that grades have over our consciousness from our earliest days. The A is an invention that creates possibility for both mentor and student."[33]

The practice of "giving an A" allows the professor to line up *with* her students in their efforts to reach their full potential, rather than lining up *against* students. The freely granted A expresses "a vision of partnership, teamwork, and relationship."[34] It is life enhancing.

The key insight from the Zanders is that all grades are a human invention. Grades often "rise and fall with moods and opinions."[35] Each grade that is issued limits what is possible between professor and student. The freely granted A lifts the student "off the success/failure ladder" and spirits him away "from the world of measurement into the universe of possibility."[36] The professor becomes less of a judge and more of a partner.

Having said all that, it is obvious that "giving an A" is not going to happen at any college or university that I'm familiar with. It is too radical, however theoretically appealing. It's interesting to note in passing, however, the words of communications professor John Watson of American University. He says, "The purpose of teaching is to cure ignorance and infuse into students a variety of skill sets. The perfectly taught course is one in which everyone earns an A. In my teaching philosophy, the grades I assign indicate how well I have taught."[37]

Even if we keep grading as we always have and keep to "business as usual" when it comes to grades, professors can help students to focus less on grades and more on learning by discussing the competencies and skills an assignment will bolster. Professors can also ask students what they think they will learn from the assignment.

As is so often the case, Weimer offers wise advice. She cites a professor who, early in the course, asks her students to think about the future professional lives they hope to live and the kind of life they hope to live. Then she asks them, in order to reach their goals, "What skills and knowledge are you going to need that you don't have or don't have enough of?"[38] Students make a list and, after every assignment or activity, they write a short reflection on how what they just did supports what's on their list.

Weimer also suggests having evolving assignments, as opposed to one-time assignments.[39] She points out that learning is an evolving process and it is good to teach students how to do more work on an already completed exam, activity, or assignment. A student might submit a draft, get comments back, work on the report again, and then submit it for more comments before submitting a final version. Professors give feedback on each draft, but no grades. Weimer suggests that "the need-to-know on the grade front is calmed by announcing that everyone has at least a B unless they hear otherwise."[40] The assignment, whether a paper, report, or exam, is graded once, at the end, with a few constructive comments. This also more closely resembles real-world projects that go through many iterations and rounds of comment and feedback from superiors and other team members.

The best professors give students opportunities to redo their assignments and to improve their grades by rewriting and revising papers and retaking exams. Why not allow several revisions, so that students can keep improving their papers and learning more? This is the essential message of educator Sal Khan's TED talk, "Let's Teach for Mastery—Not Test Scores."[41] He says that when a student gets a low grade, she should keep working on it. "You should have grit; you should have perseverance; you should take agency over your learning," says Khan. He argues that this approach will "reinforce the right mindset muscles."

Lang suggests starting small. "Select an early exam or paper and offer students at least one opportunity to revise or retake it." He writes that this sends a message about the type of classroom you run: "In this course, you are communicating to them that you care more about their learning than you do about their specific performance on this particular assignment. If the performance did not match your expectations, try again. What matters is that you learn from it."[42] The downside to this idea is when time-challenged instructors have to re-read numerous long papers.

Colleges and universities should experiment with nontraditional grading systems, such as assigning students an honors/pass/fail grade. The basic argument for letter grading is that it may push students to work, but the push comes with many disadvantages. Grades can cause more harm than good.

Replacing grades by some other assessment system that encourages learning and intrinsic motivation is a worthwhile goal. The traditional grading system should be abandoned in some sensible, careful way, so that students can focus on learning instead of their next test score.

Doing away with grades might well free students to focus on learning and to be more adventurous in their selection of challenging yet rewarding classes—classes in which they risk not doing well.

The purpose of college should not be just to get high grades, but rather to develop character. Students need to grow not only in academic proficiency, but also in emotional intelligence, integrity, self-control, self-discipline, empathy, and a sense of responsibility—attributes that are important if students are to find profound, long-term fulfillment.

This is part of a larger conversation about what determines a valuable education at colleges and universities. Getting high grades is less important than learning that fosters growth in leadership, character, and creativity. Students with a strong moral foundation, and a willingness to take educated risks, will have the greatest and most positive impact on society and make the most contributions to prosocial causes. The value of an education should be measured not in grades achieved, but by what the student goes on to become as a person.

Chapter 5

Harness the Power of Caring

One looks back with appreciation to the brilliant teachers, but with grati-
tude to those who touched our human feelings.

—Carl Jung, psychologist and psychiatrist

Teachers demonstrate that they care about their students when they make the
effort to get to know them. Why does caring matter? Study after study has
established that caring leads to more learning.[1]

Caring affects students' attitudes toward their studies and their academic
experiences. When teachers show that they care about students—by communicating respect, being warm and engaged, and treating the students with
sensitivity—they help to create an effective learning climate.

Of course, caring is not the totality of effective teaching. A good instructor
must also be enthusiastic, knowledgeable, and articulate, and must insist
on high performance standards. But when instructors show up on time for
meetings with students, respond speedily and helpfully to emails, show
empathy, listen attentively, and use students' names, the students tend to feel
more connected with the professor, more positively about the course, and
more appreciated and valued. They're also more likely to participate in class
and ask for help, both of which are behaviors that enhance learning.

CARING AS A MOTIVATOR

Caring, by both teachers and students, is a critical factor in the learning environment. The best teachers see students as whole human beings. Students do
more than think and take in information. They have emotions. They feel, and

as Dr. James Lang says, their "feelings can play a valuable role in our efforts to motivate and inspire student learning."[2]

The relationship that students forge with their professors profoundly affects their learning experiences. Dr. Maryellen Weimer points out that it isn't always easy to be caring toward students.[3] Fatigue, stress, a huge pile of papers to grade, disrespectful students, and other draining negatives are among the many reasons that caring by teachers, and showing a caring manner every day in the classroom, can be hard. But it's well worth achieving.

Likewise, Dr. Ken Bain points out that for students to learn, they must care. If they don't care, they won't be willing to do the hard work that learning requires.

In his excellent book *What the Best College Teachers Do*,[4] Bain describes what learning is—and its relationship to caring. He argues that students have "thousands of mental models" of the world—many of them deficient—that they use to understand what they hear in class and read in textbooks. When they encounter new material, they try to comprehend it in terms of something they think they already know.

When students believe professors care, they will be motivated to work harder to strengthen their cognitive abilities and stretch beyond their mental models. Lang makes a persuasive case that "paying attention to students in class" makes "a noticeable difference in creating a positive atmosphere" in the classroom and increases the number of students who participate in classroom discussions.[5]

ACKNOWLEDGING THE TOLL OF STRESS

Professors need to understand the stress students are under. That stress may derive from anxiety, learning disabilities, student debt, inferior or neglectful parents, death of grandparents, relationship tensions, cyberbullying, toxic roommates, the hookup culture, a violent society, depression, emotional harassment by other students, and other adversities.

The fact is that virtually all students face difficulties of one kind or another, obviously some far more severe than others. But everyone struggles, and everyone is called upon to be resilient. It is easier for students to be resilient—and to learn—if they have teachers who connect with them.

MICROAGGRESSIONS: INSIDIOUS STRESSORS

A 2015 study from the Harvard University "Voices of Diversity" project found that diversity on college campuses has increased, but that women and people of color still face discrimination and prejudice.[6] This discrimination often shows up in "microaggressions"—barely overt and often covert, subtle digs and manifestations of bias that are pervasive in our society and impede learning. They are tiny acts of marginalization and exclusion perpetrated by a hegemonic group on a minority that can, for example, "communicate hostile, derogatory, or negative racial slights and insults toward people of color."[7]

It is common for someone from a dominant culture (for example, white males) to unintentionally marginalize a person of color or a female. Dr. Stephen Brookfield calls these microaggressions "ingrained, seemingly instinctive behaviors that represent years of unconscious assimilation and socialization."[8]

According to professor and psychologist Derald Wing Sue, microaggressions

- repeat or affirm stereotypes;

- position the dominant culture as normal and the minority one as aberrant;

- assume all minority group members are the same;

- minimize the existence of discrimination against the minority group;

- deny the perpetrator's own bias; and

- minimize the importance or presence of conflicts between the dominant culture and the minority group.[9]

Microaggression happens all the time. And it's hard to focus and concentrate if you are beset by discrimination. The stress is especially chilling for young women living in a sexist, misogynistic culture; for minorities living in a racist society; and for LGBTQ students living in a non-inclusive society. Faculty have an important role in working to improve this situation.

In reading Brookfield's outstanding book *The Skillful Teacher*, I was amazed at how openly he talks about his struggles with his own racism. This is not overt racism (e.g., using a racist epithet or openly disrespecting a person of color). It is something unintentional and far less conscious. Brookfield's candor is inspiring. He says, "I have learned racist impulses and instincts and I will never lose these, though I can become more aware and struggle against them."[10] And he writes that "enduring White racism is embedded" in our colleges and universities.[11]

His candor resonates with me, even though I identify as a progressive, liberal Democrat. I know that deep down in my bones, I am biased and that

I need to constantly fight that. Brookfield wants to make these muffled racist inclinations public, so they can be recognized and challenged.[12]

An example of a racial microaggression would be a person not wanting to be in a study group with students of different races. Another example pertaining to women is the fact that most professors are white men and often the course material features the work of white men. My own teaching suffers from this weakness. In my area of environmental and wildlife film-making, I need to make a bigger effort to show the work of women and people of color.

Brookfield's concluding thoughts are worth quoting in full here:

> Between declaring a readiness to work in anti-racist ways and actually doing this lies an ocean of experiential contradictions. By sharing my own regular commission of racial and gender microaggressions and by talking about my own racist impulses and instincts, I hope to teach that doing this work is incredibly complex. I hope to communicate with White colleagues the deep-seated nature of learned racism and the message that as soon as you think you're making progress in combatting this you will say or do something that will reveal how racist ideology has its hooks into you.[13]

INVESTING IN STUDENTS' LIVES

Is it possible to be an effective teacher if you don't get to know your students? Perhaps, but it is much harder. Students learn much better and more easily if they know their professor cares about them and wants them to succeed, and if there is a real connection between the teacher and the student. In their book *How College Works*, Daniel Chambliss and Christopher Takacs argue that "faculty-student interactions both inside and outside the classroom have dramatic effects on student learning."[14]

Professors must not only care about students but also show that they care. And students can tell. Students are more likely to invest in a class if the professor cares about the class and the students' learning than if the professor is minimally invested, takes days to respond to students' emails, and generally exhibits a lack of energy and enthusiasm. Those professors who invest in their students' lives—by meeting regularly with them, demonstrating respect for their views, encouraging them to work hard, and so on—show caring.

Professors should be interested in their students' lives, just as committed parents are interested in their children's lives. When professors act in a way that is caring, they inevitably develop rapport with their students. This leads to students being more committed to learning and to caring about the class content. Caring and learning go together.

In chapter 9, I'll discuss how to deal with the much harder challenge of getting to know students in a large class (say, more than fifty students).

WHAT IS "CARING"?

Caring means being respectful, enthusiastic, warm, likeable, approachable, and open to questions, all driven by nothing more than a desire to have students be more motivated learners. A caring professor, by definition, creates a motivating, learning milieu in which students thrive and blossom. She makes the class engaging and inviting, not to be popular but to encourage intellectual growth. Such a learning environment incentivizes students to attend class and invest in their studies.

Steven Meyers, a professor of psychology at Roosevelt University in Chicago, wrote a cogent and well-referenced article in this area.[15] His 2009 essay, titled "Do Your Students Care Whether You Care About Them?" argues persuasively that "caring is an important dimension of effective college teaching." Students are acutely aware of whether their professors care about them, Myers writes, but professors do not typically attach the same importance to it.

He warns that caring is not necessarily easy. Some professors do care, but find it difficult to show, perhaps because students don't seem to appreciate it. Other professors don't want to get too close to their students, and yet others take the view that their job is to teach content, not to mollycoddle students.

Still, after taking all the potential negatives into account, Meyers asserts that "supportive relationships in the classroom can encourage students to become more invested in learning, enable them to extend beyond their current abilities, and form a bridge to mentorship."

Lang says that paying attention to students in class boosts their motivation to learn. Chambliss and Takacs's research arrives at the same conclusion.[16] They also emphasize something touched on earlier in this book—that teachers matter and that the best teachers are not only knowledgeable but also "exciting *to students*, accessible *to students*, and engaged *with students*."[17] They are compelling, engaging, humble, and respectful.

How can a professor show caring? I've already mentioned numerous ways. Here's a pithy list of some of those and more:

• make eye contact with students when talking;

• smile more;

• move around the class when talking and don't get stuck behind a lectern;

- encourage students to talk, participate, and ask questions;

- be humorous;

- address students by name;

- ask students for feedback on how the class is going for them;

- praise students when they do good work;

- make constructive suggestions about work that needs to improve;

- let students have some agency over the syllabus and what is learned, by giving the syllabus to them and inviting their feedback;

- be available to students and easy to reach;

- give thoughtful and substantive comments on papers and exams; and

- establish a rapport with students and the class as a whole.

Caring by professors does not compromise academic rigor, nor does it mean lowering standards. It also does not rule out criticizing poor student work or pushing students to achieve more academically. What caring does mean is being prepared to mentor students and to teach effectively.

WHY MENTORING MATTERS

On September 10, 2014, columnist Tom Friedman wrote in the *New York Times* about some research that Gallup had done to explore the relationship between education and long-term career success.[18] Brandon Busteed, executive director of Gallup's education division, told Friedman the research showed that successful students had one or more teachers who were mentors and who took a real interest in their aspirations.

Graduates who had a professor or professors who cared about them as a person, or had a mentor who encouraged their goals and dreams, were much more likely than their mentor-less counterparts to have fulfilling careers and higher overall well-being. But Gallup made the alarming finding that only 22 percent of college grads said they had such a mentor.

Chambliss and Takacs found evidence in their research that "mentors can have deep, lasting, positive results for students."[19] They go so far as to argue that academic disciplines are as much "a vehicle for meeting teachers as for ingesting important information."[20]

In other words, mentoring—or trusted advising—may matter more than conveying course content, and the highest value of a teacher may be in the mentoring relationship he offers to students. The benefit of mentoring a student lasts longer than the retention of much of the course information too. Chambliss and Takacs say that mentoring involves a significant professional connection and manifestation of concern for the student that goes beyond the "immediacies of a course."[21]

The bottom line is that mentoring is so important that students who are lucky enough to be mentored by a professor have a significant advantage compared to those students who don't. As I said at the start of this book, students should choose teachers over topics. Students should find out who the good teachers are (those who care, who are compelling, who inspire, and who love to learn and help others learn) and take their classes.

BRING CARING TO CLASS

To be most effective, professors need to integrate caring into every phase of the class, from preparation to maintaining a tone of thoughtfulness and civility in discussions, evaluations, communications, and classroom control.

WHAT TO DO BEFORE CLASS

It goes without saying that preparation and planning for class are important. The best teachers prepare thoroughly. They arrive meticulously prepared, including having backup plans and extra whiteboard markers or chalk in their pocket. They also are ready for technical contingencies and know the number to call for immediate tech support in case they need it.

One idiosyncratic thing I do in the hour before class starts is to review aloud a list of key attributes that I seek to convey in the class. This list includes words and phrases that guide my approach; they include such self-triggers as: *be enthusiastic, dynamic, caring, energized, learning-focused (not teaching-focused), professional, warm, passionate, inspiring, firm, engaging, highly competent, authoritative, get students to talk and be active, listen actively, smile, don't hurry.*

By saying these words—affirmations really—out loud and vigorously drilling them into my head, it somehow helps me get ready to teach and raises my energy level, enthusiasm, and focus.

LAUNCHING THE FIRST CLASS

In the first class, go over a few housekeeping items, such as what you want students to call you (by your first name or by "Professor Smith"), whether you allow eating in class, and whether you permit students to use their cell phones and laptops in class.

During the first class, I tell my students that I expect to learn from *them*, both during class discussions and from their research and papers. I give a short anecdote about something I learned from a student in a past class.

I write the plan for the class on the board before students arrive (or as they arrive). This helps the students know what to expect and encourages participation. As the class unfolds, I mention where we are on this plan. This practice gives me a chance to recap and answer questions. I don't have to cover everything in the plan. I remain flexible. The goal is to focus on student learning, not necessarily on covering every detail in the outline.

In the first session, I give out a sheet of paper with advice from past top students in the class on what they did to earn an A grade. Students like to learn from other students. Some of the tips are:

Work hard and persevere in the face of challenges. If you worry that you are not doing well, go and talk with Professor Palmer. I always left my talks with him with a determination to improve. Above all, have a growth mind-set—a realization that through hard work and effort, you can get an A in this class. Your capacity to learn and improve is unlimited.

As students of COMM-524, you're about to exercise critical thinking and gain important skills that can be applied not only to wildlife and environmental filmmaking, but even to fiction film and to life in general. You will be presented with a lot of information, and the more effort you put into the class, the more you'll get out of it. Make sure to take the time to form your own opinions but be open to hearing other people's as well. Be ready to engage in meaningful conversations in class, and with Professor Palmer—he's a great resource in navigating life after school.

Succeeding in COMM-524 is not as daunting as it may seem. Most students choose to take this class because they have a genuine interest in or passion for the subject. The most important thing you can bring to class is your enthusiasm and readiness to learn and work hard. You get so much more out of this class if you invest yourself in it. This means meeting with Professor Palmer as often as you can, turning in homework on time—as well as doing it thoughtfully and to your best ability—and of course coming to class. I am a quiet person, but I urge you to try, as I did, to contribute to the conversation. During my time in this class, I became very close to many people with whom I keep in touch. Contribute and work hard and this will become much more than just a class.

The secret to success in COMM-524? Adopt a new mindset about what you can achieve. This is not a course in which learning and growth are confined to

15 weeks. The finish line is not a final examination. Rather, Professor Palmer's course is an opportunity to make meaningful progress toward your personal and professional goals, whatever they may be. The knowledge you will gain, the relationships you will build, and the skills you will practice matter well beyond this class, but only if you approach them with an opportunity mindset.

FIRST-DAY INTRODUCTIONS

I recommend that students introduce themselves during the first class and say something of substance about their lives and aspirations: where they are from and their course concentration, for example, or even what they plan to do after completing their degree.[22] An effective twist on this is to have students meet and interview those next to them in the classroom and briefly present their new friends to the class.

Faculty can also use a learning management system such as Blackboard for introductions. Invite the students to introduce themselves on the discussion board.

Many students will be interested in the professor's background and experiences. In *McKeachie's Teaching Tips*, the authors recommend allowing students to ask questions about you.[23]

Author and educator Robert Magnan suggests playing "Meet Your Teacher," by distributing the syllabus and relevant handouts, giving students time to read everything, and then dividing the class into groups and having them select questions to ask you.[24]

Some professors include a brief bio in the syllabus, in part because it gives students a way to talk to parents and friends about the instructor. And of course, faculty bios can be found in the department or division website.

WRITTEN PROFILES

In addition to the introductions, I seek to learn more about my students by asking them to complete a questionnaire. This helps me get to know them better as individuals.

Here is the questionnaire I created for my filmmaking class. On the actual form, I leave plenty of space for students to write their answers:

Name as on class roster: _____

Name you want me to use in class: _____

Pronouns you use (Some students look male but may identify as female, or vice versa. Some students don't want to be called "he" or "she," but "they.":

_____

Phone number: _____

E-mail (please print clearly): _____

Undergraduate: Junior_____ Senior_____ Major_____

Graduate: MA_____ MFA_____ Program (if not film and video) ____

1. What other film or video production or writing courses have you taken?

2. Why are you taking this class? What is the purpose of this class for you?

3. What content, skills, and knowledge do you want to learn?

4. What are your career aspirations?

5. What do you feel strongly, or even passionately, about?

6. What sort of films do you like, and perhaps would even like to produce?

7. Is there an organization you would love to work for if given the chance?

8. How do you learn best? What is the best learning experience you have ever had?

9. What have teachers done in the past that helped you to learn?

10. Please tell me some more things about you:

11. Is there anything you would like to know about me?

My students fill this out in the first class and hand it in to me. I read their responses carefully, so that I have information and insights to understand them well.

ARRIVING EARLY

I recommend showing up early for every class, which provides the opportunity to connect with students as they enter the classroom. Greet them by name and inquire about their lives and interests. Be very careful to leave no one out and to treat everybody equally. Having no favorites is a particularly important rule to observe. This inclusive interaction will help to create a positive mood in the classroom.

Dr. James Lang recommends arriving early and putting something up at the front of the class for students to ponder as they arrive. For an astronomy class, it could be a photo of the cosmos, for a writing class a sentence, for a music class an audio clip, for a filmmaking class a video clip, and so on. Invite the students to look at whatever you have selected. Ask them what they notice about it and what they wonder about it.[25] This provides an on-topic focus that gets them engaged in the material right away.

I often tell my students to find someone in the room they don't know very well and talk with the person about a topic for a couple of minutes while I write the plan for the day's class on the board. I give them a topic to discuss that is related to what we are learning.

MEMORIZING AND USING NAMES

The best professors make a serious and obvious effort to learn their students' names during the first or second class. Learning their names (and having them learn each other's names) creates a warm environment that encourages learning and participation.

In a study exploring the use of student names by professors in large biology classes, more than 85 percent of the students said it was important to them that their instructors knew their names—while only a small fraction of that number said it was likely that the professor knew their name.[26]

Commenting on this study in *Faculty Focus*, Dr. Maryellen Weimer reports that students like professors to know their names, as it "positively affects their attitudes" about the course. They feel "more valued and invested" in the course and more comfortable asking for help because it is easier to talk with the instructor. Overall, this improves student performance in class.[27]

One technique that has helped me learn the names of students is the use of name tents, placed prominently in front of each student. I write the name of the student on *both sides* so that not only can I see the name of the student, but a classmate sitting behind her can peer over her shoulder and see it too.

I collect all the name tents at the end of every class and give them out at the start of the next class. This is an easy way to make sure the name tents don't get lost and to see who is missing. Reading and collecting the name tents helps me to memorize who they belong to as well.

The best professors address their students by name when speaking in class. This helps students develop a connection with the professor. I also encourage students to use each other's names rather than using pronouns like *him* or *she*. When a student says something like, "I don't agree with her comment," I encourage him to say instead, "I don't agree with Susan's comment." This enhances the sense of community and makes students feel engaged.

In addition, I take a photo of the class (this is assuming the class is under, say, fifty students). Before each class, I go over the photo, drilling myself on the names.

Chambliss and Takacs's research shows that a small action, such as using a student's name, can have a surprisingly big impact.[28] This insight undergirds James Lang's superb book *Small Teaching*.[29] Small actions can make a big difference. A simple gesture of respect from a teacher can mean a tremendous amount to a student.

Every semester, my wife and I invite all my students (about thirty) to our house for dinner. It's not a big imposition on us, and Chambliss and Takacs have found that "being a guest in a faculty home has a huge impact on the college experience of a student."[30]

MAKING THE CASE FOR LEARNING

New students may not realize the value of learning the course content, so in the first class it's worth spending fifteen minutes describing why they need to take the class and how it will benefit them.

It's surprising how many professors assume their students understand why the class is important. In fact, students often don't—and even if they do, it's worth reminding them. This is especially crucial for first-year college students who are likely to be unfamiliar with college-level work.

Some students may be extremely interested in the subject matter. For others, the class may be a third-choice elective that they need to take in order to fulfill some requirement.

Describe the benefits of the course in terms that resonate with students. Tell them, for example, how it will help them grow intellectually, make them more employable, and find a career. Explain that the course will help them to acquire valuable study skills, develop leadership and social skills in a team environment, produce items for their job-seeking portfolio, and gain skills that will enable them to be lifelong learners and find fulfillment. In other words, tell them the many ways in which the course can change their lives.

ONE-ON-ONE MEETINGS

As I mentioned in chapter 3, I tell my students that they *must* meet with me for a one-on-one, face-to-face meeting within the first two weeks of the semester.

When we meet, I discuss the students' answers in the questionnaire described above. Their answers help me know more about them. In the one-on-one meetings, I am able to learn more about each student's background, interests, and life goals. This benefits the students because I can be more sensitive to their unique backgrounds and experiences and shape my teaching strategy to be most helpful to them.

It is important to be aware of boundaries. There is a fine line between getting to know someone and prying. Be careful not to cross this line.

The best professors get to know each students' interests and concerns, and learn about their hopes and dreams. The goal is to treat all students as individuals. The payoff? It shows that you care and that you want to do everything you can to help them learn and get the most out of the course. Most students will respond in kind, by caring and putting full effort into the course.

A POSTDATED LETTER

The Art of Possibility by Rosamund Stone Zander and Benjamin Zander offers an intriguing idea that I mentioned in chapter 4 but want to describe in more detail here.[31] The authors recommend that the professor ask all students, as part of their first homework assignment, to write a letter to the professor that is dated the day of the *last* class. In it, the students describe how much they learned in the class, how they contributed to that learning, and the kind of person they became because of it.

In other words, they position themselves in the future looking back and describe vividly all their achievements in the past semester—all the ways they have changed, grown, and learned. The letter is written in the past tense. It is a work of creative imagination.

I do this for every one of my courses. Although I cannot describe with certainty the pedagogical benefits of this exercise, I believe it to be useful because it is consistent with educator and author Stephen R. Covey's admonition to "begin with the end in mind."[32]

I read the letters carefully and put them away for fifteen weeks or so, bringing them out on the last day of class. Typically, students are surprised to find that the letter they wrote months ago is very similar to the letter they would write having actually reached the end of the course. I ask students what the exercise taught them. They usually say something like, "I'm amazed how this is virtually the exact letter I would write were I to be writing it today."

Here is an example of such a letter, written by a student at an American music academy. It is included in the Zanders' book:

> I got my A because I had the courage to examine my fears and I realized that they have no place in my life. I changed from someone who was scared to make a mistake in case she was noticed to someone who knows they have a contribution to make to other people, musically and personally. . . . Thus all diffidence and lack of belief in myself are gone. So too is the belief that I only exist as a reflection in other people's eyes and the resulting desire to please everyone. . . . I understand that trying and achieving are the same thing when you are your own master—and I am. I have found a desire to convey music to other people, which is stronger than the worries I had about myself. I have changed from desiring inconsequentiality and anonymity to accepting the joy that comes from knowing that my music changes the world.

This student's candor and goals for growth are exactly what I hope to inspire in my own students as they use this assignment to set their own learning goals.

PROMOTING CIVIL DISCOURSE

In a classroom setting, civil discourse is represented by productive, energetic, sometimes impassioned discussions on any topic, with no personal attacks on students with different opinions. At its best, civil discourse in class allows critical thinking, learning, and self-reflection to blossom. It gives students the opportunity to examine underlying assumptions, consider differing views with an open mind, and identify their own biases.

Occasionally, a class may include a disruptive student. Dr. Andrea Brenner, a sociologist at American University, has made a special study of this problem and how to handle it. She defines *disruptive behavior* as behavior that interferes with or hinders the learning for other students in the class.

Brenner says that prevention is the key and that the best time to deal with classroom disruption is before it begins. At the outset, Brenner advises professors to establish an environment in which all students can learn. Students should expect a class wherein everyone treats everyone else with understanding, dignity, and respect, despite the inevitable occurrence of uncomfortable discussions.

Brenner suggests creating clear guidelines and a positive classroom environment by working out a set of ground rules early on that will govern class interactions. The ground rules might include such statements as:

- Our goal is intellectual exploration, not necessarily arriving at a judgment or conclusion.

- We will not interrupt each other.

- We will not use hurtful epithets.

- We will listen respectfully to what others are saying;

- All voices will be heard.

- We will not allow a few students to dominate the discussion.

- It's fine to disagree with each other respectfully, but it is not fine to attack others who have different viewpoints.

- We will ask for clarification when confused or hurt by something someone says.

- We will avoid sarcasm, ridicule, or bullying.

Of course, it is crucial that professors model respectful communication and exemplify the behavior and etiquette they want to see in students. Brenner says teachers must respond to disruptive behavior consistently and in a timely manner. Rather than judge or "diagnose" a student who exhibits disruptive behavior, it is better to identify the behavior—perhaps saying, "You are causing the class to become distracted from the learning objectives for today." Follow up by talking with the student about it afterward, outside the classroom. If the student does not respond to a verbal request to stop the behavior, the teacher should ask the student to leave the classroom. Finally, if the student refuses to leave and the professor may fear harm or injury, it is appropriate to call campus security.

In my fifteen years of teaching, I have never experienced any disruptive behavior by students. It is rare. But creating clear guidelines for governing classroom discussions is good practice in any case, as a way to promote and acknowledge the importance of civility in the class.

THE ONE-MINUTE PAPER

At the end of the first class, I find it very useful to give a blank sheet to each student. I explain, "This is an anonymous writing assignment that you should aim to complete in about three minutes. On one side of the paper write what you liked about the class, and on the other side write what you didn't like or what was missing for you. It is anonymous, so you can be as blunt as you want."

This exercise indicates my interest in learning from them, starts to give them some say in how the class is run and managed, and encourages them to start thinking about their learning. In addition, it allows me to shape my teaching to maximize their learning. It gives me constructive feedback on how to improve the class.

At the start of the next class, I hand out a typed list of everything they wrote (however derogatory or cutting) and tell them what changes I'm going to make. There are always a few items on the list about which I have to say, "I disagree with this and will not make the requested change," but invariably most of the suggestions are worth implementing.

* * * * *

Dr. Ken Bain's research shows unambiguously that personality plays little or no role in successful teaching.[33] The best professors might be loud and extro-verted, or quiet and retiring. Regardless of personality, Bain found that the best teachers *invest* in their students and that they do what they do because they care about their students as people and learners.[34]

There is a strong bond of trust between effective teachers and their students. Often that trust develops because teachers are not afraid to talk about their own journey and how they struggled with setbacks, confusion, lack of understanding, failures, and frustrations.[35]

Students often find it comforting to discover that professors once spent time wrestling, sometimes unsuccessfully, with the contents they are now teaching. Good teachers don't pretend to have special powers or to be far superior to their students. Rather, they show that they are fellow travelers on a path of learning, discovery, and exploration.

Chapter 6

Convey Your Passion

Throughout history the exemplary teacher has never been just an instructor in a subject; he is nearly always its living advertisement.

—Michael Dirda, author and literary critic

In the first class of the semester, students will be nervous and apprehensive, wondering what they have gotten themselves into. What kind of professor are you going to be? Friendly or cold? Approachable or standoffish? A tough grader or a pushover? Will the class feel intimidating or safe? Will they be able to keep up with the work? Will they get a decent grade? Students will be looking to the professor for a sense of the answers to such questions. Conveying your passion will provide a huge clue to them.

The last chapter talked about getting to know students, showing that you care, and the importance of caring in helping students to learn. This chapter focuses on another key to launching a successful class: showing passion and enthusiasm for both teaching and the course content.

To many teachers, the prospect of displaying emotion will be a red flag. It's common to believe that teaching and learning should be unemotional, cerebral, rational, and detached. But as Flower Darby, senior instructional designer at Northern Arizona University, argues, "Our emotions are a central part of our humanity."[1] She says to deny them is "to deny the essence of who we are."

Emotions not only inspire and motivate us. When our emotions are aroused, we pay more attention. As an example, Darby points out that seeing a photo of a wounded refugee child has far greater impact than reading a fact-filled analysis of the crisis itself. Dr. James Lang says, "When we feel strong emotions, our attention and cognitive capacities are heightened."[2]

We need to be mindful about bringing emotions, including passion and enthusiasm, into the classroom. The goal is not to be a well-liked, popular teacher. Rather, it is to promote student learning. Lang writes, "The emotions that we demonstrate to students, especially our positive emotions connected to the subject matter we are teaching, can create a strong positive boost to student motivation."[3] Students are social animals and feed off the teacher's emotions. If a teacher is enthusiastic, it will help create a better learning climate in the class.

Enthusiasm should not be confused with being entertaining. The best way to capture students' attention is by conveying enthusiasm *for the subject matter*. The professor's enthusiasm should not focus on the professor or the students but on the class content. Enthusiasm does not necessarily mean that the teacher is a jokester. That may or may not be the case, but lots of laughter in a class does not assure that a lot of learning is going on. The goal always is student learning; enthusiasm should be a tool directed solely to that end.

In a 2008 talk at America University, Professor Patrick Allitt asserted that a teacher's body language and voice must convey the unmistakable message that there is nowhere else he would rather be than right there in that room with his students. Earlier I shared an observation by Allitt that bears repeating: "My whole teaching life had convinced me that nothing works better as a classroom technique or gets a better response than simple enthusiasm."[4]

The chapter suggests how to project enthusiasm. For starters, here are fifteen things a teacher can do to convey enthusiasm and passion. They are tools to motivate students to want to learn and participate in class.

1. Capture students' attention.

2. Set intentions—both yours and the students'.

3. Establish a self-transcendent mission and sense of purpose for the learning.

4. Aim for transformative learning.

5. Encourage intrinsic motivation.

6. Give students an early success.

7. Share your professional experiences.

8. Be physical.

9. Try not to use notes when teaching.

10. Put on a performance.

11. Offer a simple invitation: Please see me.

12. Don't treat students like customers.

13. Build rapport with students.

14. Catch students doing something right.

15. Encourage curiosity.

Let's elaborate.

CAPTURE STUDENTS' ATTENTION

Capturing the attention of students is pivotal. They often arrive in class fatigued, stressed, anxious, and easily distracted. Lack of concentration and focus is endemic, aggravated by students' obsession with social media. The professor's enthusiasm can corral their attention, help them to focus, and ignite their interest in learning.

Effective teachers command attention and do not let it go. Enthusiasm is a key component of this. Enthusiasm can be projected at the start of the very first class in any number of ways, including a provocative case study, a poignant story, an inspiring and emotive visual image, or a stunning statistic from a recent newspaper article.

SET INTENTIONS—BOTH YOURS AND THE STUDENTS'

An intention is a statement about how a person wants to be in the class and what the person wants to accomplish. It describes, says coach and author Elena Aguilar, "an aspiration for how you might think, feel, engage with others, or engage in your learning so that you can be your best self today."[5]

When you set an intention, you are more likely, says Aguilar, to make choices that support it—through what you do or what you think. In *The Mindful Brain*, neurobiologist Daniel Siegel writes, "Intentions create an integrated state of priming, a gearing up of our neural system to be in the mode of that specific intention: we can be readying to receive, to sense, to focus, to behave in a certain manner."[6]

Some professors may find that having their students set intentions is too touchy-feely and not to their taste. But it can enable many students to focus, get centered, and elevate their aspirations for the class.

Examples of intentions for students might be:

- I want to take risks and contribute to the whole group discussion at least once.

- I want to connect with others.

- I want to ask challenging questions.

- I want to be accepting of my classmates and not get annoyed by their comments.

- I want to be fully present and will only check my email and phone at the break.

Professors can, and should, set intentions too, either before the class starts or when students are setting theirs.

I use—and often state—the following intentions for myself in my classes:

- I will do everything in my power to help my students learn.

- I will teach inclusively and make sure no one feels left out.

- I will be enthusiastic, stimulating, inspiring, and provocative.

- I will encourage deep thinking.

- I will enunciate clearly and talk persuasively.

- I will encourage active participation by everyone in the room and not allow a few students to dominate the discussions.

- I will use pauses and repetition to powerfully underscore key points I want to get across.

Ken Bain found in his research that "the most effective teachers generally thought more carefully and extensively about their intentions with students and let those aspirations and attitudes guide them in their teaching."[7]

Dr. Maryellen Weimer was drawn to an essay by professor and mathematical scientist Larry Lesser that appeared in the November 2010 issue of the newsletter *The Teaching Professor*.[8] Lesser came across a poem in a Jewish prayer book that expressed noble intentions for a worship space. It inspired him to write his own set of noble intentions for his classroom spaces— starting with what he intended to do and be as a teacher and mentor, and followed by his aspirations for students. Weimer says, "His intentions transform classrooms, lifting them from ordinary places to spaces of power, filled with potential. Sharing those intentions changed how his students thought about the classroom."[9]

ESTABLISH A SELF-TRANSCENDENT MISSION AND SENSE OF PURPOSE FOR THE LEARNING

Lang is eloquent about the powerful idea of infusing learning with a self-transcendent purpose.[10] He says that the most powerful forms of purposefulness occur when students see the potential for their learning to improve the world. Creating in our students a strong sense of purpose through helping others, correcting social injustices, or making a real difference in the world will drive them to become more focused and attentive in class, and more tenacious in their efforts to learn.

The process of establishing a self-transcendent mission for the learning is similar to that used for "setting intentions" as described above, except that setting intentions can include self-oriented motivation as well, such as a desire to get better grades, participate in class discussions more, or become more likable to classmates.

So, tell students why the class is important and useful, and why you find it fascinating. Explain why they should find the content compelling and why it matters. Describe the skills, insights, and strengths that they do not have now but will be able to attain by taking the class. Above all, describe why learning the content will put them in a much stronger position to help make the world less cruel, unjust, or harmful. This will give them the strength and determination to persevere through learning challenges and to grow as critical thinkers.

AIM FOR TRANSFORMATIVE LEARNING

How can the class change a student's life? One way is through "transformative learning," or learning that changes what a person thinks and does, and who he is. Such transformation is rare but can happen—and when it does, it's magical.

Suggesting this possibility to students can help them raise their ambitions and think more deeply about the amount of hard work and attention they will devote to the class. Tell them that you will do everything in your power to give them a transformative experience. This shows students that you have a profound commitment to their success.

ENCOURAGE INTRINSIC MOTIVATION

Grades are important to students, but professors need to convey a bigger truth—namely, that learning is more important than grades. We want students to be driven by their love of learning. If they are driven by grades, they run the risk of relying on superficial memorization, and gathering just enough information to squeak through the next exam. By articulating the distinction between grades and learning, teachers can help students think more carefully about their commitment to learning and what learning really means.

Filmmaker professor Maggie Stogner says she frequently makes this case to students, but often receives vigorous pushback. The students say that grades *do* matter, especially for scholarships and other funding. Stogner finds a lot of anxiety around this issue and suggests framing the discussion to emphasize that if students are fully engaged and learning, they are more likely to receive good grades.

Students want to feel that they are part of a supportive community when they are in class. They want to feel connected. According to educator Karin Kirk, research shows that students who feel they "belong" and who feel they relate well to their classmates have more intrinsic motivation and academic confidence.[11] According to students, their sense of belonging is fostered by a teacher who demonstrates warmth and openness; encourages student participation; is enthusiastic, friendly, and helpful; and is organized and prepared for class.[12]

GIVE STUDENTS AN EARLY SUCCESS

Giving frequent, early, positive, and constructive feedback can encourage students, helping them to believe they can succeed in the class. Assign tasks that are neither too easy nor too difficult. In classes early in the semester, students seem to perform best when the level of difficulty is a little above their current abilities. They are stimulated and motivated. If the work is too easy, students will get bored and restless—and perhaps lose some respect for the course. Work that is too difficult can cause students to be frustrated and anxious.

That said, it is important for students to take risks and leave their comfort zones, especially after the first couple of classes as students adjust to the expectations and learning style of the course. Professors should challenge students with more work than they think they can handle, even if this leads to poor evaluations by students.

Demand that students push themselves further than they normally might. Class work should encourage them to develop high-level critical and analytical thinking skills. Students and their parents pay a lot of money for college and quite rightly expect results.

SHARE YOUR PROFESSIONAL EXPERIENCES

Look for opportunities to tell students more about your professional experiences, relating them to the learning outcomes for the course. They can learn from your successes and especially from your mistakes. Students should know their professors are human, and that it is normal and perfectly fine to make mistakes, have setbacks, and experience disappointments and failures.

Successful people meet with failure over and over. When that happens, they don't give up. Author Peter Brown writes, "Striving, by its nature, often results in setbacks, and setbacks are often what provide the essential information needed to adjust strategies to achieve mastery."[13]

Stogner argues that relating the stories of setbacks to learning outcomes is very important. She adds that the experiences shared should be carefully chosen: they must be relevant to the students' interests, to what they are learning, and to the learning outcomes for the course.

BE PHYSICAL

An effective teacher is acutely aware of his audience, and that's much easier to do when moving around the room and making eye contact.

Furthermore, classes are much more engaging for students when the teacher moves around rather than sitting still or lecturing from a podium. So step away from the lectern. When students see your enthusiasm, they'll want to participate in the class and in learning.

Walk among the students, be physically active and animated, and use your whole body and voice to reflect your fascination with the subject matter and with teaching it. To inject energy into the room, stand up straight, with shoulders back, and move with alacrity. When professors slouch, slump, droop, or sag, they unintentionally drain the room of energy.

I never bring food or coffee into class because it sends a message that I am relaxed. If a teacher is relaxed, it encourages students to lose focus. Instead, inject what I call "productive tension" in the air through your physicality, so students know it is time to concentrate and take the class seriously.

TRY NOT TO USE NOTES WHEN TEACHING

Professors who must use notes extensively are seriously handicapping their effectiveness. Every time the teacher is looking at his notes, he is not looking at the class and is missing visual clues about how his students are feeling. He won't be as acutely aware of his audience as he should be. And he may be sending a message that he is simply recycling dusty lectures, which is a sure way to bore and disappoint students.

The more the professor has mastered the material and has no need for notes, the better. Teaching without notes frees up the professor to soak in what is happening in the class, to make constant adjustments to improve student learning, and to radiate confidence and excitement about the content.

PUT ON A PERFORMANCE

Even for an introverted professor, teaching is a performance art. Professors need to engage students, who can be apathetic, bored, and frustrated. If students are not engaged, learning won't take place.

Remember that professors are responsible for leading the class and therefore need to do whatever is necessary to make sure that students are learning. Teaching is not acting, but effective professors should seek to have a big impact on their students, to inspire and provoke them, just as actors do for their audiences.

It is hard for students to fall in love with a topic if the professor is not consciously aware of his role as a performer—as someone who has responsibilities to his audience and therefore must perform to certain standards. When you teach, you are, by definition, performing. Your words, your jokes, your gesticulation, your stories, your clothes, your movement, your smiles, your eye contact, and how often you bring students to the front of the class ("to the stage") to perform—all must be thoroughly considered for maximum impact.

Since you must perform, you have an obligation to put on the best performance possible for the sake of your students' learning. If you play the role of an engaged, vibrant, caring professor, chances are good your students will respond in like manner.

Professor and psychologist Sarah Rose Cavanagh writes, "If you teach, you are acting. Like acting, your best performance will stem from tapping into your true emotions and connecting with your audience on an authentic level. But you are still crafting an act using speech, movement, and props—and laying it before a critical audience. Your highest hope isn't that your students will approve . . . but that they'll be . . . changed intellectually and emotionally."[14]

Of course, a teacher wants to put on a "performance" that comes across to students as a warm, inviting *conversation* rather than a peroration. Professors are not performing to impress students, but to draw them into the class content and help them learn.

OFFER A SIMPLE INVITATION: PLEASE SEE ME

Professor and psychologist Micah Sadigh writes a simple message on tests or assignments of students who are struggling: "Please see me so we can discuss your performance on the test (or assignment). Let's see what we can do to improve your grade."[15] Students who have met with him have indeed done much better on subsequent tests. He reports, "I think the most important message of these meetings was to convey to them that they were not simply a name in my gradebook but that I really cared about their learning and their success."

Sadigh makes it clear to the struggling students that he and they *will work together* to find a way to improve the student's grade on future tests and assignments. This resonates with the previous chapter on caring because Sadigh, a professor of psychology, says, "A simple conversation may have far-reaching implications. In many cases, when we feel that others truly care about us, we tend to reciprocate by paying more attention to how we act in their presence." He says he has witnessed some "remarkable transformations" stemming from the simple request, "Please see me."

DON'T TREAT STUDENTS LIKE CUSTOMERS

Students today are different from their predecessors of twenty-five years ago. They are much more customer-oriented, and want to know exactly what they are getting for their education dollars. But are they really customers? They are paying for college, and so are entitled to expect certain things, such as housing and food. Obviously they are not entitled to A grades, though; that would be ludicrous. Students must earn their grades through hard work, diligent thinking, and creativity.

In class, students are learners, not customers. However, professors can still give them some control over their learning by giving them choices. For example, let them pick their lab partners or choose alternate assignments. Granting students some measure of autonomy in the learning process and class structure will lead to a higher motivation to learn. In part this is because it gives students significant responsibility for shaping their own learning and your teaching. This effect is especially apparent for students who show a lot of maturity.

Allitt tells the story of a student who arrives for class late, has an attitude, and, without any effort to conceal what she is doing, opens a fashion magazine and begins to browse. Allitt gives her about thirty seconds before breaking off in mid-sentence and walking over to stand right in front of her. In a loud and angry voice, he says, "Stop reading that magazine at once. And don't you ever again do that in my class." The student hastens to obey. "Do you understand me?" She nods and begins to blush with embarrassment.[16]

In my opinion, Allitt treated her appropriately. He treated her as a student, not as a customer. If she was a customer, he would have been less blunt and more delicate. Such half measures would not have benefited the class, or even the student herself.

BUILD RAPPORT WITH STUDENTS

Want a formula for failure to engender learning? Here it is: Rarely smile, respond tardily to emails, don't bother to learn students' names, take little interest in your students' professional and personal goals, be negative and belittling in class, seldom talk informally and affably outside class, and ignore your students when you pass them in the hallway. Act in this way and it will be challenging, perhaps impossible, to build rapport with students. It will impede student learning by not creating a climate for engaging with the class, the content, and the teacher herself.

Connect with students where *they* are, not where *you* are. Show the relevance of the subject to their personal and professional goals. To the extent possible, relate the class content to events, happenings, and news that intrigue the students. Start with an issue that students care about and know (or think they know). This is how Socrates taught. He started by focusing on what people knew (or thought they knew), and then gently challenged them to move to a new and better understanding.

CATCH THEM DOING SOMETHING RIGHT

Be alert to students doing good things and catch them in the act! If a professor sees constructive behavior by a student, it's an opportunity to provide positive feedback—one of the most powerful instructional tools. Positive feedback nurtures and cultivates behaviors that should be replicated. Is a student showing curiosity? Commend her. Is a student listening respectfully to another student with whom he disagrees? Praise him. And always express approbation with specificity.

ENCOURAGE CURIOSITY

Professor and philosopher Barry Casey says that curiosity is what drives learning.[17] Curiosity is the engine of true learning. I have already made the case that the "grades as a driver of learning" model leaves much to be desired. On the other hand, curiosity entails a hunger for understanding and meaning—the root of learning. It is alarming that Casey says he rarely sees curiosity in classrooms; he finds that students do not often go beyond asking how and where to asking why. Adam Grant, the Wharton psychologist, was once asked the best way to motivate students to want to learn, and his short answer was to cultivate curiosity—the desire to know.[18] When students are curious, they wonder about everything and keep asking questions.

* * * * *

Effective professors, through their passion and enthusiasm, create welcoming classroom environments that motivate students to thrive. They are committed to excellence in teaching. This commitment to enthusiasm manifests itself as responsiveness to students' e-mail and office visits, and a willingness to go "beyond the call of duty." When professors show passion and enthusiasm in class, it rubs off on their students, who are much more likely to become competent learners.

Chapter 7

Promote Active Learning

The educator must believe in the potential power of his pupil, and he must employ all his art in seeking to bring his pupil to experience this power.

—Alfred Adler, psychologist

The traditional model of instruction and learning dates back centuries. In it, an instructor who possesses knowledge on a given subject transmits it to students by speaking from a lectern. These days, the lecture may be augmented by PowerPoint slides or Prezi. But one thing about the model has not changed: students do not actively participate in class, except perhaps to ask the occasional question.

Richard Feynman, the famed theoretical nuclear physicist, was legendary for his brilliant and compelling lectures. Undoubtedly, a lecture can be memorable in the hands of a dynamic instructor like Feynman who treats it like a theatrical performance, captivating students with passion, intensity, and commitment, and coaxing along key messages with voice inflections, movement, gesticulations, and emotional heft. But Feynman may be a rarity. Increasingly people are questioning the effectiveness of the traditional lecture as a method for teaching and learning. Silent attention—not uncommonly, let's admit, with glazed eyes—is no longer regarded as clear evidence of learning.

In March 2018, *Science* magazine published "Anatomy of STEM Teaching in North American Universities." The article was authored by nearly thirty researchers who undertook a massive study of 550 lecturers as they taught more than seven hundred courses at twenty-five universities in Canada and the United States.[1] (STEM is short for *s*cience, *t*echnology, *e*ngineering, and *m*athematics.)

The researchers concluded that lectures are highly prevalent throughout the undergraduate STEM curriculum, and that "students in classes with traditional lecturing were 1.5 times more likely to fail than were students in classes with active learning."[2] It turns out that telling students things without asking them actively to process them results in less learning.

Lectures have their uses, but the focus should be on students actively learning. Lecturing transfers information from teacher to students without any guarantee that the students understand it. Physics professor Rhett Allain at Southeastern Louisiana University says, "Traditional lectures simply aren't effective. Research shows students don't learn by hearing or seeing, they learn by doing."[3]

David Gooblar, a lecturer in rhetoric at the University of Iowa, writes, "I sometimes worry that the word *teach* leads us astray in academe. The word suggests that our job as faculty members is to put new knowledge into our students' heads. But in my experience the best learning occurs when students teach themselves—when they discover something on their own."[4]

For the most part, students prefer to learn rather than be taught.

Journalist and science writer Annie Murphy Paul adds a crucially important point in a *New York Times* essay. She says not only that research has consistently found active learning to be superior to lectures, but also that active learning benefits "women, minorities, and low-income and first-generation students more, on average, than white males from more affluent, educated families."[5] Thus we have yet another powerful reason to move from lectures to active learning.

THE GROUNDBREAKING WORK OF ERIC MAZUR

One of the leaders in active learning is Professor Eric Mazur, a physicist at Harvard. After giving what he thought were excellent lectures for many years, he was shocked to find out that, despite his high student evaluations, his students didn't truly understand the fundamentals of physics.

They could solve difficult problems using formulas and equations (to memorize, apply by rote, and pass exams), but when his students were asked questions in simple language that required a deep understanding of fundamental concepts such as force, gravity, and momentum, they were perplexed and full of misconceptions. Mazur realized that his success as a teacher "was a complete illusion, a house of cards."[6]

He didn't know whether there was something wrong with the questions, his teaching was poor, or his students were dim. The students remained confused. He grew exasperated.

Then he did something he had never done before. He said to the class, "Why don't you discuss it with each other?" According to Dr. Craig Lambert, who writes about Mazur in *Harvard Magazine*, the class erupted in seeming chaos as 150 students started talking with each other in one-on-one conversations.[7] Within a few minutes, the students figured out the answer, indicating their understanding to the instructor by responding to multiple-choice questions with a wireless clicker device.

What happened? Mazur says that students teaching each other often are more effective than erudite professors teaching students. Professors can forget why the content is so challenging (they mastered it decades ago), whereas students who have figured out the right answer are more familiar with the challenges that beginners face. In other words, the person who knows best what a student is struggling with in assimilating new concepts is not the professor, but another student.[8]

What Mazur discovered, and then pioneered, is a way of teaching that is variously called "active learning," "peer instruction," or "interactive learning." Essentially it shifts the focus from the teacher to the students, from teaching to learning, and from lectures to discussion-based classes.[9]

Mazur and others have conducted meticulous research on active learning, and the results are overwhelmingly positive: through active learning, students learn far more than in traditionally taught classes, and retain far more knowledge for longer periods. Mazur writes, "So, evidence is mounting that readjusting the focus of education from information transfer to helping students assimilate material is paying off."[10]

Mazur reported in *Science* magazine in 2009, "Data obtained in my class and in classes of colleagues worldwide, in a wide range of academic settings and a wide range of disciplines, show that learning gains nearly triple with an approach that focuses on the student and on interactive learning."[11]

LEARNING BY TEACHING

Interactive pedagogy turns "passive, note-taking students into active de facto *teachers* who explain their ideas to each other and contend for their points of view."[12] As self-improvement guru Stephen R. Covey persuasively argued, the best way to learn anything is to teach it.[13]

Sitting passively in a class listening to a lecture and taking notes is not often an effective way of learning. What Mazur and teachers like him do *prior to the class* is distribute the lecture notes and post online video recordings of lectures. They tell students to review these materials *before coming to class*, thus liberating class time for active learning and peer instruction.

During class, active-learning professors function as coaches, encouraging students in discussions, projects, and exercises. The class is repurposed as a workshop where students can ask questions about content, interact with one another in hands-on collaborative activities, or put into practice what they learned from the video lectures they viewed outside class.

The information transfer happens *before* class, rather than *in* class, and class time is devoted to wrestling with the material and deeply understanding it. With traditional lectures, the process of making sense of the content is left to students to navigate on their own after the class. What Mazur did was to "flip" the class. He writes, "They must read material before coming to class, so that class time can be devoted to discussions, peer interactions, and time to assimilate and think. Instead of teaching by telling, I am teaching by questioning."[14]

FLIPPED CLASSES

Education is far more than the transfer of information. Information needs to be connected to what students already know—and then be carried further. As Dr. Ken Bain explains, new mental models need to be constructed and old, less useful ones discarded.[15]

In a traditional lecture, students take notes as the teacher talks. There is often little time to ruminate in any depth on what is being said. In the flipped classroom, the lectures are under the control of the student. They can watch, pause the video to think, rewind, or fast-forward, as they deem necessary. This is valuable to all students, and is especially helpful to those who are hard of hearing or for whom English is not their native tongue.

Flipping the class changes the role of the professor from detached talker to collaborator. The role of students changes from being passive consumers of education to being more responsible for their own learning, via interaction and active learning. The focus of the class changes from passively listening to learning, and is elevated from simple exposure to material toward a fuller understanding of it.

In terms of Professor Benjamin Bloom's revised taxonomy, flipping the class means that students are doing the lower levels of cognitive work (gaining knowledge and comprehension) outside of class, and focusing on the higher levels of cognitive work (application, analysis, synthesis, and evaluation) in the classroom where they have the support and help of their classmates and the professor.[16]

There are challenges to making flipped classes work.

The first is motivating the students to watch the video lectures before class begins, so they arrive in class ready to take advantage of the discussion, interactivity, and individual guidance.

A second challenge is to assume that active learning is always causing students to learn. Discussions and collaborative learning exercises can easily turn into busy work, which keeps a student busy but has little value. It is important continually to ask if students are really learning in discussion-based classes. Is active learning moving students from engagement to a deeper understanding of the content? Is it making them curious to know more?

A third challenge is for the faculty. They are used to having all the attention on them as they stand at the front of the class and lecture to students. Reframing this role to allow more active learning means sharing control of the class with the students. That can be scary.

Dr. Maryellen Weimer says,

> We don't know which of the many active learning approaches (group exercises, use of wireless clickers to communicate with the professor, online discussion, hands-on experience, etc.) works best with what kinds of content and for what kinds of learners. We've got lots to learn, but we definitely know enough to challenge ourselves and our colleagues to step back from lecturing and move forward with approaches that feature students taking action.[17]

Flipped classrooms currently are having their biggest impact on STEM subjects. In part that is because teachers of subjects in the humanities, such as philosophy, literature, and history, have been using flipped classes for decades. Students read texts before class, then come together for classes in which the professor and students talk about different ways of interpreting the material.[18]

THE CASE FOR ACTIVE LEARNING

Flipped classes may not be to every instructor's taste. Some professors enjoy lecturing and argue that it is the only way they know how to cover the material. However, as Weimer writes, "Study after study, not just in the STEM fields, but pretty much across the board, have reported findings that favor active learning approaches over lectures."[19]

A professor may successfully "cover the material" by lecturing, but that success is of little consequence if students are not learning. There will be times, even in fully flipped classrooms, when it makes sense for an instructor to lecture. Based on the evidence, though, there should be fewer lectures and more discussion-based classes founded on active learning.

Making students more engaged and more responsible for their own learning means that students are likely to learn more. Because they understand the content more deeply (having worked with it and made it meaningful to them), they will remember it longer. And if students enjoy the learning process more (because, for example, they experience the frisson of mastering a new concept), they are more likely to want to continue learning.

All those reasons support the view that lectures should be replaced to a large degree by active learning and discussion-based classes. We need, as Weimer says, "to move away from instruction devoted to teacher-transmitted content and teacher-directed learning and toward student-centered teaching."[20]

Most students learn best when they are reacting to lectures with questions and comments, participating in class discussions, and performing active learning exercises. Professor and psychologist Dr. Angela McGlynn writes, "The more students are active learners—that is, the more involved they are in the learning process—the more they'll learn and remember."[21]

In his 2016 book *Excellent Sheep*, essayist and critic William Deresiewicz writes,

> I myself became a decent teacher only when I started to relinquish some control over the classroom—stopped worrying so much about "getting my points across" and recognized that those moments of disorder that would sometimes occur, those spontaneous outbreaks of intelligence, were the most interesting parts of the class, for both my students and myself. We were going somewhere new, and we were going there together.[22]

We now have overwhelming evidence that effective pedagogy involves active students interacting with their professor and fellow students, solving problems, debating different viewpoints, asking questions, testing ideas, collaborating with each other, analyzing issues, creating a product, evaluating evidence, or generating hypotheses.

This requires a dramatic shift in focus from what the teacher says to what the student is doing.

Teacher and students together, not just the teacher alone, are creating a climate of learning, inquiry, curiosity, engagement, and enthusiasm.

When students engage in active learning in class, instead of passive listening, they begin to see the classroom as a place of excitement and discovery. This will help them become lifelong learners.

CHARACTERISTICS OF ACTIVE LEARNING

Active learning helps to make teaching more learning-focused and student-centered (instead of being focused on the teacher). Here are nine questions to ask yourself when assessing how much active learning is happening in your class.[23]

1. Do students discover things for themselves, or does the instructor tell them what they should know?

2. Do students learn from each other, or only from the instructor?

3. Do students have some say in how the class is designed and conducted?

4. Are students encouraged to collaborate rather than compete?

5. Are students encouraged to think about their learning rather than their grades?

6. Are students actively engaged, enthusiastic, and participating in the discussions, or are they mainly passive?

7. Do the students talk more than the professor?

8. When students make mistakes, is it treated as a learning opportunity?

9. Is the class helping the students ultimately to become autonomous, independent, self-directed learners?

The most important characteristic of the flipped class is its emphasis on students being actively involved in their own learning and actively participating in class. Even if an instructor lectures—and lectures can readily be broken into segments to allow for questions, discussion, quizzes, and interactive exercises—the key is to make the class focus more on students learning and less on the professor talking.

THINK-PAIR-SHARE

One of the best ways to encourage class discussion is to pose a question and then ask students to write freely on the topic, in silence, jotting down their ideas and notes to help them organize and formulate their thoughts.

After two or three minutes of brainstorming on their own, ask them to form pairs (I usually add "with someone in the class you don't know very well," to encourage everyone to get to know each other) and ask the pairs to discuss their thoughts about the posed question.

Allow those conversations to last about two or three minutes (the class will be gloriously energized and cacophonous for that period) and then bring the class back to order for a plenary session. Don't wait for hands to go up, but call on students by name, so that the extroverts don't dominate the discussion. It is essential at this point in the process to give students time to respond. A period of silence and time for thinking is perfectly fine. Accept the silence with equanimity and even encourage it.[24]

This system, which has been used by teachers for decades, is called "think-pair-share." History professor Kevin Gannon writes, "What I like about this technique is that students tend to provide deeper and more analytic answers having had the time to think and write before being asked to share. . . . This is a fairly simple technique that brings much larger results, in the form of richer and more sustained discussions with a wider range of participants."[25]

NONTRADITIONAL LECTURES

Lectures do not have to follow the traditional model—and the most effective lectures break this mold. Here are fourteen ways to make them more learning oriented, and help students stay focused and attentive, and to link what's covered in lectures to what they already know[26]:

1. Arrive five minutes early and talk with students as they enter the room, especially those who are reluctant to talk in class, so as to show them that you are approachable, encouraging, and not intimidating.

2. Start class by asking a student to summarize the main points from the last class. This practice provides continuity, helps students who were absent to catch up, and allows students to become more comfortable with oral communication. During the first class, let the students know about these oral summaries, so they can come to class prepared.

3. Before starting a lecture, ask the class to write for one minute on "what I want to get out of this lecture." This helps to activate their working memory and remind them of relevant prior knowledge.

4. Then capture their attention by telling them a poignant story, a shocking statistic, or something that will amaze them, and connect it to the content you're teaching.

5. Instead of giving, say, a one-hour continuous lecture, divide the presentation into perhaps four parts. Stop after each part for a short period of questions, discussion, or writing. I often ask my students to stand up and stretch.

6. At these breaks, give a summary of what you have said so far to help students organize their notes.

7. Also at these breaks, pose a provocative question, such as, "What's the most controversial statement you've heard me say so far?"

8. Take the opportunity at these breaks to check how well students are understanding your lecture. Don't do this by asking if anyone has any questions; if you get no questions you may misinterpret the silence as an indication that the students understand the lecture. A better approach is first to ask students to write down a question or two, and pair up with a student sitting next to them to compare ideas. Then ask the class for questions.

9. Ask the students to respond to questions using clickers. (For example, project four statements on a screen and ask them to select the most important one or the most erroneous one.)

10. In the lecture give examples that are vivid and compelling and that link directly to students' interests. Ask the students for examples of how they might apply what they are hearing in the lecture to their own experiences and their own lives.

11. During the lecture, sporadically call on individual students by name to answer questions without first asking for volunteers. This is the traditional law school model, and I recommend it because it keeps the whole class awake and alert. Never go for more than three or four minutes without getting a student to speak or respond in some way. Never let students get overly comfortable. You want them to be on their toes, knowing that you might call on them at any time to answer a question. Be kind and encouraging but be a benevolent dictator. Create productive tension in the class.

12. Design your lecture to build suspense toward resolution of a conflict, or find the answer to a mystery, conundrum, or enigma posed at the start. Throughout the lecture, the students will (ideally) pay rapt attention, trying to work out what the resolution will be.

13. At some point in the lecture, move to the back of the room and talk from there, so that all the students who are trying to hide in the back row are now in the "front row" and suddenly conspicuous. That movement creates a sense of dynamism, energy, and enthusiasm.

14. At the end of the lecture, or at the end of each part of it, ask a student to summarize what you have said, in coordination with point 6 above. This is often called a "minute paper." Or give the students five minutes to write a summary of the main points in the lecture without looking at their notes.

MORE EXERCISES IN ACTIVE LEARNING

Here are more ways to promote active learning[27]:

1. Hold small group discussions (groups of two to four students), with a specific focus, such as analyzing an issue or a problem raised in the lecture.

2. Use case studies (real-world examples from your discipline) to help students analyze and apply information.

3. Use journals to give students an opportunity to observe their own ongoing learning and reflect on gaps in their learning.

4. Use video clips, TED talks, and short documentaries to stimulate class discussion.

5. Experiment with role play, in which students take on specific roles or perspectives to problem solve and think critically.

6. Ask students to do post-exam analyses, often called "exam wrappers," in which they analyze the results of a graded exam to discover "their individual patterns of mistakes and areas for improvement."[28]

7. Ask students to give oral presentations.

8. Set up debates between student teams to challenge students to present opinions different from their own.

My American University colleague Professor Elizabeth Cohn at the School of International Service uses the following active learning exercises in her classes[29]:

1. Brainstorming
   The purpose of brainstorming is to elicit a lot of information in a short amount of time or to generate new ideas. Cohn says this technique is

quite effective and often overlooked in the classroom. The professor asks a question and tells the students that the class is going to brainstorm the answer. The professor writes all answers on the blackboard—regardless of whether they are good or correct. Students are not allowed to criticize what anyone else says, though their answers can contradict other answers. Once a thorough list of answers is on the board, the professor works with the information, choosing an approach that supports the intended learning outcome. If the goal is to elicit facts, any answers that are incorrect are crossed off—following an explanation of why it is wrong. If the goal is to teach conceptualization or theorizing, students are asked to group the answers in categories of theories (usually no more than five). If the goal is to teach analysis, the students are asked to prioritize the answers and explain why some are more significant than others.

2. Quick write or free writing
   This exercise to quickly jot down key points aims to stimulate thinking, generate ideas, and provide time for students to collect their thoughts before speaking in class. As indicated earlier when discussing the "think-pair-share" technique, allowing time to think and prepare leads to better student comments in class discussions.

3. Pause2Reflect (P2R)
   P2R is a technique that provides time for students to think about lecture material or discussion comments. Either the professor or a student can request a P2R to give students four or five minutes to write in their notebooks or laptops. Students are not asked to share their thoughts, as they are with a quick write.

4. One-minute lecture
   At the end of class, the professor gives students ten minutes to prepare a one-minute lecture. Doing so helps them analyze and reinforce the most important points of the lecture, which in turn helps them to remember more of it. The professor reviews the lectures and might ask the authors of one or two of the best ones to present to the whole class at the next class or later.

5. Draw it
   Students take a few minutes to make drawings to "map out" the information that has been covered. The exercise calls upon them to think visually about a concept, by identifying actors, relationships, and processes without using words. Cohn says it enables all students, especially visual learners, to analyze and better understand complicated ideas.

Dr. Stephen Brookfield suggests "the appreciative pause."[30] He says one of the least practiced behaviors in discussions is "to show appreciation for how someone has contributed to our learning." Near the end of a discussion, the professor calls for a pause of a minute or so and the floor is open for anyone to acknowledge another student (*not* the professor) for helping advance the learning in the class. For example, a student might express appreciation for a comment that clarified the relationship between two ideas.

I also like to let my students take more control of their own learning by allowing them to counter-offer when I give a homework assignment. For many assignments, such as those that focus on learning important, specific content, this won't be appropriate. But where it is, I allow a student to say, "Instead of homework assignment X, would it be possible for me to devote an equal amount of time, if not more, to assignment Y because this will be more helpful in my education or career?" On the syllabus/assignment sheet, I note with an asterisk which few assignments are open to such substitution.

I also recommend including a variety of writing assignments throughout the semester: informal and formal, in-class and out-of-class. These include: "thinking" pieces, interpretive essays, research papers, reports, and journals. Writing has a major role not only in student learning and engagement, but also in promoting critical thinking and intellectual curiosity. As English professor Christopher Sten at the George Washington University says, "Students not only learn to write, but they also write to learn." It's important to teach students how to write and make them do it often.

ANONYMOUS FEEDBACK

One of the most powerful ways to encourage students to take responsibility for their own learning is to find out how they see the class and then respond to their concerns. For years I have used frequent—every couple of weeks—anonymous surveys to try to get inside the heads of my students and see the class through their eyes. I believe that surveying them only at the halfway mark and end of the semester is not nearly enough to give students true agency over the class.

Professor Stephen Brookfield, author of *The Skillful Teacher*, argues that "the key to being a good college teacher is regularly collecting data from your students concerning how they are learning, week in week out, and then using that information to guide your decisions."[31] He says that teachers need a constant awareness of how students are experiencing their learning and perceiving the teacher's actions. Without this knowledge, our skills as teachers may be wasted or misfire.

Instructors must ask students frequently how the class is going for them—what they like and what is missing for them—and make the surveys anonymous so the feedback is honest and candid. If the surveys were not anonymous, worries about possible retribution and retaliation by the professor would color students' comments.

Here is my questionnaire. It was inspired by the questionnaire Stephen Brookfield uses.[32] I leave plenty of space after each question for students to write their comments.

ANONYMOUS CLASS FEEDBACK

Please leave your name off this survey. Don't feel you need to answer every question; leaving a space blank is fine. I'll share all the answers with the entire class. Your answers will help me make the class more responsive to your concerns. Thanks for taking the time to do this.

1. When do you feel most engaged with what is happening in class?

2. When do you feel most distanced from what is happening in class?

3. What do I do as the teacher that you find most affirming or helpful?

4. What do I do as the teacher that you find puzzling or confusing?

5. Do you have any other feedback that would help me make the class best meet your needs?

The students fill out the survey, and I then ask one of them to collect them all to ensure anonymity.

I type out all the answers and send a copy of all the answers to the whole class. I'm careful not to leave out any comments, however wounding. Transparency at this point is very important to building trust.

In the next class, I go over the comments, particularly focusing on the negative ones. I report to the class on what I learned from the feedback and the changes I intend to make as a result. I make it clear that I welcome candid and constructive feedback from students and I make sure vigorously to implement the changes I promise to make.

It is essential to address the results of the survey openly and honestly. Occasionally I tell the students that I disagree with a suggestion and am going to ignore it (e.g., if they ask for easier quizzes or less homework.) But invariably students make comments that cause me to change and improve how I teach.

I find this process very helpful. It gives me consistent awareness of how my students are experiencing their learning and perceiving my teaching. It helps me find out what is really going on inside their heads and hearts. If contentious issues arise in the feedback, we talk about them in class in a way that makes everyone feel heard and respected.

The main benefit of this frequent feedback is that it gives students more input into their learning, and it helps me to detect very early any serious problems that need to be addressed before they get out of hand.

I writhe with angst when I read the negative and critical feedback and see all the things that are going wrong and all the mistakes I am making (e.g., "You talk too fast and I can't understand you"; "You rush too much and I hate it when you rush"; "You don't explain the assignments clearly and I get confused"; "You give us too much busy work and I'm not learning enough about topic X"; and "Your grading seems arbitrary and inconsistent"). But the feedback ultimately helps me be a better teacher and helps my students become better learners.

Working through these evaluations also provides a chance for me to model constructive ways of dealing with stinging feedback without getting defensive and upset. It is an opportunity to show that the course matters more to me—that the students matter more to me—than any temporary discomfort I might feel.

This exercise empowers my students and sends the message that I care about how they are doing in the course, and that I am open to making changes for their benefit. Students feel they have a direct impact on shaping the class and their learning. They become more active learners.

Chapter 8

Support and Encourage Quiet Students

You will either step forward into growth or you will step back into safety.

—Abraham Maslow, psychologist

The last chapter made the case for making classes as interactive as possible. It discussed the importance of transforming students from passive observers to active players—getting them to ask questions, take quizzes, work in twos or threes on analyzing issues, and so on. Students learn more and retain more when they are actively involved.

But what about quiet students who resist, even resent, active learning? Many of these students would rather sit unnoticed listening to a lecture than endure a class with active learning. In fact, at first blush it is easy to confuse a quiet student with an unmotivated student.

This chapter probes why and how to draw out quiet students. And as part of the solution, it describes how to deal with students who are the opposite of quiet—the loud, vociferous, extroverts who, if not checked, can absorb all the energy in the room and sideline other students. When self-confident and loquacious students dominate the classroom conversation (perhaps permitted to do so because the teacher is so grateful to have a vigorous discussion), quiet students may sink even further into obscurity and silence. This is not acceptable. Gregariousness should not bestow an unfair advantage on a student in terms of learning.

THE RESPONSIBILITY TO HELP QUIET STUDENTS

I believe professors have a moral responsibility to protect the soft-spoken and encourage shy and diffident students to speak and be heard. It isn't just a nice thing to have a hitherto quiet student talk occasionally. Rather, teachers have an ethical obligation to think about the quiet students—the ones who are forced to listen to their talkative peers—and find ways to give them space to learn and participate, not be excluded or marginalized.

Professors fail to do their job if they ignore quiet students and assume that students who appear quiescent and subdued are happy, self-sufficient, and content being left to their own devices.

Many quiet students deep down *want* to be encouraged by their teachers to participate in class. They *want* to have their voices heard. If a professor allows them to get away with *not* participating, they may feel, at some gut level, let down.

Most students know they benefit from working in groups and participating actively in class. Some of them will even say, as one did to me, "Please help me participate more in class. Don't let me get away with being a quiet dormouse. I want to learn how to speak up." Reserved and quiet students know that being able to speak up confidently and cogently will help them as they continue their educational and professional lives.

WHY STUDENTS ARE QUIET

Students who don't participate in class discussions and who resist speaking up in class may not simply be introverts. Dr. Todd Zakrajsek, who teaches in the Department of Family Medicine at the University of North Carolina at Chapel Hill, says there are many reasons a student might be reluctant to participate in class discussions, including the following[1]:

- **Fear of failure**
  Some students don't want to be seen making a mistake in public and would rather stay silent than take the risk.

- **Lack of interest**
  It's possible that some students are not interested in the subject matter and have no desire to think about it, let alone talk about it in class.

- **Lack of information and knowledge**

Students may not speak up because they believe that they are ignorant and have nothing of value to contribute. They also may keep quiet if they haven't done the homework and don't fully understand the question posed.

- **Unconscious bias by the professor**
  Without intending to do so, teachers may project cues that make some students feel disrespected and marginalized. These students are disincentivized from participating. Often the students are people of color, international students, women, or members of some other group that does not feel fully accepted.

- **Cultural differences**
  Some students (e.g., Asian women) come from cultures where it is considered socially unacceptable for them to challenge the authority of a teacher, to contradict someone else in public, or to appear contentious and argumentative. They may well have been taught that to be meek, humble, and silent in class is the only proper way to behave. Karin Fischer, a senior reporter at *The Chronicle of Higher Education*, writes, "American educational culture emphasizes critical thinking, drawing conclusions, and classroom participation. Those may be foreign concepts to students schooled in systems that stress rote memorization and esteem for one's teachers."[2]

- **English proficiency issues**
  Students for whom English is a second language may be self-conscious about the way they speak—their accent, for example, or their limited command of English.

- **Shyness**
  If students are shy and uncomfortable around other people, speaking to others can be vexing and difficult. Shy people often feel awkward, withdrawn, self-conscious, and easily embarrassed around others. They fear being judged and are highly sensitive.

- **Introversion**
  Yes, some students prefer to do things alone or with a small group they know well. They are not necessarily shy; they may interact very capably with others and have good social skills. But they find social interaction exhausting. Introverts prefer working alone and usually choose to think through and plan carefully what they want to say before opening their mouths and talking. In contrast, extroverts are energized by social

interaction and talk freely because they seemingly enjoy finding out what is going to come out of their mouths next.

It is obvious that students in each of the above groups have learned for different reasons that there is safety in not speaking. Different approaches are needed to encourage them to participate in class.

TEMPERAMENT IS NOT THE ISSUE

The goal of professors is for students to be outstanding learners. The temperament of students—whether extroverted or the opposite—should be irrelevant. Dr. Maryellen Weimer argues that good learners have the following characteristics,[3] none of which are tied to temperament.

- Good learners are curious and love to learn new content;

- Good learners pursue understanding diligently and persistently, and don't give up easily;

- Good learners recognize that learning isn't always fun and sometimes can be boring, tedious, and tiring;

- Good learners don't want to fail but know that failure is part of the process of learning. They accept setbacks and struggles with equanimity;

- Good learners make new knowledge fit with what they already know, expanding their understanding;

- Good learners never run out of questions and are never satisfied with what they already know; and

- Good learners share what they've learned and look for opportunities to teach others what they have learned.

PROFESSORS SHOULD BE DISRUPTIVE

I don't agree with teachers who say that their job is to respect their students' temperament and not make the students feel uncomfortable, whether they are extroverts or introverts (I'll use this term to identify quiet students, whatever their reason for being quiet). Introverted students need encouragement from their teachers to speak out, and extroverts need to be told to give other students a chance to talk. Both of these changes will cause discomfort for the affected students. It's worth it. As I wrote earlier, professors must be benevolent dictators and ensure inclusivity and equity in the class.

Instructors have the responsibility to give every student a chance to participate, and to make the classroom inclusive. Quiet students must be given the opportunity to get involved in class discussions. Extroverts will benefit as well, by hearing the ideas of their classmates.

One way for professors to do this is to intentionally disrupt the usual pattern of the most extroverted students, the ones who tend to dominate class discussions. Both this chapter and the last chapter describe plenty of ways to interrupt the process, thereby leveling the playing field and making participation more balanced.

Disruption should happen early and as often as required. Why early? Because the longer a student remains silent, the harder it is to bring him into the discussion. The sooner the habit of silence is broken, the better.

WHY GET QUIET STUDENTS TO TALK?

Teachers may ask, "Is this really such a big deal? Aren't quiet students small in number? Are quiet students really something faculty need to worry about?"

In my experience, it *is* a big deal. Large numbers of students characterize themselves in a classroom setting as quiet, reserved, intimidated, self-conscious, shy, introverted, or experiencing something in their lives that leads them to shun talking in class. Nicki Monahan, a facilitator in faculty development at George Brown College in Toronto, Canada, says, "In every classroom there are a significant proportion of students who would identify themselves as introverts."[4]

The introverts may be voluble and exuberant with their friends, but in class they clam up and go quiet, preferring to listen and observe rather than participate.

Author Susan Cain, an expert on introverts, writes, "It's not always the biggest talkers who have the best ideas,"[5] and Dr. Maryellen Weimer points to five other reasons it is important to get quiet students to talk.[6]

1. Students learn content when they talk about it; attempting to teach something to someone else is a good way to learn it and an effective way to make the material meaningful.

2. Talking lets students learn from each other: it can be easier for students to learn from each other than from the professor. As discussed in the last

chapter, it is sometimes easier to explain something you've just learned. Instructors can forget how challenging the content can be because they learned it so long ago.

3. Talking gives students the opportunity to practice using the language of the discipline. Invariably the jargon is extensive and the best way to learn the new vocabulary is to use it in conversation.

4. Talking connects students with the content. When a student talks to another student about the content, it is the first real step to working in this new field and can give the student a sense of ownership.

5. Talking connects students with each other. Students get to know each other, and research by educational researchers Chambliss and Takacs[7] shows how important this is.

WAYS TO HELP QUIET STUDENTS

The first step is to establish expectations for students. I recommend making it clear to the class at the start of the semester that you expect them to ask questions and to participate actively in their own learning. I state in my syllabus that I expect them to come to class prepared to contribute their insights and knowledge, and that we will all learn from each other. I tell them that participation in class will raise their grades. I emphasize that I expect them to participate in class discussions, and that these discussions are an opportunity for them to practice interpersonal skills crucial to their future success—listening, empathy, enthusiasm, emotional maturity, and consideration for other people's concerns.

Here are other ways to help quiet students:

1. At the start of the semester, allow quiet students the option of participating in class discussions by reading out loud something they have already written, instead of talking extemporaneously.

2. Some professors arrive before class and move the chairs into a circle or semicircle. This seating arrangement encourages participation and a sense of community.

3. I call on students constantly, so that everyone gets an opportunity to speak. I don't only call on those who raise their hands. This keeps all

students awake and on their toes. They know I might call on them at any time. They can't get too comfortable, inattentive, or lethargic.

4. I don't allow long-winded or loud students to dominate the class conversation. For example, I might say, "Thank you, Susan. I want to hear more from you, but first let me hear from others in the class who have not yet spoken. It is important that everyone be heard from."

5. Listen actively, to reinforce student participation. This is done by maintaining eye contact; paying full attention to the student speaking; and nodding, smiling, or otherwise acknowledging the student as he is talking so he knows you are paying attention and are fully committed to understanding what he is saying.

6. Look for ways to find something, however small, to compliment so that the student feels encouraged. In other words, give critical and incisive feedback but also look for ways to praise the student for at least one observation so that the student feels supported.

7. Use active listening; say back to the student what you think you've heard her say and ask if you've understood her.

8. Meet with quiet students during office hours to get to know them and discuss strategies to help them feel comfortable speaking up in class or actively participating in other ways. I had one shy student who hated to come to the front of the class to talk. At the same time, she was an excellent student and wanted to overcome her fear of public speaking. She and I worked out a plan that allowed her to present from her seat instead of coming to the front of the class the first few times. This helped her, and she made great progress talking in class.

9. All students, even the most extroverted, benefit from being given time to process the question posed by the professor, and then more time to decide how best to respond. History professor Kevin Gannon recommends mentally counting off "ten seconds after asking a question . . . to allow for students to think and respond. If the silence persists, then we can go back and rephrase or clarify the question, but it's essential for us to show our students that silence and time for thought are not only OK but encouraged."[8]

10. In fact, it's a mistake to pose a question and *not* give students time to think about it before answering. Posing a question and giving time for

students to ruminate in silence can especially encourage introverted students to participate because they can think about what they want to say before the discussion begins. I will sometimes open the discussion by saying to a quiet student, "Helen, you looked like you were thinking hard about this question. Any thoughts?"

11. Call on quiet students precisely because they do not enjoy talking to a large group. Part of a professor's responsibility is to encourage learning, and an important skill to learn is the ability to talk in public. It makes quiet students feel uncomfortable, but discomfort is often the price of learning.

12. I believe many quiet students are grateful for the opportunity to talk, because that is often an opportunity denied them by their garrulous classmates who normally seize all the discussion time for themselves. Once a quiet student has tasted the success and pleasure of talking in class, it usually becomes less exhausting and nerve-wracking for them to speak up in the future. The habits of silence and passivity slowly get eroded.

13. It may be worthwhile to share in advance with some quiet students a question you are going to pose in class, and even tell them you'll be calling on them in class to answer it. This way they can prepare their answer and be ready to participate.

14. A good way to help quiet students is to ask the class to work together in small groups to prepare a presentation or an analysis of some kind. This could be either in or out of class. Many students who feel intimidated by a class discussion are more at ease in relaxed, small group settings.[9]

15. Professor Leena Jayaswal, a photographer and filmmaker at American University, says that when a shy or introverted student writes a particularly good paper, she often mentions the student's name during class discussion. She says, "Well, Fred brought up a great point in his paper when he mentioned X. Fred, do you want to add more?" Jayaswal says this helps build confidence.

16. Professors need to go out of their way to show they value participation by students. One way to do this is later in the class or online to bring up something constructive a student said in class, as a way of showing you were listening and appreciated the comment.

17. Look for ways to point out the added value of a student's comments, for example, by referencing something the student said earlier and how her new comment adds a new dimension in some way.

18. Writing students' comments on the board is another way to show that you value the contributions made by students. Quiet students especially will appreciate this kind of recognition.

19. Dr. Stephen Brookfield recommends using social media to pose questions to the class, find out what they are thinking, and gauge how well they understand the material.[10] He says this democratizes the classroom because on social media "it is much harder for a small clique of students to dominate the discussion and dictate its direction."[11] He adds, "Nobody's voice is 'louder' on the screen. So those who don't usually get heard have as much chance of their contribution determining the direction of the class as anyone else."

20. Brookfield also points out that, for students who are introverts or who speak English as a second language, social media provides time to process and frame a response or question. They have time to think through how they want to express their thoughts.[12]

21. Focusing on student strengths is a potent approach for helping quiet students. Educational researchers Beverley Myatt and Lynne Kennette, both from Durham College in Oshawa, Ontario, make the case that professors tend to offer feedback that focuses on how students can improve. But Myatt and Kennette point out that "helping students to understand what they already do well is a powerful strategy for increasing engagement and decreasing negative emotions."[13] They suggest that instructors offer three genuinely positive comments for every constructive criticism.

22. Alternatively, Myatt and Kennette recommend that each student identify for the professor a strength (such as analytical skills or lucid exposition) that he thinks will help him in the course. The professor can then look for opportunities to reinforce that strength throughout the semester during discussions, when grading homework, and in meetings during office hours.

It is not that we are trying to change introverts into extroverts. Not at all. Rather, we are trying to give abundant learning opportunities to all students, regardless of temperament.

GRADE FOR ENGAGEMENT

If you grade for participation, make it clear to the class that you are not focused solely on recognizing students for speaking at length, looking intelligent, or making brilliant, off-the-cuff points. Rather you are looking for *engagement*—that is, more subtle and nuanced ways in which students can enrich class discussion. Such practices, which will be more appealing to the quieter members of the class, include:

• listening carefully and actively;

• responding to others;

• asking questions;

• showing appreciation to others for learning insights;

• building on comments made by others;

• pointing out similarities and difference in observations made by others;   ·

• synthesizing and summarizing comments from others to assure that they are understood;

• asking for clarification;

• pointing out a new resource, such as an article, book, or website;

• posting a useful comment on the class chatroom or an online class forum;

• requesting a minute of silence so that everyone can slow down and absorb what is being discussed; and

• writing thoughtful journal entries that are shared with the class.

In short, engagement is the key, rather than participation. Not all engagement involves talking in class.

* * * * *

The most fundamental step that professors can take to help quiet students is to create a learning climate where students feel inspired to take risks and to share in learning.

Constructive class participation happens when the professor creates an environment of trust and belonging in the class—a sense of community. Students will participate in discussions if they feel they belong to the class and that they have friends there. They want to feel safe, respected, and cared for, and that it is okay for them to make mistakes and learn from that process. The atmosphere must feel inclusive and trusting so students feel their views are heard and valued.

There is one word in the last paragraph that perhaps should be challenged, and that is the word *safe*. Yes, we want our students, especially the quiet ones, to feel safe in some sense, but let's deconstruct that word a little.

If feeling safe means never feeling uncomfortable when wrestling to understand new concepts and ideas, never feeling stretched and challenged to do new things (such as talking in class), and never feeling the need to question assumptions and existing mental models, then safe is not what we want for students. That kind of safety leads to complacency, mediocre standards, and even smugness.

We want students to feel safe in the sense of being treated with civility and respect. They may not—and should not—always feel safe as in free of stress and challenges. It is impossible to learn without experiencing some healthy stress arising from being challenged to grow in new ways.

Learning isn't always safe and comfortable, nor should it be. Students must take risks, and that includes quiet students being courageous and pushing themselves to be vocal and active participants in class, with the help of a caring and enthusiastic professor.

For a student who is prone to being quiet, it takes grit and fortitude to speak in public. That display of character should be recognized and lauded overtly by the instructor in one-on-one meetings with the student during office hours.

To repeat, the best foundation to bring about discussion in class by not only vocal students, but also reticent, shy, or taciturn students is for the professor to do everything in her power to produce a learning environment that brims with trust. Students need to know that their ideas, opinions, and suggestions are important and welcome and will be taken seriously and considered with respect.

Students in this high-trust atmosphere know they will be listened to, responded to, and never disrespected, mocked, or belittled. In such an environment, all students get the message loud and clear that they are important and highly prized members of a hardworking and bonded community of learners.

If professors are understanding, creative, flexible, caring, and accommodating, quiet students can thrive and blossom in class.

Chapter 9

Make Large, Lecture-Based Classes Feel Smaller

A teacher who is attempting to teach without inspiring the pupil with a desire to learn is hammering on cold iron.

—Horace Mann, educator and politician

Lectures are usually the primary teaching strategy for large classes. However, learning in such a setting presents many challenges. One is that the lecture hall can seem to students to be quite impersonal and even unwelcoming. It is almost impossible for the instructor to get to know all the students and learn their names.

Nor is the environment conducive to discussions. Even vocal, assertive, and self-confident students may hesitate to respond in a large class when the professor poses a question and waits for a response.

In teaching a large class, it is not easy to get everyone to pay attention and learn. Even if the lecture is engaging, at the back of the room a significant number of students inevitably will be texting, scrolling through Twitter, checking Instagram, shopping online, or dozing off. They are checked out and not paying full attention to the instructor.

Even for students who are conscientiously paying attention, large classes can be difficult because the experience often is passive; they don't have any opportunity to measure their understanding of the material. At the same time, it is hard for professors to know how students are doing and if they are grasping key concepts and ideas.

What can instructors of large classes do to stop students from feeling like nameless numbers that no one cares about? How can the students be helped to feel connected and have a sense of belonging? The key is to enable them to be more active, thus making large classes *feel* smaller.[1]

101

THE CHALLENGES OF TEACHING A LARGE CLASS

In sum, the challenges of teaching a large class include

1. getting the students to attend, arrive on time, pay attention, participate in class, feel enthusiastic, stay throughout the class, and do the homework;

2. diminution of faculty/student interaction and the lack of contact between instructors and students;

3. the likelihood that students will be unable to get to know each other well[2];

4. the lack of discussion and of active learning opportunities;

5. the increased level of passiveness by students;

6. managing all the paperwork, including collecting and handing out tests, quizzes, and other assignments[3]; and

7. The difficulty on the part of professors to assess whether students understand the principles and concepts being taught.[4]

DISCUSSION-BASED LEARNING

There are many ways to transform a lecture into an active learning experience for students. Professors should start by making it clear at the beginning of the semester that students are expected to ask questions and to interact with each other and with the instructor during class.

Professors Rosealie Lynch and Eric Pappas teach a three-hundred-student general education critical thinking course at James Madison University. They have opted to ground their large classes in human connection and informality.[5] Large- and small-group discussions occupy a central role in their course as an important means of facilitating development of critical thinking skills. This means that they do not need to use learning management systems like Blackboard or Canvas or other platforms to facilitate discussion.

Lynch and Pappas don't suggest that instruction in a large class can equal the effectiveness of a smaller class, but they do claim that their group discussion techniques preserve many of the characteristics enjoyed by students and faculty alike in smaller classes. Those characteristics include increased familiarity among students, greater accessibility to the professor, more frequent in-class dialogue, personalized feedback, critical thinking and writing skills development opportunities, and small-group work.[6]

One discussion-based technique that can work well in a large class is inspired by the "think-pair-share" approach discussed in chapter 7: working from the individual student outward. Discussion develops organically in small groups and is not expected to bloom as soon as the professor poses a question to the entire class.[7]

The first step is for the professor to pose a question and put it on the screen or board so that students can refer to it. He asks all the students to reflect on the question in silence for a couple of minutes and write down their answer. Then the students work in pairs to share their thoughts with a partner and select a response that represents both students (or synthesize one from the responses of both students).

As history professor Kevin Gannon says, now "students . . . are explaining and defending their ideas to others, which leverages some of the learning potential that we know can emerge" from students teaching each other.[8]

In the next step, each pair of students joins with another pair and repeats the process. After those four students have discussed and defended their answers to the question, the group must select a response that speaks for all four. They also select a spokesperson to represent the group and present their thoughts to the entire class.

Gannon writes, "The process by which students explain and defend their position to peers contains all sorts of cognitive benefits, including deeper understanding and better retention of the material." He adds that using this technique can "create a class that hums with conversation rather than drones with lectured monologue."[9]

The inclusion of "think" time and the initial opportunity to talk about a response with a single peer alleviates the stress many students feel about responding to a question from the professor.

This technique may not be easy if the room has theater-style seating, because that setup makes formation of small groups difficult. But it is still possible. Students sitting next to each other can form discussion pairs, for example, and students in one row can engage with those in the row in front of them.

MORE STRATEGIES FOR ACTIVE LEARNING

Active learning does not depend exclusively on student interaction. Here are other techniques an instructor can use to promote dynamic learning in large classes:

1. Start the first class on time, introduce yourself, and tell the students something interesting about yourself, such as your research interests and what drew you to the subject in the first place.

2. Describe your teaching style, how you like to be treated, and how you want the students to behave. For example, tell them what to call you, whether you mind being interrupted for questions, how often you want discussions, and how you like to conduct discussions.

3. Introduce students to each other to make them feel more comfortable and at home. They will more likely contribute to discussions, request help, admit confusion, and learn from other fellow students if they know each other.

4. Send students an outline of what the class will cover. This tells them what to expect, so they can think over what they already know about the topic and remind themselves of their existing knowledge. Leave blank spaces where they can fill in material provided in class lectures. Students are able to use the outline as a guide for taking notes, but not as a substitute for attending class.

5. Before beginning a lecture, describe to students how the session will be organized. A brief outline posted on the board or screen at the beginning of class will help students get organized and geared up for what is coming.

6. Stop every ten minutes or so and pose engaging questions to the students, especially questions that require higher-level thinking skills. Encourage students to think about their answer for a minute or so, and then call on specific students to respond to them. Asking questions and giving quizzes gives students practice in remembering the material.

7. Ask students to work in pairs or small groups to answer some questions posed in class. (This can be handled as think-pair-share or not.) While the student discussions are going on, the professor and teaching assistants circulate through the room to help.

8. Promote real-world applications of whatever you are teaching, so students can see that the content has relevance to society and to their possible future careers.

9. At the end of the lecture, ask students to take out a sheet of paper and compose a "one-minute paper" summarizing the key concepts and main points covered. The professor may choose to collect the papers and review them to assess whether students understand the material.

10. Ask the students to write a short paragraph on a topic they are finding difficult to understand. This is sometimes called a "muddiest point paper."[10] Collect the papers to see if there is wide agreement on what students are finding most baffling and confusing. Share the results with the class and describe how you will respond to the problems identified.

11. At the end of each class, summarize the important points that were covered in the lecture and give students some idea of what you'll be covering in the next class.[11]

When students are engaged in class through the use of teaching techniques such as these, they tend to learn more. The key is to get students directly and actively involved, instead of allowing them to be inert, inactive, and anonymous.

INTERACTION VIA TECHNOLOGY

Hand-held clickers or smart phones with such apps as SurveyMonkey allow students to vote in class. For example, the professor might put several statements on the screen and give students a few seconds to vote for the one they think is invalid.

Questions that can be presented in multiple-choice format are well suited to clickers. Students are asked to select a response, and the results can be displayed in real time. This has the benefit of coaxing widespread student participation in the intellectual process of thinking about the multiple-choice question.

What matters here pedagogically is not the vote but the discussion that follows. The vote (via the clicker) is a way of provoking student engagement with the content by asking them to make their best choice from several options. The discussion reveals the critical thinking, the evidence, and the arguments, and explores why students made the choices they did.[12]

Clickers can be used to gather individual responses from students or to gather anonymous feedback. When every student in a large class is given a clicker, the professor gains class-wide student involvement and feedback, and a quizzing tool.

Other effective uses of technology include setting up a class newsgroup or an electronic mail list, so everyone can easily communicate with each other, and creating a course website that contains practice problems, answers to sample exam questions, a glossary of terms, and other items helpful to students. Twitter or text-message-based feedback and online quizzes also encourage student engagement when classes are large.

LECTURES THAT COMMAND ATTENTION

Instructors must speak compellingly whatever the size of the class, but it becomes particularly important when the class is large.

We've all suffered through talks by middling lecturers who speak in a monotone, read their notes and slides out loud, repeat what was in the reading, don't stop for questions or exercises, have little rapport with the students, use no eye contact, and speak in a confusing way. It is a draining, dispiriting experience for students to endure.

Here are some proven techniques for livening up a lecture:

1. Add variety by using video clips, music, animations, cartoons, demos, and the occasional guest speaker.

2. Make the class interesting, informative, fun, and relevant to students' lives. Tell stories to engage students, especially stories about your own experiences where you struggled and perhaps failed several times. This can help illuminate the ideas and concepts that you are teaching and help bring the learning to life for students.

3. Don't speak to the class when writing on the board and facing away from the class. That is not good for any class, but especially harmful in large classes, where it is so easy to lose connection with the students. And when you write on the board, write briefly, legibly, and not in cursive.

4. Don't get stuck behind a lectern. Walk around the room and up and down the aisles. This will make the class feel smaller and encourage student participation. Have as little as possible blocking the space between you and the students. Lead the discussions from different points in the room to give the students a feeling of being in the middle of the action rather than simply observers. Don't give the impression of speaking only to students in the front of the room or to a select group or population of students.

5. Smile when appropriate. Be conversational.

6. Know the material so well that you barely need to use notes and are therefore free to look at the students as much as possible. Eye contact is powerful.

7. Show your enthusiasm. Allow your love of teaching and your passion for the content to show clearly in your body language, gestures, movement, voice, and eyes.

CLOSING THE TEACHER-STUDENT GAP

It is challenging in a large class to have meaningful interactions between the professor and every student. This difficulty can impede student participation. Professors can do some things to bridge the teacher-student gap. Try these[13]:

1. Even though a large class has many students, learn their names as much as you can and use them as much as possible. Use name tents or name tags to help you.

2. Prior to class, contact several students and inform them that they will be called on to answer one or more questions. When class begins, select each of these students, in random order, to answer questions and lead the discussion.

3. Arrive early for class and stand by the door welcoming students and chatting informally with them.

4. Stay after class to talk with students and answer questions. Anything you can do to create rapport with the students in your class is beneficial and is likely to lead to more engagement.

5. While adhering to high academic standards, be kind, gentle, affirming, supportive, and patient. If students see you as intimidating, aloof, arrogant, harsh, or abrasive, they are more likely to disengage and stay distant.

6. Create a comfortable climate but be firm and don't let students run over you. It is better to start out being quite strict, formal, and hard-nosed, and then, as appropriate, ease off a little as the class unfolds.

7. Do everything you can to promote a high level of trust and respect in the room. Students are more likely to ask questions and talk willingly with

a classmate if they have trust that the professor and their peers won't embarrass or laugh at them.

8. Fear of peer judgment is powerful and can readily shut down students. Helping students get to know each other by having them work in pairs or small groups will build trust in both you and their classmates and will encourage students to participate more.

9. Don't allow any student to dominate a discussion and discourage quieter students from speaking up. Professors must protect shy and introverted students from being interrupted or marginalized by louder, more vocal students.

10. Set out a box by the door for feedback—questions, thoughts, suggestions, ideas, opinions, commentaries, critiques, and so on. Begin or end your lectures with items from the box. Encourage students to contribute. Show that you value their input.[14]

11. Encourage students to use your office hours. For large classes, it may be physically impossible to meet with every student individually. An alternative is to ask the students to meet with you in groups of four, six, or even eight. This helps students to get to know each other, and helps you get to know them. As a fallback, assign students to meet with a teaching assistant (if you are lucky enough to have one) or another faculty mentor.

The above actions taken by the instructor can help students feel more bonded with the professor and therefore more inclined to do the required reading, ask questions, and be actively engaged in the class.

OBTAINING FEEDBACK

We discussed in an earlier chapter how important it is to find out how students perceive the class. We talked about distributing an anonymous survey to students to obtain candid feedback, and the need to do this frequently instead of the usual one-time end-of-semester surveys.

Surveys are obviously more challenging to do with a large class, if only because reading all the responses becomes incredibly time-consuming. I recommend giving the anonymous survey to a different portion of the class (say, twenty students) each week. Reading the responses from twenty students is feasible and useful.

Another approach recommended by Dr. Stephen Brookfield is to ask all the students to complete the anonymous survey individually and then read their responses out to each other in small groups. Or the groups can take each question on the survey in turn, and any students who want to respond can speak up. One person in the group then summarizes the main comments on one form and hands it in. So in a class of two hundred with, say, groups of five, the instructor would receive forty surveys, a manageable number to read, assess, and respond to.[15]

Asking throughout the course for candid feedback empowers students by signaling that you want to listen to their concerns and to take them seriously during the semester, and not just at the end when it is too late to act on them. If you adjust your teaching because of feedback from the students, let the students know. They will appreciate having some influence over what is going on in the class.

* * * * *

Students learn more in large classes when they are actively learning and engaged. If they feel invisible and anonymous, there is a real danger that they will disengage.

If the professor tries conscientiously to give an inspiring, intellectually stimulating, and informative presentation, broken up with questions, silent time for thinking and reflection, group exercises, discussions, and time to work on problems, then students, even in large classes, are more likely to engage with the class and learn the content. The key is to require students to become active learners by incorporating a wide variety of activities into the class.

Chapter 10

Add Variety to Your Class

The essence of teaching is to make learning contagious, to have one idea spark another.

—Marva Collins, educator and activist

Effective instructors add variety to their classes to keep students alert and energized. That means professors must be not only knowledgeable, caring, and enthusiastic, but also a little unpredictable—not unpredictable as in mercurial or impulsive, but rather as in creative and fresh.

To be unpredictable, professors must constantly look for ways to introduce a multiplicity of teaching activities that are new (or at least interesting) to students, thus keeping them engaged.

Here are some ideas:

- stretching and moving

- games

- role-playing

- humor and improvisation

- mindfulness and contemplation

- lessons on success and fulfillment

- large-scale innovation

- "in the spotlight"

- guest speakers

- field trips

- networking

- showing relevant videos

STRETCHING AND MOVING

It's a good idea to take a stretch break every thirty minutes or so. Sitting for more than two hours (or even forty-five minutes) is too much for anyone, so once or twice during the class ask all your students to stand up and stretch for about a minute. This has the twofold benefit of breaking things up—creating a breather—and helping to keep their bodies and minds awake.

I will often continue teaching while the students are stretching, touching their toes, or rolling their necks and shoulders. Having students stand up and get out of their chairs even while the teaching continues revitalizes the whole room.

GAMES

Consider occasionally introducing a short game into the class. Games are a fun break from the intensity of class and can help build a sense of belonging and community. Such games, which last no more than a few minutes, help students to get to know each other, to remember each other's names, and to bond. They can also increase students' motivation and desire to learn, especially when they are related to the learning outcomes of the course, as they should be.

More specifically, games

- set a positive tone for the class;

- loosen things up and enable students to feel less tense;

- get students out of their chairs and stimulate them to become active;

- help the instructor seem more approachable;

- help students get to know each other and build relationships;

- give students something to talk and laugh about; and

- give students something to look forward to.

Stacey Beth-Mackowiak Ayotte, a professor of French at the University of Montevallo, asks, "Is there a place for games in the college classroom?" and answers with an emphatic yes. Ayotte writes, "It is not always easy to get each student to participate on a daily basis, but I've found that when I incorporate games into the classroom, new attitudes emerge and new personalities blossom."[1]

But she cautions that games are not just fun for the sake of fun. She says, "They should be designed to reinforce or review topics covered in class, they should be organized, and they should be used to add variety to our college classrooms."[2]

I start my first class each semester with a brief game involving beach balls. I bring to class five beach balls, and after briefly introducing myself I ask all the students to stand up. I then toss out the beach balls and ask them to keep the balls up in the air without allowing any of them to hit the ground.

Everyone plays, including me. Invariably laughter erupts in the class as the balls go flying everywhere and students chase them. After a minute or so I collect the balls and ask the students to go back to their seats.

I ask, "Why do you think we played that game?" Students tentatively call out their answers. They say such things as "to loosen us up," or "to help us bond," or "to help us relax," or "to encourage us to work together." "Yes," I respond, "all those are good answers." Then I add that the game is also a metaphor for the course on which they are embarking with me.

Each ball represents a key activity—showing up for class, doing the homework, coming prepared to participate, making presentations, passing the final exam, working hard, and so on. I tell them that they need to do all these things to succeed in the class. If they fail on any of these activities—if they allow a ball to hit the ground—they will not do well.

I tell them that the game is also a metaphor for their life at college. They need to keep in touch with their parents, learn all they can, manage their money, make and maintain friendships, eat healthily, keep fit, get good grades, and so on. All these "balls" must be kept up in the air and performed successfully.

Another game I play early in the semester is called the "circle game." This game is essentially a way for the students and the professor to get to know each other. The game also helps students see similarities and differences, so they can appreciate them more.

I have all the students stand in a circle, so they can see each other. Then I say, "When I read a category, if you identify with it and feel comfortable sharing, please step into the center of the circle until I read the next category. Some of the categories are fun and others are more serious. Our goal is to see what we share with others in the group and to appreciate those voices who are absent or outnumbered in the class. I'll join in, too."

Next I say, "Step into the circle if you . . ."

- are a grad student;

- were born outside the USA;

- feel uncomfortable with networking;

- enjoy speaking in public;

- often feel over-stressed;

- are an only child;

- love dark chocolate;

- are a parent;

- are a vegetarian;

- are fluent in a language other than English;

- are a twin;

- eat pizza more than once a week;

- plan a career in the [add the appropriate name of an industry or field];

- are an immigrant;

- are married;

- keep a daily journal;

- have a personal mission statement;

- serve or have served in the military;

- can do a handstand or cartwheel;

- live on campus;

- like to cook;

- worry about finding a job after you leave college;

- like to dance;

- worry about how well you'll do in this course.

The whole game is played with a lot of impromptu humor, but it has a serious purpose beyond everyone getting to know each other better. If certain groups are not represented in the class, how will their perspective be included in class discussions? Professor and psychologist Angela Provitera McGlynn suggests that the professor can also point out to the class that these categories, by themselves, limit our understanding of the identity of a person.[3]

A game that helps to address personal identity involves a student introducing another student's non-obvious trait. Students form pairs, and the instructor tasks them with learning one thing about their partner that is not obvious by looking at the person. Then, they briefly introduce their partners to the class.

Another game can be used to help students learn each other's names. The students form a circle, and the professor selects one to start the process. That student says, "My name is Bob Smith." The next student says, "My name is Susan Weinstein, and this is Bob Smith." The next student in the circle says, "My name is Emily Luang, this is Susan Weinstein, and this is Bob Smith."

This continues around the circle, with each successive student having to remember more and more names of their class mates. I usually end by taking the final turn and going around the circle of students pronouncing everyone's name from memory. The game is handled with levity and is viable only for small classes (say, under thirty students).

ROLE-PLAYING

Professor Richard Kenney Jr., who directs the Social Work Program at Chadron State College, uses role-playing as a learning activity, not only to add variety to his teaching but also to help students take more ownership of their education. Several times a semester, he invites professional social workers to his classes; the professionals role-play clients that his students may encounter in their careers as social workers.

He writes, "Role-plays may include clients experiencing addiction, domestic abuse, or mental health issues. Students assume the role of a social worker and, as a group, are responsible for assessing the problematic situation, determining client needs, and formulating action plans."[4]

These realistic role-plays are designed primarily to have students work together to solve problems. Students build on each other's questions and determine a plan of action to help each of the role-playing clients.

A similar method using actors called "standardized patients" has been part of medical school education for decades.

HUMOR AND IMPROVISATION

Humor is another good way to bring variety into the class. It is true that education is exceedingly important, but important issues don't have to be treated in a gloomy, somber, or cheerless way.[5]

Humor doesn't directly lead to learning—or at least, I've not been able to find any research showing it does. Nor does it suddenly make esoteric or difficult ideas easier to grasp and less unfathomable, complex, or nuanced. But humor does seem to help make a class more enjoyable, less tense, and more memorable. Those effects, in turn, seem to produce in students a greater willingness to work hard, to be more persistent in their efforts to learn, and perhaps even to retain more content. At least, this is how I see it. Humor improves the student *experience*.

Educational expert Dr. Maryellen Weimer is a strong advocate of using humor in the classroom. She writes, "Humor connects teachers and students. It creates that sense of community, how we're all in this together, how we all make stupid mistakes and need to laugh at our foibles. It keeps students interested and attentive. Some of us think it helps put students at ease— encouraging discussion and engaging exploration of topics and issues."[6]

Humor has a dark side. If an instructor starts believing that her performance skills are more important than what the students are learning, a line has been crossed. Weimer calls this "performance teaching."[7] The focus is on what the professor is doing rather than what the students are learning. Of course, humor that belittles or mocks students or others is obviously inappropriate and should be rigorously avoided.[8]

Humor can take many different forms. It doesn't have to be original or produce big guffaws. If a teacher wins a little smile, that is victory enough. Alissa Klein and Christian Moriarty are not comedians (they are academics at the University of South Florida and St. Petersburg College, respectively), but they use humor as a teaching tool. Their priority is teaching, not humor, but they argue that "the more difficult it is to engage students and the more important the concept, the greater the potential for comedy to be helpful."[9]

Professors can use original humor (and take advantage of low student expectations) or tap humorous material from other sources, such as short videos from YouTube, funny memes, or cartoons. Klein and Moriarty write, "When you make the class more fun, you make the content more memorable, and improve the student experience. Students are more positive about the class and more engaged, which aids in retention of information."[10]

Improvisation (improv) skills can be useful when a professor wants to add variety to the class. "Yes, and . . ." is the foundational building block of improv. Professor and improv comedian Beau Golwitzer argues that this technique can help with class discussions and brainstorming. In improv, when a performer is on stage with a scene partner, both actors do their utmost to support each other's choices in order to create a scene together. The "yes, and . . ." signifies that each performer builds on the partner's ideas rather than argues with them. Golwitzer says using this technique in class puts him in "an affirmative rather than combative mind-set."[11] An instructor draws from the students' ideas and builds on them rather than saying they are wrong.

Professors don't need to be standup comedians or improv artists, but the occasional joke or levity can help with information retention, as well as student stress alleviation, participation, and engagement.[12]

MINDFULNESS AND CONTEMPLATION

Mindful-based or contemplative education gets students to become more aware of their thoughts and feelings, lowers their stress, and encourages them to be fully present. The basic idea is that, in the silence, students are more open to learning.

One example of this way of adding variety to a class revolves around the notion of "beholding." According to Professor Andrew Reiner of Towson University, in a classroom setting, beholding is a mindfulness technique to help overwhelmed and overstimulated students to stop multitasking and silently focus on, for example, a graph, a painting, a formula, an equation, a photo, a word, a phrase, or a topic.[13]

Reiner reports that multiple studies at the University of Virginia found that students would rather accept an electric shock than sit quietly alone with their own thoughts for up to fifteen minutes.[14] Stillness and silence are often anathema to students, but they are essential to learning.

As with humor, there's been limited research on mindfulness in education, so the benefits of beholding are not yet fully evidence based. We should regard any claims of the pedagogical benefits of mindfulness with some skepticism. Yet common sense and intuition support, at least for me, being open to the real possibility that beholding and contemplation are helpful to students in their learning.

LESSONS ON SUCCESS AND FULFILLMENT

Another way to introduce variety into a class is to look for an opportunity to discuss how the course content fits into the question of what it means to lead a fulfilling and successful life.

I ask students to write personal mission statements describing the kind of life they want to lead, but there are many other ways to approach this topic. The basic goal is to get students to reflect on their lives, to discuss what really matters to them, to think about how to find purpose and meaning in their lives, to explore their life goals, and to think about their values.

For example, consider posing one of the following questions to students:

- What is the best way to use this course to shape the person you want to become, so you can contribute in a meaningful way to society and help other people?

- How can this course and its content bring more purpose and focus to your life?

- How does this course help you to build a vision for your life that is inspiring?

The essential idea is to step back from the immediate content of the course and give students a chance to think about what they are learning and how it might affect their ability to live a successful and honorable life.

It is important to teach students to periodically spend time quietly reflecting on the question of whether their lives are heading in the right direction. Teachers want students not only to learn the content they are teaching but also to see the class as a building block to becoming their best selves.[15]

LARGE-SCALE INNOVATION

Variety in class can take dramatic, large-scale form. This type of innovation is appropriate where the course would benefit from significant redesign incorporating major student involvement, or where the course has goals that are very different from those of a traditional class.

For example, an instructor could invite his students (usually grad students) to help design and teach the class. The syllabus becomes the starting point for the class, not the end point. The professor and students work together to build on the original syllabus and change it to make it stronger. They incorporate changes and additions from students that are designed to improve how the class is managed, the class schedule, what its learning objectives are, what the learning experience is like, and how the learning will be measured and assessed.[16]

The idea is to develop more student ownership and commitment to the class. The professor intentionally surrenders some control of the class, but in exchange has students who are excited by the opportunity to have some agency over their learning. Many professors will not be comfortable with this idea and will see it as self-abnegation or even irresponsible. It has, however, worked for me.

Another type of large-scale innovation is epitomized by a class my colleagues and I created at American University called "Producing Environmental Films for Public Television" (COMM-568). In this class, the professor essentially converts the class into a film production company, with all the challenges that come with producing a professional film in fifteen short weeks. The class creates the film for Maryland Public Television (MPT), one of the major PBS stations in the country. MPT and other PBS stations broadcast the thirty-minute student-produced film at prime time.

Filmmaking classes normally involve an instructor teaching the class about editing, cinematography, screenwriting, directing, and so on. In COMM-568, the students instantly become producers, writers, directors, shooters, researchers, editors, and social media producers—all as a part of "*568 Productions.*" The goal is to produce a thirty-minute film that meets strict public television editorial and broadcast standards. The instructor (Professor Mike English, who is also a top producer at MPT) is the film's executive producer, assigning its premise and storyline, and constantly channeling and adjusting class talent, effort, and direction.

Over the semester, the student filmmakers write, produce, shoot, and edit a topical documentary that investigates a timely conservation issue. In doing so, they gain invaluable hands-on experience and also a deep understanding of how difficult—but also how satisfying—it is to create a professionally produced film that offers insights into important environmental issues facing people today. In effect, students become players in the real world and make the class into an organization that does something useful.

Dr. James Lang describes another example of large-scale innovation not unlike COMM-568. It involves a class on microfinancing—providing small business loans to up-and-coming entrepreneurs in developing countries to help them start small, successful businesses.

Cary LeBlanc, a professor teaching a marketing class at Assumption College, decided that instead of running a traditional class, he would enlist his students to create a microfinancing program. In other words, LeBlanc's students would learn about microfinancing by creating and implementing a program. The class moved out of the narrow confines of the classroom and into a more public arena with a more public purpose.

Lang describes this as a "heady" prospect because the students would, with help from LeBlanc, launch a real-world microloan program and thus directly change "the lives of men, women, and children halfway round the world."[17] Lang says LeBlanc's class created an incredibly powerful learning experience for the students.

"IN THE SPOTLIGHT"

I recommend an activity that I call "in the spotlight" to inject variety into class. The instructor invites a student to come to the front of the class, and for a few minutes he interviews her about her life in a non-intimidating and friendly way. The dual purpose is to have the student practice oral communication and to have the class get to know the spotlighted student better.

Questions can be related to class material; an American history professor, for example, might ask, "Why didn't President Lincoln move faster to fire General George McClellan in the Civil War?" More general or student-oriented questions work as well. The professor might ask, "Can you tell us about a turning point in your life?" or "What would you like to be doing in five or ten years?" Other possible questions include:

1. Do you think of yourself as a creative person? In what ways?

2. If your house were burning down, what items would you save and why?

3. Who has been the most positive influence in your life?

4. What do you consider to be one of your biggest accomplishments in life?

5. What goal did you meet that you found particularly difficult to achieve?

6. What would your ideal professional life look like?

7. If you could do anything with your life, what job would you choose?

8. Who are your heroes?

Remind your students it is always their choice as to what to share and at what depth.

GUEST SPEAKERS

Inviting guest speakers to visit class is a wonderful way to add variety and to give students a deeper understanding of the content the teacher is helping them to learn. Guest speakers also give students a chance to meet successful professionals in the field and to learn vicariously from their experiences.

Guest experts can present new perspectives and fresh approaches. A guest could be a community leader, a scientist doing innovative work, the principal investigator for a research study, or anyone thinking creatively in the course discipline. Students get a chance to learn about the guests' professional lives and how the guests conduct their work or research.

If getting guest speakers to visit class in person is too difficult for whatever reason, then Skype, Zoom, FaceTime, Google Hangouts, and other online tools can help.

Professor Gillian Parrish teaches poetry and composition at Washington University in St. Louis and uses Skype for live interviews with book authors for her creative writing courses. She does this to shrink the distance between "the students and the authors by pulling back the wizard's curtain between the exalted 'author' and the ordinary person who did the everyday work of writing."[18] Another purpose for Parrish is to "provide students with an opportunity to vicariously experience the writing process at the level of an expert."[19] Through these conversations, students learn that true experts are students themselves and constantly learning.

I find that interviewing guest speakers in front of the class works well, with questions coming from both the instructor and the students. It keeps the conversation more informal, requires less preparation time for the guest, and keeps the focus on the learning outcomes for the class and on the issues and concerns most important to the professor and students. In other words, conducting an interview with a guest speaker helps the experience to be more student centered.

Guest speakers may come with some negatives. They may repeat content students already know, talk too long, talk over the heads of the students or at an inappropriate introductory level, or deliver information that is disconnected from the course's learning outcomes.

The professor might speak with a guest before the class event to assure that the speaker's contribution is useful and productive, that it advances the learning outcomes, and that it is aligned with the class material. Professor Randy Laist, a professor of English at Goodwin College, recommends that the teacher encourage the guest expert to tailor her remarks "toward specific learning goals that the students are actively pursuing."[20]

He also recommends not asking a guest to stay for the entire class period; it is valuable to have time before the presentation for the students to prepare questions, and time afterward for the students and instructor to reflect on what was learned.

My AU colleague, communications expert Professor Rick Stack, says he finds guest speakers highly useful to his students. He advises his students to collect guest speakers' business cards because this is a relatively easy way to expand their professional networks.[21]

Stack says that students also should be encouraged to write thank-you notes to speakers. This is both a matter of courtesy and a technique that will make students memorable and stand out in the minds of visiting experts.[22] What's more, the ability to write a good thank-you note is an important skill to have.

FIELD TRIPS

Science professor Kiho Kim at American University recommends that professors introduce variety into their classes by planning field trips and excursions whenever possible. He says he finds interacting with students in a non-classroom environment more engaging because the students tend to feel more relaxed.

Kenney says one way he keeps his teaching relevant, fresh, and creative is to take his social work students to art shows and museum exhibits on campus. He says he's learned that art can speak to students in a way that many lectures cannot. It also connects the students to parts of campus and subjects being taught that are unfamiliar to them but that enrich their lives.

One art show featured works by an artist who painted young adults experiencing issues such as isolation or abandonment. Kenney asked his students to select one of the individuals in the paintings as a potential client, and then to imagine how their client would respond to several questions relevant to their uniqueness. Kenney says the subsequent discussions "were profound and powerful."[23]

NETWORKING

I recommend giving students an occasional three-minute "networking" exercise. Before it starts, stress the importance of networking (making contacts and meeting key people) to their careers. Particularly for grad students, a class may contain future creative or business partners, so students getting to know each other is especially important.[24]

Then tell them to stand up, move around the room, and find a student they don't know or don't know well. Give them an exercise, such as discussing a question relevant to the class content, that will provide an opportunity for them to get to know one another. If time permits, another approach is to have the students give quick reports to the class on what they learned from each other.[25]

SHOWING RELEVANT VIDEOS

Because I teach filmmaking, showing clips and videos in class is so routine that I take such screenings for granted. But, as Stack reminded me, in practically every other discipline, showing relevant footage from a film is a welcome break from the typical lesson plan.[26] Not only does it jazz up the class, but it can also increase learning by covering substantive information that supplements content covered in lectures.

* * * * *

Adding variety to a class can increase learning. The goal of all the activities described above is to help students become more engaged and involved in their own learning. It is important for them to feel a responsibility for what happens in the class, and not to assume that the professor alone is responsible for what they learn. Students should not be passive observers of what is happening in the class. Another great benefit of using a variety of activities is that it keeps the teaching and the learning process fun and engaging for the instructor too.

Chapter 11

Finish the Semester Strong

Education is not the filling of a pail, but the lighting of a fire.

—attributed to William Butler Yeats, poet and playwright

As a semester unfolds, fifteen weeks can seem interminable. Toward the end of the semester, professors and students become increasingly busy: faculty rush to get through their remaining content, and students prepare for finals. Both students and instructors can get stressed, cranky, and exhausted.

This chapter contains ideas to help professors complete the semester strongly and tie up loose ends, without fatigue or looming burnout compromising their energy, enthusiasm, and level of caring.

It may seem that some of the ideas discussed in this chapter fall outside the instructor's responsibilities. For example, helping students prepare for the real world may appear not to be part of the instructor's duty, but rather the job of the university career center or the students' parents. A professor hired to teach, say, chemistry, may believe that teaching chemistry should be his prime focus.

These are fair points. Nevertheless, implementing one or two of the techniques described here might keep interest and energy high for both professor and students, and enable students to become productive and employed members of society. This chapter covers the following ideas:

- interleaving;

- employing useful prompts;

- requesting short status reports;

- preparing students for the real world;

- polishing up soft skills;

- fine-tuning digital footprints;

- reaching out to parents; and

- taking care of yourself.

INTERLEAVING

When students study for quizzes, they tend to focus on material most recently covered in class, or wrestle with one kind of concept, problem, or skill at a time. Similarly, when professors review material in class, they usually focus on the most recently covered content.

The problem with this approach is that in real life (or even in exams), problems don't arrive in neat packages in the sequence they were covered in class. They arrive all mixed up and out of order.

Dr. James Lang points out that interleaving deals with this issue head on. It involves two related activities that promote high levels of long-term retention: spacing out learning sessions over time and mixing up the practice of skills being taught.[1] Assignments and homework should ask students to tap into the ideas and content they learned earlier in the semester. In other words, teachers should keep returning to previously covered material.

When giving quizzes, always include a few questions related to material presented earlier. This reinforces material in an ongoing way from the start of the course to the end. When students regularly revisit content covered in earlier classes, the search, reminder, review, and reconnection to what they already know helps them remember and understand it more deeply.

Dr. Maryellen Weimer calls interleaving an "evidence-based study strategy." She acknowledges that students won't like it because it is challenging for them. It makes studying harder, but it also makes understanding and remembering easier. Weimer states that the payoff comes on the exam, in the courses that follow, and in the work that students will be doing in their real-world careers.[2]

Students feel more positively about interleaving if teachers explain the reasons for it—including how beneficial it is to their learning and long-term success.

Lang says that interleaving improves long-term retention in all areas of learning, "from retention of facts to the mastery of higher order cognitive skills."[3] He advises that an interleaved approach to learning "should overlay all of your course design and teaching practices."[4]

EMPLOYING USEFUL PROMPTS

One technique that helps students think and learn on a deeper level comes from B. Dietz-Uhler (from Miami University) and J. R. Lanter (from Kutztown University). In 2009, these two psychology professors authored a set of four prompts to promote critical thinking:

1. Identify one important concept, research finding, theory, or idea that you learned while completing this activity.

2. Explain why you believe that this concept, research finding, theory, or idea is important.

3. Apply what you have learned from this activity to some aspect of your life.

4. Articulate what question(s) the activity raised for you. Tell what you are still wondering about.[5]

These four prompts actively engage students in the course content and can be used to energize them and the professor throughout the semester.

Weimer points out that the question set can be versatile.[6] For example, the four questions can be used to review what happened in the last class, to summarize an in-class discussion, or to dig deeper into a reading assignment. They can even be used to encourage students to reflect on their learning over the whole semester. (What's one important idea you learned this semester? Why do you believe it is important? How does what you learned in this course relate to your life? What new questions has this course raised for you?)

Dietz-Uhler and Lantern found that the four prompts had a clear effect on student learning.[7] Critical thinking scores were significantly higher when the questions were used. Weimer writes, "Sometimes I think we gravitate toward fancy techniques—the ones with lots of bells and whistles. [The four question set] showcases a simple but useful way students can interact with the content."[8]

REQUESTING SHORT STATUS REPORTS

As the semester winds down, ask students to submit short status reports about papers and projects well before the due date. Offer feedback to make sure that they are on the right track.

Feedback can focus on how students can improve their work, expand their thinking, add nuance, elucidate their arguments, or incorporate source material in a more powerful way. It also reinforces the role of the professor as an engaged and caring educator.

PREPARING STUDENTS FOR THE REAL WORLD

Look for opportunities throughout the semester to remind students why the class is important and how it relates to their future lives. Call attention to the links between the content they are learning and the skills they will need post-graduation.

For example, when students use oral reports as part of their assignments (such as presenting in class or contributing to class discussions), point out that being able to talk about their ideas and thoughts cogently, clearly, and concisely is a skill that is directly transferrable to work situations.

Find time, even if it is just a few minutes, to discuss students' professional development. Occasionally add into the homework some broader questions about future careers, such as, "What is the job you'd ideally like to be doing in five years, and what steps are you taking to achieve that goal?"

I don't want to minimize the importance of learning technical or "hard" skills (including mathematics, writing, engineering, and foreign languages). In my field, for example, I teach the hard skills of animation, cinematography, editing, interactive media, trans-media, participatory media, and immersive media. I help build student competence on digital devices, social media, mobile apps, and augmented reality. I help my students create meaningful and purposeful media through visual and aural storytelling. Other fields offer their own unique sets of skills, techniques, and knowledge.

But in addition to hard or technical skills, students must learn professionalism. Professionalism involves civility, courtesy, a solid work ethic, networking, and strong communication skills. Professionals acknowledge and learn from mistakes, act as team players, consistently give their best effort, always treat others with respect, and keep their promises. These are the kind of people that employers want to hire.

In his bestselling book *How Children Succeed*, author and journalist Paul Tough argues that simply teaching cognitive skills such as math and reading to young kids isn't nearly enough.[9] He contends that the most important things to develop in children are non-cognitive skills—that is, character traits such as integrity, self-control, self-discipline, focus, resilience, efficiency, ambition, perseverance, and resourcefulness. What is true for children is also true for college students.

POLISHING UP SOFT SKILLS

All the technical skills in the world won't help students if they can't find jobs or can only find jobs that painfully under-employ them and don't use their full potential. Yet that demoralizing situation seems to be the case for far too many students.[10] Many talented graduates lose out on jobs because they lack so-called "soft" or basic life skills, such as self-discipline, resourcefulness, leadership, professionalism, collaboration, lifelong learning, resilience, persistence, and integrity. Whenever possible, professors should teach students how to sharpen those soft skills to help them develop that extra edge necessary to effectively compete for jobs.

Young people need to know how to take initiative and be life-long learners; how to be adaptable, resilient, and resourceful; how to be ambitious, confident, and assertive; and how to live with honor and integrity.

More specifically, five vital strengths that students need are:

* *Leadership*: The capability to assume a leadership role when necessary is a skill much sought after by employers.

* *Interpersonal skills*: These invaluable skills include being able to converse with others, ask questions, and maintain eye contact in face-to-face communications.

* *Collaboration*: Most careers require collaboration, which means having the ability to listen to others and accept constructive criticism from them.

* *Time management*: Everyone needs to be organized, make priorities, stick to them, work productively, and get multiple assignments completed by established deadlines.

* *Problem-solving*: This involves the life skill of dealing with unexpected issues calmly and with astuteness and insight.

Professionalism in digital communication is important, too. It is amazing to me how many adults are terrible at using email and other digital correspondence.

Their replies are slow and obfuscatory, their subject lines are unclear, and their follow-up is weak or nonexistent. With help from professors, students can learn to do better than this.

FINE-TUNING DIGITAL FOOTPRINTS

Students live online, but they sometimes don't appreciate the importance of the digital footprint they leave for future employers to find and judge. Inappropriate posts in social media can lead potential employers not to hire people.

History and psychology professor Dawn McGuckin at Durham College in Canada recommends that students google themselves, so they can see what a future potential employer would find.[11] She also suggests that teachers encourage students to create a powerful and professional online identity, not one marred by irresponsible social media use.

REACHING OUT TO PARENTS

Near the end of the semester, select the top half dozen students in the class. Ask their permission (that's very important) to call their parents and tell them how well their son or daughter has done in the class.

Once the student gives permission, call the parents and tell them that they can be very proud of their child for, say, the diligence, creativity, and tenacity they have shown. The parents will be delighted to receive this call and are likely to respond with how proud they are of their child. This message, in turn, is one the professor can convey to the student. For a few of them, it will be the first time that they have heard their parents express such a pride so publicly, and they will feel very moved.

In the April 2018 *Reader's Digest*, Indra Nooyi, chairman and former CEO of PepsiCo, describes why she began writing notes, not to her employees but to their parents. When she got the top job at her company, she visited her mother in India, and her mother arranged for scores of family members to come by the house to visit. Each of the visitors gave a brief hello to Nooyi, but then went to her mother to say, "You should feel so proud that you brought up this daughter, and you brought up your child so well."

It was then that Nooyi realized the visitors were focused on praising not her but her mother, for the good job she had done raising Nooyi. It made Nooyi realize that she had never told the parents of the people who reported directly to her what a great job they had done. So she wrote to each employee's parents, "I'm writing to thank you for the gift of your son, who is doing a wonderful job at PepsiCo." I believe there is a lesson for professors in this.

When he taught American University undergraduates, systems dynamics professor John Richardson got permission from his students to send a copy of the course syllabus to their parents, with the suggestion that they discuss the course with their children when they came home for vacation. Richardson found that parents typically appreciated his gesture deeply.

Richardson also always provides students with copies of his recommendation letters and suggests to students that they share them with their parents.

TAKING CARE OF YOURSELF

Professors can get burned out and stuck in a rut. They can feel uninspired, stressed, and jaded. Taking care of yourself when dark moods cloud your life is crucial. A sabbatical, retreat, or vacation can help to recharge your pedagogical batteries. In addition, simple daily habits of exercise, eating healthily, and getting enough sleep can help, as can sharing your feelings with a trusted colleague, mentor, or friend.

* * * * *

Completing the semester with energy and enthusiasm is often challenging because the stress levels on both faculty and students can be punishing. If you feel exhaustion, fatigue, or stress begin to damage your attitude and mood in class, head off trouble by using some of the ideas shared in this chapter.

Taking good care of yourself is particularly important. You can't take care of students and give them the care and attention they deserve if you as their professor are undernourished physically, emotionally, mentally, or spiritually. You must take care of yourself before you can take care of anybody or anything else.

Chapter 12

Be Responsive to Students

Have you ever really had a teacher? One who saw you as a raw but precious thing, a jewel that, with wisdom, could be polished to a proud shine?

—Mitch Albom, author

Professors should be responsive to students, not in the sense of kowtowing or truckling to them, but by treating them with respect and dignity. Responsive professors make it abundantly clear to their students that they are eager to know about any problems or worries the students have with their learning, so that they can assist. This chapter explores the following ways of achieving that goal:

- being responsive to e-mails and calls;

- managing office hours effectively;

- providing substantive feedback;

- using grading rubrics; and

- encouraging attendance in class.

BEING RESPONSIVE TO EMAILS AND CALLS

I recommend that professors respond promptly (within twenty-four hours) to all student emails and messages. Add the professor's office or cell phone number (whichever is best for receiving calls) under the name at the end of the e-mail so that students can call if they wish.

Answering emails congenially and quickly helps to build trust. Professors Steven Corbett and Michelle LaFrance, both from George Mason University, suggest communicating with students "in ways similar to how you would communicate with your close colleagues."[1] Treat students with the same thoughtfulness, professionalism, and respect that you expect to receive.

If you can't fully respond right away, write a brief response saying you will do so by a certain time and date. Or say something like, "Let's talk about this before class tomorrow," or, "Good question—please raise it in class tomorrow so I can explain it to everyone." The point is to be responsive and not let more than a day go by with no answer. Nobody likes to be ignored.

Teachers who don't answer email promptly risk damaging their relationships with students. Every unanswered email represents a dissatisfied student. That student is waiting for a response—guidance, advice, acknowledgment, feedback, encouragement, information regarding a website, a research paper, or something else—and is frustrated, disappointed, even insulted when no response comes.

I send an unsolicited e-mail to all my students within a few hours after each class ends, commending them where appropriate, thanking them for their enthusiasm and diligence, thanking individual students for their contributions, urging them to maintain their hard work and creativity, and reminding them of their commitments, assignments, and homework.

MANAGING OFFICE HOURS EFFECTIVELY

Office hours give professors a chance to meet students and get to know them better. Students often are motivated to work harder for professors they get to know.

It is important to be in your office when you say you will be there. Treat office hours as the serious commitment they represent. Few things will alienate and annoy students more than finding an empty office when you said you would be there.

During office hours, leave the door open to indicate that you welcome students and are not busy with something else.

I like to have a sign-up sheet on my door so that students can schedule a meeting for a specific time and day and know they won't have to wait. In addition, I keep some blocks of time open for students who want to drop in.

Schedule office hours on days and at times that are convenient for students. Before and after class often works well. A few students may find it impossible to visit during posted office hours because of other commitments or other classes. When that is the case, do your best to find other times to meet with them, or use the phone or Skype instead of an in-person meeting.

Getting students to come to office hours can be challenging. Make it clear that you are eager to see them one-on-one. Encourage students to drop by, even if they don't have specific questions.

I advocate *requiring* students to meet with instructors regularly throughout the semester. As mentioned in chapter 3, I insist that my students see me for a one-on-one meeting in the first two weeks of class. Once students have made one visit and not found it intimidating, they are more likely to come back for more one-on-one meetings.

In office meetings, give students your full attention. Don't take phone calls. Encourage students to come with an agenda and questions, but not to feel obligated to do so if they have more general reasons to speak with you.

PROVIDING SUBSTANTIVE FEEDBACK

Assessing and grading papers, reports, and exams is exhausting, and sometimes tedious. But students typically attach a great deal of importance to their work, so the professor's comments and feedback, and especially the grade, mean a lot to them.

Try to return papers quickly—within a week after they are handed in. That way, students receive feedback while the assignment is still fresh in their minds. Ideally, students should absorb feedback and process it before submitting the next assignment.

Do your best to provide meaningful and meaty comments on homework assignments. Students want rigorous, critical, and detailed feedback that is presented in a constructive and encouraging manner. The more critically encouraging your comments, the better.

Instead of writing "Great job" or "This needs work," provide specific feedback describing what is good about what the student has done, what needs more work—and why. Providing constructive feedback and written comments is the most vital part of grading projects and papers, because it fosters learning. The comments should be a cogent mixture of encouragement, praise, criticism, and suggestions for improvement. Even a poor paper should receive some positive comment if possible.

Criticize the paper, not the person. A comment on a piece of homework might begin, "This paper missed the point," instead of, "You missed the point." It is vital to remember that the teacher's goal is to help students to learn, and degrading them shuts them out.

Never be contemptuous, curt, or disparaging. Never be mocking or caustic. All these behaviors can cruelly distress a student. Your comments are emblematic of your respect for the student. They are your way of telling him that you know he can do much better and that you have confidence in his ability to learn and master the course content.

Some feedback will be *summative*, explaining and justifying why the student got the grade she did and outlining the strengths and weaknesses of the work. Most feedback, however, should be *formative*, indicating how the student can improve and that she is capable of improvement. The idea is to encourage a growth mindset, fostering creativity, hard work, and intellectual striving.

Dr. James Lang writes that, after becoming familiar with the research on growth mindset, he has eschewed giving students such feedback statements as "You are really a talented writer." Instead he tries to use language that encourages growth and learning, such as "Excellent work—you took the strategies we have been working on in class and deployed them beautifully here," or "You have obviously worked very hard at your writing, and it shows in this essay."[2]

The language the professor uses can indicate to students either that they have fixed abilities, or that they can get better. The latter is far better because it conveys to students that their hard work and genuine effort can lead to rapid academic growth. They will be surprised and delighted by how swiftly they can become better students and grow academically.

Journalist and professor Amy Eisman at American University argues that if one student is particularly adept at a skill, point it out and have an expectation for the student to be the "expert." Don't just say, "That was a well-written paper." Instead, indicate exactly what about the ideas or wording or structure of the paper made it stand out. Eisman says this raises the student in the esteem of classmates and encourages the student to stay abreast of the topic.

USING GRADING RUBRICS

Rubrics are one way to give students a grasp of how their work will be graded. Well-crafted rubrics lucidly define the criteria you are using to evaluate assignments. Share them with students when the assignment is handed out so that they know in advance what behavior and skills you are seeking to teach and what you consider important.

Stephen Brookfield says a successful rubric provides students with specific and visible indicators of what they should be doing.[3] Of course, the rubrics must be in sync with the syllabus.

ENCOURAGING ATTENDANCE IN CLASS

Some professors believe it is the students' responsibility to attend class. After all, they are adults. That argument has merit, but I've found that students are more likely to attend class if they know I take roll. Most students feel that their professors care about them more when they keep track of attendance.

I recommend contacting students who do not show up to class to find out why they didn't attend and if they need help. Show that you care.

I tell my students that if their parents or siblings or out-of-town friends are visiting, these guests are welcome to sit in on the class to see what a typical class is like. Before making this offer, professors should check first with the university or department to make sure such visits are allowed.

* * * * *

We all know that powerful economic and cultural forces drive students to attend college or university. They want to obtain an education that will help them to find and succeed in their first job out of college.[4]

Charles Dorn, a professor of education at Bowdoin College, observes that, in addition to providing opportunities for enhancing career prospects, "colleges and universities have historically encouraged students to expand their aspirations in the direction of serving the public good."[5]

Dorn says that colleges should help students think seriously about more than a career. He argues that a college should expand a student's "understanding of the world as well as his personal ambitions," and equip "him to live well while fostering an awareness of his responsibility to others."[6]

Helping a student find a job and helping her simultaneously become an effective citizen are not incompatible. As educational expert Bethany Zecher Sutton says, "Critical thinking, problem solving, working in diverse teams, ethical reasoning, communicating—these make both good employees and good citizens."[7]

Sutton adds, "Higher education has a responsibility . . . to ensure that the students who come to our institutions actually do have an educational experience that prepares them for more than a job—in fact, for more than a career."[8]

Professors have a responsibility to do their utmost to see that their students have an educational experience that prepares them for life and to contribute to society, in addition to preparing them for a job and a career.

Instructors must, of course, create syllabi, reading lists, lesson plans, lecture notes, homework assignments, quizzes, exams, field trips, and so on. But they need to remember to attach more importance to learning than to academic success. The goal is to advance experience, knowledge, and wisdom, and not just focus on grades.

Working with students is challenging, but it is also a significant privilege. It is not a job so much as a calling. Students want to be challenged by their instructors, while being inspired by the instructors' enthusiasm, and fortified by their caring.

Teaching is one of those rare professions that provides the opportunity to reinvent yourself and redesign your job on a regular basis. Every semester you can begin anew.

Professor John Richardson, a former American University colleague who taught most recently at the National University of Singapore, brought to my attention the following poem. In his book *Ethics for the New Millennium*, the Dalai Lama writes that he repeats the poem at the end of each day.[9] Richardson says it is particularly relevant to professors, and to all who want to pursue teaching as their life's work.

May I become, at all times, both now and forever
A protector of those without protection.
A guide for those who have lost their way.
A ship for those with oceans to cross.
A sanctuary for those in danger.
A lamp for those without light.
A place of refuge for all who lack shelter,
And a servant to all those in need.

Chapter 13

Other Professors and Students Give Their Views on How to Excel at College Teaching

PROFESSOR DENNIS AIG

Formulating a proposed film's through line or "spine" is one of the most difficult tasks for new filmmakers. Instead of articulating an underlying thematic idea, students inevitably lapse into loglines or synopses that summarize a series of actions or events. Often the problem is that finding the through line usually involves a process of trial and error that takes the filmmaker through the film's narrative until there is a realization of what the film is *really* trying to show.

One technique I use to ease the students through this often difficult but necessary give-and-take is to treat the class as a de facto "writers' room," so the filmmakers can help one another figure out the true purpose of each proposed film. I serve as a kind of referee, saying something is either moving us toward our goal zone or may be an intellectual fumble. (I carefully never say any idea is completely wrong because, as all filmmakers know, the very worst ideas can lay the groundwork for much, much better ones.)

Recently, one student proposed a film about the remarkable powers of crystals, a subject whose possibilities range from healing stones in the patchouli-scented head shops of the 1960s to ultra-high-tech lasers in massive contemporary factories. After about 15 minutes of discussion back and forth with her class colleagues, the student director finally said, "My film is really about how the invisible often transforms the visible and concrete." As one, the class (including me) cheered. Touchdown!

PROFESSOR EARL BABBIE

I have formed the conclusion that whenever my students are having trouble understanding some topic, there is probably some piece of that topic that doesn't completely make sense to me. More than once, I have cancelled class in mid-stream, promising to take up the topic again at our next meeting. Then I spend some time reexamining the topic by myself. Eventually I find something I didn't thoroughly understand, or something that didn't quite fit together. It's as though I were building the transcontinental railroad and the eastbound and westbound tracks didn't meet. Once I have cleared away my own confusion, the students get it easily, even though I'm not presenting the topic all that differently. I've urged students to tell me when they don't understand because I always end up getting smarter.

The first time I taught research methods to a class of 200 students, I was committed to carrying on a conversation rather than simply lecturing. So, in the first class, I told students that I wanted them to speak out, ask questions, discuss topics, and so forth. I could tell by the looks on their faces that it wasn't going to work, and I told them I understood that it might be a bit intimidating to speak up in such a large class. The breakthrough came when I asked for examples of why they might not want to speak out. One student said, "I'd worry that I was asking a stupid question." Another worried that he'd ask about something I'd already covered. My favorite was when I asked a young woman to repeat what she had said; she was afraid she wouldn't speak loud enough to be heard. Very soon, students were conversing about the topic so much that I had to cut off the discussion, which was a common need throughout the rest of the semester.

Teaching research methods to a class of 200 students, I found I could illustrate many concepts by using the students as research subjects. For example, I'd have the whole class move to one side of the classroom to help me create an index of, say, the degree to which they were NFL fans. I'd begin by asking all those with a favorite NFL team to move toward the back of the room, while the others would move forward. Then I'd subdivide each of those groups by asking if they could name three NFL coaches. Now there were three groups with two subgroups joining in the middle. Once I was satisfied with the index, I'd validate it by asking another question and have the "yes" students remain standing and "no" students sit down. In other exercises, I used devices such as contingency tables and selected samples.

PROFESSOR NAOMI BARON

Get out of the classroom! Wherever you are teaching, discover ways of incorporating the resources of your surroundings into the learning experience. A biology class might study the local flora and fauna. An art class might interview a local artist. A history class might record oral histories.

One of my most memorable teaching moments was in a course I offered on the history of English. We had been talking about the impact of the printing press on the language as well as on literacy. The conversation began with Johannes Gutenberg's development of moveable type in mid-fifteenth-century Germany. So I had an idea: Bring the class to the Library of Congress, where they could witness the birth of printing in the Western world. On display were two bibles, facing each other. One was an original Gutenberg Bible—printed. The other was a copy of the Great Bible of Mainz—done entirely by hand, at about the same time.

Walking back and forth between the two, students marveled at how the writing, vellum, and size of the two books looked identical. The class had read about the fact that it had taken many years before printing really changed the look and feel of books. Yet standing in the presence of these two bibles, students absorbed the lesson firsthand. Even now, years later, former students remind me of the impact of this visit.

My university happens to have the city of Washington, DC, that it can draw upon to extend the classroom. But wherever you are, get creative. You—and your students—will generate terrific ideas that make for enriched teaching and learning.

CRYSTAL BERG, GRADUATE STUDENT

It is an unfortunate misconception that "those who cannot do, teach." Without fail, all the best professors I have had are the ones who do both—they teach to spread knowledge and appreciation for a subject they feel passionate about. Monotonous droning puts students to sleep, while excitement is contagious.

ROBERT BOYD, GRADUATE STUDENT

One day I asked my ornithology professor whether it would be possible for a bird of flight to grow as large as the fictitious giant eagles, seen in the fantasy series *The Lord of the Rings*. Rather than ignoring or chastising me for my admittedly outlandish question, this professor was willing to consider it. More important, he turned this question into a learning opportunity, tying it back into the day's lesson plan. This professor's open mind helped fuel my interest in ornithology, making me more invested in the course and the presented material.

Some of my best professors realize that knowledge learned in the classroom should be honed in the field. These professors find a healthy balance between academic work and hands-on experience. In addition, they draw on their own unique life experiences, allowing them to teach the material in new and engaging ways.

PROFESSOR ELIZABETH COHN

It's the last day of class in my first-year seminar, which explores American values, beliefs, and structures, and I've planned a lecture to sum up the key lessons for the semester that began in August. Over the weekend, I had spent several hours polishing what I thought was a pithy lecture, and I'm excited to share my final thoughts. Entering the classroom, I observe that the classroom is quiet, and students look exhausted by their end-of-semester obligations.

I decide to put some energy into the room by showing the opening scene of Aaron Sorkin's TV drama *The Newsroom*, as it touches on one of the course themes. Besides, Sorkin's dialogue is far wittier than mine and can capture their attention. In the clip, a nervous student asks, "Why is America the greatest country in the world?"

After resisting an answer, the lead character, a newscaster named Will, launches into a three-and-a-half-minute history lesson on America, its reality and its promise. I can see that students are waking up. To help them gather their thoughts, I tell them to pair up and share their reactions. The energy level in the room goes from 2 to 10.

The first student I call on, Kim, says, "That student in the clip was 'August Kim' and Will is 'December Kim'"—meaning that she saw herself in that nervous awkward sophomore girl at the beginning of the semester and now identifies with the confident, educated news host.

I drop my plans for the day, write "August Kim" on the board and ask students to share what they had thought of America at the beginning of the semester. And then I add a column for "December Kim" and the board is covered with ideas from the students. They are reflecting on all the key themes of the course.

I add a few ideas, or probe for deeper understanding at a few points. They are demonstrating how much their thinking has changed and showing what they have learned. I add a third column, to analyze the two lists, exploring why their notions of America when they began the course were incomplete or inaccurate. An hour later we are all energized and 80 percent of what was in my lecture notes was covered, though I never lectured. It was a terrific way to end the semester.

What is the lesson here? Teaching requires reading the room, picking up on the energy level of the students, and meeting them where they are. I always come prepared with a plan, but teaching requires adapting as necessary to make a positive learning experience for those students at that moment.

Teaching requires me to be flexible, and confident that I can handle the direction of the conversation, wherever it goes. And it requires trusting that students can, with my guidance, pull together key points of course material, and remembering that a lecture isn't always needed.

* * * * *

I encourage faculty to hold group office hours for students in the same course. I find that it not only is more efficient for me to do so, but there's also pedagogical value for my students. For example, the week before a paper is due, I schedule two 2–3-hour blocks of time when students from a course are encouraged to attend my office hours. I usually meet with two to seven students at a time, and students will rotate in and out, depending on their schedules.

Group office hours are good for me, because I can answer common questions all at once. I can also give individual attention to my students but in a more efficient way. And it helps build community for my class and develop peer mentoring so that students look beyond me for learning assistance.

The experience is very good for the students. Seeing classmates struggling helps students realize they are not alone in sorting through their ideas, and this is emotionally reassuring for them. While it can raise self-doubt about whether students feel as capable as their peers, I have also seen student confidence grow when a student is able to offer suggestions to a classmate.

It's wonderful to observe the peer-to-peer advice being given, and see students sharing phone numbers for further assistance. If peer advice is off the mark, I am available to follow up.

While some students say they prefer individual appointments, once they see that I can give them personal attention in the midst of a group, they are fine. And as one student said to me at the end of group office hours, "This is fun, in a weird way." It is great fun, as we work together to help each other learn.

* * * * *

Colleagues often lament that we spend so much time giving comments on essays, and are not sure that students learn from them—or even read them. I agree. So, I require my students to *show* that they've read my comments and have tried to learn from them by applying my comments in their succeeding essays.

The directions I give on the assignment sheet are: "*Demonstrating Learning*: Before you start writing, review my comments on your first essay so that you can think about what you need to work on as you write your second essay. Once you've written your second essay, review my comments on your first essay again. Using footnotes, show on your second essay where you have demonstrated that you applied what you learned from my comments."

To carry out this exercise, students have written footnotes including comments like, "My thesis statement is more complex because . . . ," or, "I included more evidence to support my point than what was in my first essay," or, "This paragraph now has only one point, which is . . . ," or, "I edited this paragraph to be more concise," or, "My Works Cited format is now correct."

Students say that the process of doing this helps them focus on what they need to learn, and that they can see that they were learning, which helps build their confidence. For this exercise to work, it's important that faculty feedback be formative, meaning that it gives specific ways that writing can be improved, much as a coach gives pointers on how to improve performance.

For example, if the paper's structure is problematic, you need to explain how it could be improved. Some students need a lot of direction so, in addition to specific comments, including a summary statement of one or two points at the end will help students identify the key areas to address.

ANNA CUMMINS, CO-FOUNDER, THE 5 GYRES INSTITUTE

I have had the tremendous privilege throughout my life of having many extraordinary, life-changing teachers—teachers who dressed up in Shakespearean costumes, jumped onto tables à la *Dead Poets Society*, gave thoughtful feedback on every piece of writing, challenged the status quo, sang songs to illustrate mathematic equations, and in general approached their subjects with passion and exuberant charisma.

But if I had to pick one story that illustrated memorable teaching, it would be an art history course (not my field) that I took from Stanford Professor Jody Maxmin, whose reputation as a magician in the classroom is legendary.

I immediately understood the buzz about her teaching. Her ability to relate Roman and Etruscan art history to modern-day politics and culture is dazzling, her depth of knowledge brilliant, and her classroom presence is so engaging that I invited both my parents to attend one of her lectures.

Early in the class, I lost a friend to a tragic, unexpected accident. I went to Professor Maxmin's office hours for an academic-related question and found myself instead opening up about my grief. And over the course of a conversation ingrained in my mind now 22 years later, she inspired me to channel my sadness into a project for the class.

Being mentored toward a productive outlet for an incomprehensible loss was not only deeply healing. It also impressed upon me a sense of the timelessness of human emotions across history in a way that I will never forget.

Passion for one's topic is certainly a critical ingredient in great teaching. Adding to this a unique ability to observe, listen deeply, and relate academics to a student's real, lived experience remains in my mind the mark of exceptional teaching.

PROFESSOR LAURA DENARDIS

One of the most memorable professors I ever had said, "I can't teach you anything, but you can learn everything." The idea behind this philosophy is that a great professor creates the conditions in which students themselves think, analyze, critique, and learn. In cyber policy, the area in which I teach, part of students' intellectual self-discovery involves determining where they stand on some of the most consequential and complex issue areas of the contemporary era: government surveillance online versus individual privacy, freedom of expression versus public safety, and national security versus the free global flow of information. As a starting point, my tradition is to walk into every first class meeting and tell students, "My own aspiration for the course is that, when you look back at college, this class will be the one you remember as the most intellectually transformative."

Students become most engaged in a cyber policy area when they enter it through a real-world problem to which they already have personal exposure, such as cyberbullying, digital data breaches, or illegal file sharing of movies and music. Personal student experiences are an excellent foray into policy areas—defamation, intellectual property law, privacy terms of service—that can otherwise seem disembodied. Once students become interested in a cyber policy topic, determining their position requires exposure to the underlying technologies, grounding in the history of the issue area, and developing a critical understanding of the economic, social, and political stakes. It also requires an evidence base and empirical research. Critical reasoning occurs best through writing, and I invite students to present written arguments on all sides of an issue, then making a reasoned case establishing their own stance.

Beginning each class with a student-led "Cyber Policy in the News" segment has helped me understand both how interested students are in real world issues directly affecting them and also the value of ongoing engagement outside of the class. What is most rewarding personally is watching students establish their own evidence-based positions on cyber issues. This bodes well for our digital future!

ADITI DESAI, FORMER GRADUATE STUDENT, NOW FILM AND MULTIMEDIA PRODUCER

Nervous sweat dripped down my forehead as I set up a tripod for my first solo shoot in graduate school at the DC-based nonprofit Suited for Change. The fact that my professor, Bill Gentile, accompanied me added to my anxiety. He settled into an empty office while I worked through my shot list. Every now and then, I paused to review footage with him. Within half an hour, I was at ease and was able to sincerely appreciate the instant feedback. As the day progressed, my work improved, thanks to Professor Gentile's recommendations. Direct one-on-one attention from a professor is invaluable.

After we wrapped for the day, each student showed the footage to the entire class for further critique. We did similar in-class reviews throughout the semester. Progressing in any field requires mentorship and constructive criticism. Professor Gentile built this in throughout his documentary course and I know my final film was much stronger for it. I still use many of the tools and techniques that I learned in that course in my work today.

SIRJAUT KAUR DHARIWAL, GRADUATE STUDENT

For me, a good professor is passionate about the subject, takes the time to get to know the students, and recognizes that not everyone has the same learning style. This takes effort but will help bridge the gap between a professor in the front of the room and a student sitting in the back of a lecture hall.

Instead of dull PowerPoint presentations, the professor can cover some interesting and thought-provoking topics through round table discussions, and can apply flexibility in project formats. Students will not only learn the material but understand it and realize their true potential in the field. This, in turn, sparks curiosity and the desire to learn more.

During my undergraduate career, the professors and teaching assistants who stood out to me were the ones who recognized that learning is different from memorization, and who engaged the class in ways that motivated students to experience the subject with the same fervor that the professors have themselves.

PROFESSOR DANIEL DREISBACH

A technique I learned and began practicing several years ago involves calling on a student at the start of each class to take a few minutes to review the material covered in our last class, specifically identifying two or three points the student regarded as the most important to come out of that class. (I sometimes invite other students to add a point or two to this list.) I find that this exercise engages students in classroom activities from the very start of the class period, reminds the entire class of where we are in the course, brings students who missed the last class up to date, and gives me some insight into whether the students accurately discerned or, perhaps, misunderstood what I had hoped to convey in the previous session.

PROFESSOR BARRY ERDELJON

While critiquing student assignments, it became obvious to me that students were just going through the motions. I realized that they were completing their assignments by applying minimal effort at the last minute prior to class.

So, in the next class, I asked students to review each of their classmates' assignments to determine which was the best, second best, and third best. Each of the students' choices had to be defended using the assignment grading rubric. Choices were tallied to determine which assignments were most often chosen. Because they knew this could potentially happen again, the work of the students suddenly became much improved. Interestingly, friendship and popularity had no bearing on student choices. In any given class, any student would deservingly have assignments selected as the best.

Never has there been a class designation as "best assignment" that I have had to disagree with. The need for students to use the grading rubric has increased attentiveness to assignments. Classmate peer review has resulted in students taking assignments more seriously, and perhaps a healthy dash of competitiveness brought out the best in each student.

* * * * *

After years of mumbling, pointing, and avoiding using student names I faced up to the fact that I am unable to remember names. While enviously watching colleagues call on students by name in large classrooms, it dawned on me that I needed to do something about my inability to remember names; it was potentially having a negative effect on my ability to teach. The answer, it turned out, was a simple click away. Seeing my cell phone lying on the teaching podium one day, I snapped a photo of my class. Adding students' names to a print of the photograph gives me an easy-to-use cheat sheet. An occasional quick glance at the photo allows me to call on students by name.

STEPHANIE FLACK, CONSERVATIONIST AND CONSULTANT TO NONPROFIT ORGANIZATIONS

You never know where life will take you. I entered college not knowing what I would end up studying but I had a love of biology, thanks to an exceptional high school teacher named Dr. Barbara Grosz. Dr. Grosz taught biology at Pine Crest School in Fort Lauderdale, Florida. Her own love of biology and her clear, compelling teaching style launched hundreds of careers in the sciences.

As a first-year student at Princeton University, I signed up for a biology class on the evolution of sex and intelligence. It sounded fascinating—who wouldn't be interested in those topics? At the time, I did not know that this single class would set me on a path to my future career, in large part due to the mentorship and role model of the professor who taught it.

The class was offered by Dr. Alison Jolly, a renowned primatologist and conservationist. Dr. Jolly belongs in the pantheon of perhaps more widely known, pioneering women primatologists—Jane Goodall, Dian Fossey, and Birutė Galdikas. That trio was collectively known as "Leakey's Ladies," after anthropologist Dr. Louis Leakey, who sent them out to study the great apes in their native habitats.

Here was a field in which women were leaders and ground-breakers—including my professor, Dr. Jolly, who earned wide respect for her work as a researcher, writer, and conservationist in Madagascar, home of the lemurs she studied for decades.

Dr. Jolly was, in fact, jolly. She was a kindly, big-spirited American with a slight British accent, picked up from years of marriage to a British economist and from living abroad in the UK and other parts of the world.

She used her own and her colleagues' research to bring to life concepts of ethology, the study of animal behavior as an evolutionarily adaptive trait. She drew parallels between nonhuman and human primate behavior, presenting studies on subjects ranging from the evolution of monogamy to infanticide to the value of play.

Dr. Jolly also opened my eyes to the dire condition of not only primates but also the world's diversity of wildlife and natural areas, which were (and still are) being lost at a dramatic rate. I was hooked, and I had found my calling.

Dr. Jolly supported my learning both within and beyond the classroom. With her support, I received a summer internship at Bucknell University to study primates—tiny, red-bellied tamarins; mischievous squirrel monkeys; stately Japanese macaques; and lumbering hamadryas baboons.

In my later college years, Dr. Jolly became my independent study advisor, providing guidance and support as I worked on my senior thesis on mountain gorilla conservation. She took me on trips to New York City and Philadelphia to meet and engage with other primate conservationists. Her mentorship broadened my worldview and ultimately led me to graduate school in environmental science and a 20+ year career in nature conservation.

Dr. Jolly passed away a few years ago, but I will always remember and be grateful to her and the other teachers who encouraged me and helped me become the person I am today.

PRESIDENT AND PROFESSOR LES GARNER

My two most rewarding teaching experiences took place at Cornell College, where I was president for 16 years. Both of the courses I taught took advantage of Cornell's distinctive One-Course-at-a-Time academic calendar to offer students the opportunity to immerse themselves in the subject matter, both in classroom discussion and in rich experiences outside the classroom.

I co-taught the first course, "Seminar in Community Service," with Professor Helen Damon-Moore. Cornell's academic calendar is structured so that students take one course for a three-and-a-half-week term. In our seminar, students were in class for two days per week and engaged in full-time community service three days per week. In class, we discussed short stories and social and political science pieces on the nature of community. Students then tested concepts from the reading in their community service work. For the students, the application of concepts provided an epiphany in the realities of community life. It was sometimes jarring. I remember that after a day of working with single-parent families, one student found it difficult to return to campus, where her dinner tablemates, who were not students in the class, were discussing where to hold the weekend party. I witnessed all the students broaden their awareness of what it means to live in community.

The second class, which I taught with Mike Conklin, Cornell alumnus and long-time reporter for the *Chicago Tribune*, was focused on the economics, politics, and social aspects of contemporary Chicago. After a week of background reading and classroom discussion, we spent two weeks in Chicago. Our "classroom" was backstage at the Shedd Aquarium; on stage at Chicago Shakespeare Theater; in public and private offices; and in neighborhoods. At the end of the course we asked the students to propose a strategy to the mayor on a topic related to the future of the city. Their proposals were very insightful and, in some cases, nothing short of amazing. One student concerned about neighborhood decline identified a vacant lot between subway and commuter rail lines and built a scale model of an intramodal transportation center designed to be a catalyst for neighborhood revitalization.

My conclusion is simple. When I treat students as co-learners and empower them with a high degree of control over their learning environment, I learn much more from them than they learn from me.

PROFESSOR BILL GENTILE

I know that grades are important. But they are not the only measure of success. I have taught students who have graduated with perfect grades, but who have failed to reap the maximum benefit from their time at American University.

I believe that the students who most succeed at this (or at any other) university and get the most out of the university experience are those who identify early on the faculty members who will be able to best address their goals and ambitions—and who then approach those faculty members to forge professional and personal relationships with them.

These students research and identify the faculty members who most effectively bring to the table whatever it is that the students want and need to succeed; who engage those faculty members inside and outside the classroom.

The most valuable lessons often are those that a student learns outside the classroom and away from textbooks. Those lessons are all about contacts, context, experience, connections, background, perspective, example, inspiration, friendship, and the wisdom shared by professors as the practitioners of our craft away from the confines of the university. Those are the lessons that students absorb over the course of extended contact with instructors.

Case in point: During Spring Break in 2017, I brought one of my graduate teaching assistants to Mexico, where we produced the pilot episode for a documentary series about freelance foreign correspondents. The student shot the video and, over the course of nearly a year, edited the trailer and the one-hour pilot, helped me with script-writing and narration, and even participated in the crowdfunding campaign to finance the film.

In his assessment of that experience, the student wrote that his participation in the endeavor was "the single biggest professional opportunity of my life."

Though highly respectable, this student's grades are not perfect. But he graduates from the university with so much more.

* * * * *

None of the courses that I routinely teach at American University are required. All are electives that I've created for the School of Communication and that I have built on the foundation of my own experience as a journalist working mostly in foreign countries over the past 40 years.

These courses include "Backpack Documentary," "Foreign Correspondence," and "Photojournalism and Social Documentary." These are not easy courses. For example, the syllabus for my foreign correspondence course sets the bar for my expectations of student performance as they learn about the craft that I have practiced for many years:

> Foreign correspondents are noted for their dynamism and creativity, passionate intellectual curiosity about the world and about people, a conviction that their work can affect change, and a burning desire for self-expression. Not everyone can be a successful foreign correspondent. It demands determination, talent, physical as well as mental stamina, and courage. It also demands the ability to collaborate with colleagues in a positive, constructive way. This characteristic is so crucial that it sometimes overshadows raw talent as the key to success in the real world.

Students occasionally approach me to express interest in this class but also to confess they are afraid they won't measure up to its demands. And I tell them never to let fear undermine their goals—or their lives. The university experience should be about testing oneself, I tell them. Pushing oneself. Exploring one's capabilities. Getting to know and to understand oneself. Once you do that, I explain, you can play to your strengths and circumvent your weaknesses.

Fear is a natural and sometimes beneficial emotion. But, I tell students, never, ever, let fear dictate the kind of life you want to live.

* * * * *

Each semester, students ask me for a letter of recommendation because they are applying for a job or an internship. I get a lot of these requests, usually after a student has been in one or more of my classes. And my standard response is:

> Happy to do so, but please send me a rough draft of that letter, which should include the information most pertinent to your application. I'll review, add or subtract what I believe is appropriate, and send back to you what to include with your application.

So my first assignment at the end of the very first class is for students to write that rough draft of a letter of recommendation. It forces students to articulate and to project their performance during the semester. Just as my own syllabus is my legal and moral contract with students, this rough draft is a student's moral contract with me.

This exercise also gives me a chance to measure a student's projected performance against the reality of that performance throughout the semester.

* * * * *

On week seven or eight of the 15-week semester, I hand out 3 x 5-inch note cards to the students. I ask them to list the "good, the bad, and the ugly" of the class. I stress that this exercise is anonymous, that the students should *not* put their names on the cards. I also tell them that, at the beginning of the next class, students will read the comments out loud in front of the whole class. So, the comments should be honest evaluations of the class and the instructor—but not offensive or vulgar.

I leave the room for 20 minutes, during which students jot down their evaluations and drop the folded cards in a hat, which I collect at the end of the class. At the beginning of the following class, each student pulls one card out of the hat and reads out loud whatever is on the card. As a group, we discuss each of the anonymous comments.

The benefits of this exercise are many. Students have the opportunity to air complaints and concerns about the class, and I have the opportunity to respond in a constructive and informative manner—and to adjust the course accordingly.

This exercise also allows students to understand the challenges that I, as the instructor, am faced with, as students may have vastly different opinions on any given component of the class. I have to find common ground among those differing opinions.

PROFESSOR JENSON GOH CHONG LENG

The teaching tip I have for teachers is *to always take time to reflect upon your teaching philosophy and do so deeply and often.*

Our teaching philosophy governs everything we do as teachers. Until we are clear about it, we will not be able to distinguish whether a teaching practice is good or bad.

My philosophy was formed through a candid conversation with my wife in 2012. I recall the time vividly, as it was when I had made the decision to become a teacher. After listening to my decision, my wife made a surprising statement: "Do you know that all teachers are evil?"

I exclaimed, "How can a teacher be evil?"

She explained patiently, "As teachers, we always have this preconceived worldview about what we are teaching or about life. We are always eager to download all of this into the innocent minds of the young, hoping to leave an indelible imprint in them. How do we know that this will not lead them to their eventual 'demise' in life and career? Especially in our [Singapore's] education system, we often teach our children that there is only one correct way to solve a problem and there is only one path to success, the path that is defined by our society. If we are not careful, we are doing harm to our children rather than helping them, aren't we? That's why, in some ways, all teachers are evil."

How profound.

Guided by the philosophy I developed from this conversation, I believe that teaching should not be about imprinting our viewpoints upon students. Teaching should be about providing a safe and conducive environment where experiences and viewpoints on a subject can be shared openly without fear of being ridiculed. It is also about creating the opportunity for students to question and decide what to assimilate into their own knowledge and/or lives.

To build this environment, I design rapport-building and collaborative learning activities that form a scaffold to deepen the trust and camaraderie between me and students. Some noteworthy examples include playing People Bingo, sharing jokes/stories with a moral lesson at the start of every class, and collaborative learning activities grounded upon a purposefully designed play activity (such as Lego Serious Play).

Some may argue that this is a waste of teaching time. In my view, *the creation and maintenance of this environment is far more important than the teaching of the subject matter.* When effectively leveraged by teachers, deep learning in students will likely happen. This, in turn, will increase students' intrinsic motivation to learn more about the subject matter.

A reinforcing cycle of learning is developed. Teaching of any subject in this environment becomes increasingly fun, engaging, and effortless. More important, deep and lifelong friendships among students and teachers eventually will form, enriching the lives of teachers and students alike. How meaningful life can be if this should happen often.

PROFESSOR JOSEPH GRAF

As I gain more experience teaching, I think much more about teaching the whole student, and not just the material on the syllabus. In the past few years, I have talked a lot more in my classes about doing meaningful work and striving to get the most out of your life and career. Indeed, I sometimes think those class sessions are the most important of the semester.

PROFESSOR MARTHA GULATI, MD, MS, FACC, FAHA, FASPC

In medicine, an outstanding professor is often someone you see as a role model. You appreciate how they care for patients as much as you enjoy learning from them. So much of medical school education is bedside learning, so our role models often are excellent teachers with an amazing bedside manner who are loved by their patients.

One of the best professors I had was someone who loved his job and made the joy in his work contagious. Turns out he was a cardiologist (surprise, surprise, I too am now a professor and cardiologist). He was able to bring out the elegance in cardiology with its simplicity. He taught me that it wasn't necessary to memorize anything; rather, the doctor should work out the physiology from what was happening to the patient.

He made what many find complex easy to my mathematical brain, taking first principles and working from there to determine what was going on with the patient. Additionally, he was wonderful with his patients—and to me. All of this directed my wish to be like him and do what he did.

The best teachers are the ones who not only make something complicated simple because they truly understand it but also reflect the joy in what they do. Particularly in medicine, I think the best professors have huge followings because everyone wants to work with people who enjoy their work and make caring for patients not necessarily work, but a passion.

SARAH GULICK, FILMMAKER

I had strict professors with high expectations, and hilarious professors with a great sense of humor. When I think about the professors that inspired me and that I learned the most from, there were many different teaching styles and personalities. The one thing I experienced from all of my outstanding professors was respect.

In lecture courses, they came prepared, organized, and knowledgeable; respecting my time. In writing-based courses, they read my work and provided insightful feedback; respecting my efforts and helping me improve. In many of my creative courses, they were facilitators; respecting my ability to think for myself, be challenged, and grow. That respect encouraged me to do my best and to live up to their expectations. When a course started from a place of mutual respect, it felt like we were on the same team, there to learn and better ourselves and our communities.

ELIZABETH HERZFELDT-KAMPRATH, GRADUATE STUDENT

I think there are many ways to engage students in learning. One of the most successful teachers I had was my sixth-grade teacher, and I believe her methods are worth exploring even at the collegiate level.

We had a unit on how the heart worked. Every student was required to gain an understanding of the complexity of muscles that pumped the blood through valves from chamber to chamber, bringing oxygen-deprived blood into the heart and pumping oxygenated blood to every part of the body.

My teacher took a multi-layered approach to helping all 25 of us learn. We started with the textbook, and when that wasn't the most engaging my teacher brought out a huge homemade floor mat that was a map of the heart. We were to walk through the heart as the oxygen-deprived blood enters through the superior vena cava into the heart, and all the way to where the oxygen-rich blood leaves the heart through the aortic artery.

Once our entire class passed that interactive test, we had the exciting opportunity to dissect a cow's heart to physically see the elements we discussed and physically walked through.

What I learned in that unit stays with me today, I still know the right atrium from the left ventricle, and that the pulmonary valve controls blood flow out of the ventricles. But I think the biggest impression my teacher had on me during this unit was that she shared her own personal story of her son being born with a hole in his heart that caused irregular heart palpitations. This wasn't a life-threatening condition, but it did illustrate how crucial it was to understand how the heart works so that doctors were able to address the condition.

PROFESSOR GREGORY A. HUNT

I once attended a workshop on teaching given by Professor Chris Palmer in which he said that teaching must encourage "enthusiastic and motivated learners," that is, foster active learning. Active learning occurs when "students are actively engaged in building understanding of facts, ideas, and skills through the completion of instructor directed tasks" (*Active Learning Handbook* by Daniel Bell and Jahna Kahrhoff, Webster University, 2006). I have two tools for creating an active learning environment.

1. Set up teams of students to discuss specific assignments.

The first class I hold in a course begins with students interviewing each other. I break them into small teams (usually three to four per team) and have them interview each other, personalizing the interviews by asking questions about a favorite activity or drawing out "fun facts."

One team member, a chosen volunteer leader, then presents the teammates' biographical information to the entire class. The purpose of these group interviews is to allow the students time to get to know each other and to create discussion groups for future assignments.

Teams are extremely important, as they embody an active learning environment.

To engage in active learning each week, teams are required to propose discussion questions. The leaders organize their teams to review the reading assignment for the week and then launch discussion of the issues presented in the assignment. Each team is graded.

During the last half hour of class, all students break into small groups, which are then led by individual members of a presenting team. By creating discussion questions and then leading these small group discussions, students must be actively involved in learning the material.

This system also requires students to apply the material and to learn from their fellow students. My role as the professor is to support each group, and to monitor and facilitate the group discussions. A few minutes before the end of class, I have each group present to the entire class the most essential elements of their discussion. This summarization requires them to pay attention during the discussion, understand what is discussed, and apply the material.

2. Personalize the learning environment by interviewing each student during designated office hours during the first month of the semester.

In Palmer's teaching workshop, he said that the goal in teaching (and in the interviews) is to treat every student as an individual. I have found that I learn a great deal from these interviews regarding a student's background, interests, learning issues, professional goals, and academic constraints.

During the interviewing process I hear about personal situations that may present learning challenges for my students; they may, for example, be single mothers with children, be participating in internships, have jobs, or face financial constraints. Some students are "Dreamers" under the law and others may be illegal immigrants. Knowledge of these issues assists me in working with students during the academic term. This also gives students the ability to know me as a person and not only as their professor. It opens the door to communication and understanding throughout the semester, and engages students in learning.

PROFESSOR LEENA JAYASWAL

The best practice I use in my teaching is making sure my classrooms are inclusive. I start right away with a statement in my syllabus about the importance of diversity and inclusion. Because of this statement, the students know that I am open to comments and suggestions with varying perspectives. I use readings, examples, and class discussions that cover multiple viewpoints.

In my "History of Photography" course, I speak in each lecture about the canons in the field, but I also make sure to include lesser known photographers. We discuss the reasons the work of these photographers was not typically publicized. Because this course is only one semester long, there is no time to delve into the histories of non-Western photography. To broaden the course, however, I give two assignments to students to expand their knowledge. I create groups that study specific groups, such as feminist photographers, queer photographers, black photographers, and Asian photographers.

I ask the students to choose a group they do not identify with, hoping that this will give them insight into a different group. The students then write an 8–10 page research paper on that topic. The students also pair up with someone else in the class who has chosen the same topic. The two create a short video on the topic for the entire class to view. The one thing I ask them to do is to find an expert to interview for the video. The experts can range from current photographers working in that movement to academics or art historians. The students can record interviews with people around the world.

A few years ago, one group decided to interview Endia Beal. The very next year, Endia Beal was highlighted by *Time* as a photographer to watch. My students reached out to her without knowing how famous she was about to become. The class assignment was a great lesson for these two students and others; they learned about topics they would not normally explore in depth, learned to take risks, and made discoveries.

PROFESSOR KIHO KIM

I am most excited about incorporating experiential learning into my teaching. I do this in two ways: field trips to complement classroom instruction, and independent research in my lab. Whether field trips are to local organizations such as NGOs and government offices or to exotic locations such as the

Galápagos Islands or Cuba, student participants become fully immersed in these experiences because they engage all of their senses and attention.

Often these trips have an impact on students' professional trajectories. After visiting a well-regarded conservation organization, one student professed that she would one day work there—which she went on to do.

Independent research also fully immerses students, but in very different ways, requiring them to narrow their focus in order to address a question that they are motivated to answer. A good research project allows a student to explore ideas, acquire skills, and solve problems. My lab is composed of a number of students, so that they become part of a supportive learning community. One recent graduate told me that being in the lab was key to keeping him in college.

GABY KREVAT, GRADUATE STUDENT

An outstanding professor makes a sincere effort to get to know the students, encourages students to schedule/visit during office hours, asks them how class is going, and takes note of each student's long-term educational/professional goals. Additionally, an outstanding professor makes himself available for extra help that may be needed in class, or offers the student advice on where to seek extra help. An outstanding professor is clear about his expectations for class but is also empathetic. The professor challenges students by not giving easy grades and by offering written feedback on important assignments.

When I was an undergraduate student studying political science, one of my professors took note of my profound interest in a specific topic covered in class. Throughout the semester, I frequently visited my instructor during her office hours to discuss the material in further depth, and she gave me additional graduate-level reading assignments she thought I would find interesting.

I'm extremely grateful that my professor sensed my desire to learn and challenge myself beyond the expectations of the introductory class. Toward the end of the semester, she suggested that I do an independent study project with her, so I could explore topics discussed in class in more detail and receive academic credit.

SHANNON LAWRENCE, RECENT GRADUATE STUDENT

The most outstanding professors I have had emphasized that learning is not a one-size-fits-all process. Each student learns in a different way, and it can be frustrating when a misunderstanding of material in the classroom due to a teaching style discourages some students from learning. When professors are willing to adapt their teaching to different learning styles, they can help their students achieve success.

When I was an undergraduate, I struggled in my advanced ecology course, which required knowledge of some advanced mathematics. Early in the semester, I earned a poor grade on an exam. Despite the fact that I took diligent notes in class and studied hard, I was not understanding the material.

I began attending weekly office hour sessions with my professor, hoping to improve my course performance. At the beginning, my sole purpose was to improve my letter grade on my next major exam. I was so frustrated by my low grades that I was closing myself off to the learning process.

During my office hour visits, my professor spoke in depth with me about my struggles in class and my desire to improve. The lecture format wasn't working for me; I was gaining nothing from copying equations off the board in a class that seemed to turn nonnumerical science scenarios into mathematical equations with no explanation. I wasn't able to learn by simply observing.

So, my professor decided to work through different ecology models and to explain how they translated directly to mathematical equations. He ensured that I was engaged at every step of the process, challenging me to think critically instead of passively observing. It made a big difference.

The one-on-one approach did wonders for my understanding of the material. By the end of the semester, I not only mastered understanding the course material but ended up with a top grade!

ASHLEY LUKE, GRADUATE STUDENT

I have always valued professors who take pride in their work, because I've seen how difficult teaching can be. My undergraduate professors were influential in pushing me to reach my goals through hard work and through always doing my best.

An example was Professor McClure. She showed a strong desire to see me succeed and reach my full potential. One semester I took a majority of the communication classes required for my degree. Professor McClure's communication class vividly stood out because of her pleasant attitude, approachability on class assignments, and constructive criticism in class. Many students dreaded standing in front of class to give a presentation on a topic of their choice, but for me that class was the most engaging of all that semester. Professor McClure let her students, like me, be vulnerable in the pursuit of our dreams.

I looked forward to my class with her each week because of how she engaged the class on presentation delivery. More important, she gave us the room to develop as students, allowing us to make mistakes. We understood that this was our opportunity to turn uncertainties and weaknesses into successes through hard work, resolving doubts, and delivering the best presentations in class when it was show time.

I recognized her commitment to our learning through every presentation, because she recorded our presentations and provided us with a copy to review. As nerve-racking as it may have been for me and other students to prepare to speak in front of the class and then have to look over our mistakes on camera, the process conveyed her dedication to help us reach our full potential in the class, and to translate that into any other area where we might need improvement.

Achieving an A in the class took hard work, but it wasn't impossible with the support of Professor McClure and in the environment she cultivated for learning. I realized that each presentation was ultimately a step forward in developing my confidence in public speaking. Through her teaching, Professor McClure helped students like me be comfortable with "failing forward" in achieving our goals in school.

DAVID MULLINS, RECENT GRADUATE STUDENT

During my senior year as a film and media arts major in college, I took a course on environmental filmmaking. We received our homework assignments at the end of the first class with the option to personalize any or all of it. I presumed this meant applying our individual experiences to the readings or planning to make an environmental film about a subject that was meaningful to us.

I met with the professor to discuss this, and I remember him asking me, "What would you like to get out of this semester? What would help your career the most?" This was a freeing moment, as the traditional guidelines of homework vanished. The professor made it clear: The student came first. I could develop skills to progress in my field as much as possible before graduation.

I said I was beginning the script for a comedic television pilot, and it was a lofty goal of mine to have a completed copy by the end of the semester. He quickly agreed that this would be my main homework, and he would help me along the way. I walked back to my apartment, thrilled about the assignment.

I spent the next several months pitching my ideas to fellow students, diving deep into comedic character motivation and storytelling, and setting my own schedule for writing and rewriting. Every draft I submitted was thoroughly reviewed by my professor, who provided serious, constructive notes. I stayed up late reading them and revising, acting out my favorite parts. I was working hard at what I loved.

In class, I learned about project management, close collaboration, and industry standards for production. We explored ethics, morals, and how to make an honest film. I obtained an in-depth look into areas of filmmaking I would not have seen had I only taken a scriptwriting class. I could produce what I wanted on my own time and learn the professional techniques during class. I got the best of both.

By the time I was ready to graduate, I had completed a rough television screenplay, fulfilling both a personal and professional goal. The entire process—the ability to connect personally to a task, the collaboration, and how seriously I could take something so funny—is still with me to this day. It was all because the professor had the confidence in us both to be creative in our approach to his teaching and in my ability to flourish.

PROFESSOR GEMMA PUGLISI

Give students the opportunity to take risks, be creative, and push the limits in class projects. Help them think outside the box and support their creativity. As professors, we are there to guide and mentor them to use their talents and creativity. All of this can lead to exceptional successes that endure long after the students leave a classroom.

Several years ago, students in my "PR Portfolio/Campaigns" class, a course where students deliver real public relations services for clients including marketing, media, and events, proved this so perfectly. Our client was an organization that provides food and support for families in need right outside the nation's capital. Students organized food drives, worked with local supermarkets to support the cause, held a panel discussion, and, to raise awareness, put together a simple radio announcement that they sent to local stations right before Thanksgiving.

After the semester was over, I received a letter from the nonprofit thanking me and the students for their work. (The client also sent a note to the president of the university.) It turns out that several months after the students graduated, a local radio station aired the public service announcement and a local car dealership donated $25,000 to the organization.

Creativity, pushing the limits, and being there to guide are rewarding—not just for the students but the professor as well.

PROFESSOR JOHN RICHARDSON

Asking students to create and present a project that embodies the most important course outcomes has proved to be a powerful teaching tool with multiple benefits. Most often, the "outcomes" are motivated by a question. An obvious application is courses in dynamic systems modeling: "Create and defend a model responding to an important public policy question that interests you." However, the challenge is also applicable to a more general quantitative research methods course: "Create an answer to an important question, engaging the practice of international development, that statistical analysis demonstrates is 'true.'"

In a late Middle Ages history class, one might ask, "Why did feudalism not limit the growth of a strong central government in France, as it did in England?" My international development public policy students are asked to describe a project they might create and lead that would "make a difference." Jacqueline Novogratz's *The Blue Sweater: Bridging the Gap Between Rich and Poor in an Interconnected World* (New York: Rodale Books, 2009) offers examples.

I introduce project assignments with examples of excellent projects completed by students in previous classes. I may even ask students from a previous class who produced outstanding projects to come in and describe their work, share "tips" and, if appropriate, offer themselves as coaches. In addition to providing excellent projects as examples, I provide rubrics that describe my expectations clearly and that the examples I share with students exemplify.

Many class sessions and assignments are designed and characterized to students as intermediate steps on the path to completing great projects. I tell students I want them to be so engaged with their projects that they will have dreams about them as the semester progresses. Some report that they do.

Often the final class sessions, when students present their projects, are times of affirmation and celebration. In my graduate public policy modeling class, offered at Singapore's Lee Kuan Yew School of Public Policy for several years, I invited private sector managers and Singapore government officials to visit the campus, listen to the students' presentations, and pose questions. Knowing that these "outsiders" may be in the audience provided students with additional motivation.

Obviously, this project approach will not work for every subject in every setting. But as the examples above seek to demonstrate, I believe it is more widely applicable than one might think. For myself and my students alike, the greatest benefit of this project-oriented approach is that it enables me to constitute myself as coach (and even as cheerleader) rather than as policeman or referee. Often coaches must administer "tough love," but team members know that they and their coaches are partners in a common endeavor.

PROFESSOR GIANNA SAVOIE

I have found that one of the most effective teaching methods is "flipping the classroom," in which the student synthesizes the material by becoming the instructor. For example, instead of posing questions to my students based upon a particular lesson, I will ask *them* to come up with questions for each other based on the material, and then we discuss. I find that this approach fosters deeper attention and understanding of the subject matter and provides a valuable means of seeing how different people may interpret a work.

Another thing I do, in my graduate writing class in particular, is to randomly pair my students up and have them provide the first draft of their final paper to their partner. The partner must critique and provide constructive feedback on the other student's work (as I have done for them throughout the course of the semester) to help move the student to a final draft. I grade them on the quality of constructive feedback and on evidence of synthesis of what they have learned over the course of the semester, as shown via their comments on their partner's work.

I then grade the final paper itself, taking into consideration the way in which each student has assessed and incorporated the partner's feedback—if it has indeed moved them to a stronger final paper. I have not had a case yet where this exercise hasn't strengthened the work and made students more confident in their own writing.

PROFESSOR SAM SHELINE

One of the most important traits I've noticed in effective teachers throughout my education is that they encourage students to create projects about topics that excite them. It took me much longer than I would like to admit (until most of the way through college!) to realize that—when the assignment and teacher allow it—choosing a topic about which I'm truly interested can make all the difference in the world. I was more motivated to produce quality work, and spent more time and energy on that work, if the topic engaged me. And therefore, I ended up learning more. I remember feeling that motivation as a student, and today I see it in my own classroom because I've applied this lesson to teaching as a visual media professor.

Effective teachers also let their own passions and interests shine through in their teaching. All my favorite teachers have been personally dedicated to the subjects they teach, and their dedication has made learning from them easier and more enjoyable. The student-teacher relationship is, in some ways, like many other interpersonal relationships in that it feels good to make someone else happy. As a student, showing interest in and aptitude for a subject that a teacher has a deep connection to makes that teacher happy. As a teacher, it's fulfilling to see students respond with curiosity and dedication to a subject that I'm connected to and trying to teach.

Almost every one of my favorite teachers has been more flexible than average. Teachers should understand that not all students learn the same way or take the same knowledge from the same assignment. Helping decide how to shape or change an assignment or even a course was a rewarding experience for me as a student, and having my students help me tweak or design assignments and courses has been quite rewarding as a teacher.

PROFESSOR RICK STACK

[Kids] don't remember what you try to teach them. They remember what you are.

—Jim Henson, American puppeteer

Just as breakfast is considered by many to be the day's most important meal (or at least among the top three), so too the initial class of the semester can set the proper foundation for a course. I have two first-class assignments that accomplish critical objectives.

While the students are still settling in, I ask them to ghostwrite a recommendation letter for themselves from the perspective of someone who knows them well. To facilitate the process, I describe a four-paragraph formula and turn them loose for 20 minutes. Their submissions tell me how well they write, what their interests and ambitions are, and what they think of themselves. It's a quick way to get to know who's taking the class.

I weave findings from these self-reference letters into subsequent class discussions. If I've learned that Suzy is interested in sports marketing, I'll localize the lesson to show how a theory applies to the hometown team. If I know Bobby is interested in literature, I'll discuss the social impact of a prison book club.

As each student's passions become known to the class, a sense of camaraderie develops. Classroom cohesion grows as students gain an appreciation and respect for each other's interests. That bonding elevates the group dynamic. As the comfort level rises, the stress in the room subsides. When students know how to joke with each other, they are freer to express opinions. When students accept learning as a cooperative venture, there are no "dumb questions." As the anxiety of being judged fades away, even shy students become fully engaged. A classroom in which students genuinely like each other is characterized by an unmistakable joy. Learning flourishes.

My other opening class exercise is intended to gently jolt the students from their vacation slumbers. I jokingly apologize for making them think on the very first day of school. Before the chuckling stops, I ask them to draft a syllabus for the course. First reaction: I've never done that before! Once they pick their jaws up off the floor, I ask them what they think the key elements of the course should be. Attach a Roman numeral to each week with a corresponding topic, I advise. Under that, list the resources that could help explain that subject matter (i.e., book, journal article, video, website, guest expert, field trip). If they're still stumped as to what the course content might be, I hint that they peek at the textbook's table of contents.

It dawns on them that they can venture out of their comfort zones and figure things out. They're also put on notice that I intend to take a creative approach to challenging their resourcefulness. Let the semester commence.

* * * * *

Students don't care how much you know until they know how much you care.

—John C. Maxwell, American author and leadership expert

At the start of the semester, I like to pose the following question to my students and have them write out their answers: "What are your passions?" I tell the students not to limit themselves to academic interests. Be it ballet or bowling, botany or burgers, I want them to dig deep and identify what drives them. Then I make this point: You tell me what you're passionate about and I'll show you how to incorporate that into your communication studies to earn a living you'll find fulfilling, rewarding, and fun.

This exercise accomplishes two things. It gets the students thinking about what's important to them, the first step in exploring their values. It's also my attempt to address John Maxwell's observation that students won't care about how much you know until they know how much you care. As I customize my instruction to their individual aspirations, the students get the idea I care about them.

* * * * *

Professors must aspire to be informative and entertaining. The instructor's role as information deliverer is obvious. The entertainment aspect confronts what many educators may not want to admit, and newbies might not realize. But in this age of ADD-addled/social media-obsessed students, being entertaining is more critical than ever in conquering the problem of short attention spans. Another way to think of it is this: Being informative + being entertaining = being engaging.

My mother was a teacher of all things Jewish—Sunday school, Yiddish theater, senior citizen choral groups, bar and bat mitzvah lessons, to name a few. She also taught Hebrew school. For the uninitiated, these are after-school sessions for kids from about 2nd grade to 7th grade, leading to the more intense bar mitzvah preparations. Exceedingly rare is the child, especially the boy, who wants to sit through Hebrew classes for an hour or two after being in school all day. My mom, 5 feet tall on a good day, was not above standing on top of her desk and jumping up and down to share her enthusiasm for a breakthrough learning point. Talk about entertaining! Her example inspires me as a professor.

PROFESSOR CHRISTOPHER STEN

Reading a book like *Moby Dick* can be a challenge; teaching it can be a challenge, too. A semester is only so many weeks long, and there are other works by other authors to consider in any nineteenth-century American literature course. There's never enough out-of-class time for reading, or in-class time for discussion. And because it's such a daunting task for students to get started on the book, they need to dig in right away and not put off the reading until they hear what the professor might have to say in class.

To help my students meet these challenges, I do two things: (1) I provide them with a "map" or outline describing Melville's thematic organization of the book, divided into sections for each of six class meetings over three weeks (preparations for the hunt; the players and rules of engagement; pursuit/capture/killing the whale; securing the oily treasure; and, finally, the fate of the hero) and highlighting prominent themes in keeping with the overall structure of the book as the journey or quest of the hero; and (2) I require students to write a one- or two-page essay on one of the chapters assigned for each of our six meeting days.

In other words, they read about 15–20 percent of the book and write a short paper for each of the six class meetings devoted to *Moby Dick*. The amount of writing they do (just 5–10 pages total over three weeks) is not as important as the frequency: They are expected to come to every class with a short essay in hand. To make sure students concentrate their writing on the more significant or puzzling chapters of the book, I provide a list of four or five chapters to choose from for each day's reading. This procedure also helps to promote class discussion when we meet to go over the reading assigned for the day, since several students will inevitably end up writing on the same chapter or chapters.

Before students even begin to read or write about the book, I encourage them to dig into the chapter they choose to write on—to think and ponder and explore. I urge them to not simply describe what happens but to analyze and explain the significance of the action or of the chapter as a whole, while also looking for Melville's jokes and puns, his buried or symbolic meanings.

One of the advantages of this kind of assignment is that if students don't get the hang of it the first time, they can learn from their mistakes and recover with plenty of time to do better on the remaining short papers. I always return each set of papers at the next class meeting, with comments and a grade, so students can quickly see where they need to improve.

Another advantage of having students do a series of short papers like this is the cumulative learning that can result from these exercises—the sharpening of critical reading and writing skills that students can experience over time while we all engage with the novel and push through to its tragic, apocalyptic conclusion. And, in the end, they will have a set of papers that can serve as a record of their experience of the book and (hopefully) of their progress in becoming more adept and skillful interpreters of Melville's epic.

PROFESSOR MAGGIE BURNETTE STOGNER

When I began teaching, I assumed my job was to stand at the front of the room and impart knowledge with an air of authority to a class of neophyte onlookers. This was due more to ignorance than arrogance. I had a vast amount of experience as a filmmaker and was eager to share it. I prepared each lecture with the dedication of a speechwriter, ready to wax eloquent about film aesthetics, historical context, best practices, and the latest cinematic techniques. There was just one problem. The more I lectured, the more the energy in the room seemed to dissipate. Waves of polite boredom and stifled yawns washed across students' faces. Admittedly, I was not the most polished speaker, but I honestly did not understand why there was such a pervasive lack of response.

The challenge was clear: How could I engage students more fully? I began exploring different approaches and pedagogical practices. I thought about what worked when I was in college, which courses were the most memorable and why. I asked my parents, both teachers, for advice. I sought guidance from my colleagues at American University and other academic institutions. I talked with students and carefully read through their course evaluation comments. It was the beginning of an ongoing inquiry that continues to this day.

Though it continues to evolve, here is my list of ten techniques for engaging students:

1. **Show enthusiasm.** I was off to a good start in this department. A genuine passion for what you are teaching goes far. The students feel and appreciate it. It just isn't enough by itself.

2. **Move around.** By moving around the classroom, you create an energetic atmosphere that holds the students' attention. No antics and no intimidation. (I remember well a teacher in high school who would suddenly turn and throw chalk and erasers at sleepy students.)

3. **Use eye contact.** Students are not a sea of faces over which you should stare at some spot in the distance above their heads. See and connect with each student in the class. Eye contact is a way of letting students know that you are talking directly to each and every one of them and, in return, expecting their undivided attention.

4. **Use students' names.** This simple technique for connecting with each student is by far the most challenging for me. I remember faces perfectly, but not names. To compensate, I ask the students to use name cards, I review their roster photos before class, and I quiz myself afterward.

5. **Employ storytelling.** At the heart of who we are as humans is our desire to create and tell stories. Share your professional and life experiences, and let students share theirs as well. Bringing humanity into the classroom serves everyone well.

6. **Mix it up.** Over the years, I've created an array of techniques and tools. I mix up the more traditional lecture, small group and class discussions, student-led presentations, and pop quizzes with creativity exercises, mock debates and media interviews, brainstorming sessions, collaboration and team-building practicums, group critiques, and more in-class, experiential filmmaking workshops.

7. **Ban digital devices.** It may sound draconian, but there is no way to fully capture students' attention if they are multitasking on their smartphones, iPads, laptops, etc.

8. **Address life issues.** Inclusivity, gender identity, sexual harassment, and other issues are not external to the classroom. Students are affected by what is going on in their lives, and helping them navigate tough issues by modeling humane approaches in the classroom is part of every teacher's job.

9. **Meet outside the classroom.** One of my favorite graduate school professors would sit beside an old oak tree on the Stanford campus doing the day's crossword. Students would stop by, sometimes to discuss a problem, other times to help work the puzzle.

10. **Ask questions!** This is the most radical change I made from when I began teaching. No longer do I stand at the podium lecturing to a room full of politely bored faces. Today, I view teaching as a collaborative journey with students. It is my job to prompt enquiry and discussion so that we might all continue to learn together. So, here's my question for you: What techniques do you use?

PROFESSOR SCOTT TALAN

I believe in the Four C's of teaching: Content, Community, Connection, and Communication. Content is important, of course. The community you create in class is vital to how much content students learn. Related to this is the connection you forge with students in general and each student as an individual. Communication encompasses the connection and effective transmission of information. Not just information but a feeling. A story.

I recall saying to a group of students, "Geography is destiny," and then explaining why I believe where they live (city, zip code, country, etc.) will determine so much of their life ahead. A short while after I first said this, I was in downtown Washington, DC, when a student saw me and shouted, "Geography is destiny." This is just one small story about how the words that teachers speak can be remembered by students who hear them.

GRANT P. THOMPSON, FORMER ADJUNCT PROFESSOR AND ENVIRONMENTALIST

Most of my years of formal education were spent in the pre-computer, pre-Internet days, when learning took place with a professor standing in a classroom lecturing, asking questions from time to time, and supplementing what he or she taught by assigning reading assignments from a book or two selected to represent an entire body of information in the field. Students were mainly passive sponges of information and viewpoints that traveled from lecturer to pupil.

In smaller classes, you were kept on your toes by occasional questions or discussions. Studying astronomy at Pomona College under Professor Paul

Routley was a completely different, somewhat terrifying, but electrifying experience. Routley held the revolutionary idea that students didn't really understand astronomy at a deep level if they were unable to explain concepts in their own words. By forcing each of us to assume the role of professor from time to time, he guaranteed that we were more than robots regurgitating canned lectures. "If you can't teach it, you don't understand it" was his motto.

A second experience that shaped my perception of teaching occurred when I taught energy policy to a small class at Dartmouth College. My students were horrified that I asked them to write a short paper each week. They accused me of failing to understand the burden that being forced to write placed on them. Even more appalling, they soon discovered that I would routinely return their papers to them marked up with corrections, questions, suggestions, and hints, and I had the audacity to ask them to rewrite the papers in a final draft! I recall one student—who went on to become a leading geologist—years later confessing that she kept a doll in her dorm with my name on it and with pins that she stuck into tender parts. But she also reported that being forced to write and rewrite was the single best experience of her college years.

AMELIA TYSON, GRADUATE STUDENT

I believe college professors have something to learn from teachers of grades K–12. Take Mrs. Anderson, for example. She was the best teacher I ever had between first grade and undergraduate school. In second grade, I struggled with mathematics and reading, and dropped behind my classmates significantly. Enter Mrs. Anderson. Instead of berating my academic deficiencies, she made me feel worthy. She made me see that I wasn't the problem. Through her, learning became a joy. By fourth grade, I had caught up with my classmates. To me, her approach to teaching was brave. Brave because it was so different from most other teaching methods. I wish her approach to teaching were replicated by university faculty.

Mrs. Anderson established an atmosphere of true friendship and encouragement as a fundamental classroom element. She combined that with the view that people are not empty vessels into which knowledge is poured, but dynamic beings with the capacity to understand both simple and profound concepts. She was devoted and dedicated to students' growth. She was patient with the learning process. That was apparent through her willingness to sacrifice her time and energy for the improvement of others. Thank you, Mrs. Anderson.

PROFESSOR ANGELA VAN DOORN

Early in my teaching career, I attended a conference and was struck by the assertion that, while I thought my job as a professor was to teach about my field and expertise, in reality 30 percent of my job was actually to teach students how to learn.

This was a light bulb moment for me. I had been frustrated with constant demands for study guides. Many students were accustomed to getting detailed lists of exactly what to memorize for the exam, and thought I was mean when I did not provide them with a study guide. With my newfound insight, I realized that these requests arose from the fact that students were struggling with identifying the key concepts in the material and with how best to learn the content.

I immediately went home and started rethinking my lectures and assignments. To prepare students for the first exam, I interspersed examples of exam questions throughout the lecture.

I also created an assignment that required students to prepare their own study guide a week before the exam. I discussed several different review options and study techniques, including flashcards, outlines, and mind maps, and allowed them to choose the options that worked best for their perceived learning styles.

I then had students share and quiz each other with their study guides. I collected the assignment and was surprised that many guides were packed with unnecessary details that resulted in a voluminous amount of content to study, while others lacked even basic details. I then posted my own study guide for the material and had students write a short response in class identifying how our guides differed.

After the exam, I posted an exam wrapper (see the example below) that students could use to reflect on their study habits (such as time spent studying, reading the textbook, and/or reviewing notes). I offered to discuss it with them individually to suggest strategies for the next exam. Prior to the second exam, I again assigned a study guide and had students share their guides in groups, but did not provide a guide myself.

For the final exam, I encouraged the students to make a study guide, but did not require it. Most students continued to create their own exam guides, and the average test scores of my students increased compared to the previous semester. I also have never had another request for a study guide!

I observed that information is always more interesting to students if it is personally relevant to them. I ask students, "Why do we need oxygen? Where does the electricity come from when you turn on the light switch?" Most students don't know the answers to questions such as these. The explanations make the course content more relevant to their lives and their understanding of the world.

Post-Exam Reflection (Exam Wrapper) for ENVS 150

This activity is designed to give you a chance to reflect on your exam performance and, more importantly, on the effectiveness of your exam preparation. Please be candid in your responses.

While studying for this exam, how many points (out of 100) did you expect to earn? _____

After completing this exam, how many points (out of 100) did you think you had earned? _____

How many points did you earn? _____

Approximately, how many hours did you spend studying for this exam? _____

How many days did you review the material? _____

How many days before the exam did you start studying? _____

Have you missed more than 3 classes? _____

Did you feel that you understood the material? _____

Did you study enough? _____

Could you have studied "smarter"? _____

If yes, how?

What percentage of your test preparation was spent in each of these activities (the numbers you enter below should add up to 100)?

_____ Reading chapters for the first time

_____ Rereading chapters

_____ Reviewing PowerPoints from class

_____ Reading over assignments

_____ Reviewing information from the "You should be able to" summary slides

_____ Quizzing yourself on vocabulary

_____ Outlining and note-taking

_____ Reading through notes taken earlier in the class

_____ Talking about the material with a classmate or friend

_____ Identifying important ideas and concepts

_____ Other – explain _____

Carefully look over your exam and estimate the **percentage** of points you lost due to each of the following (the numbers you enter should add up to 100, no matter how many points you lost):

_____ Careless mistakes

_____ Misunderstanding the question

_____ Not being familiar with vocabulary/terms
_____ Not understanding concepts
_____ Not fully answering the question
_____ Not reading the chapter that the question was based on
_____ Not reviewing the "You should be able to" slides
_____ Not understanding what information or ideas were important
_____ Rushing/poor time management during the exam
_____ Other – explain

If you are not satisfied with how you did on the exam, describe three things that you plan to do differently in preparing for the next exam. For instance, will you spend more time studying, change a specific study habit, try a new one? Please describe. If you are happy with how you did, list three things you did that you feel helped you earn a good grade, and that you plan to keep doing in the future.

1.

2.

3.

What can the instructor do to help support your learning and your preparation for the next exam?

KENT WAGNER, GRADUATE STUDENT

Good professors should get to know their students and find out what they are passionate about. If they know one another well enough, then it is more likely a professor will be able to help a student as he strikes out toward his chosen career path. Not *every* professor needs to make a connection with *every* student. But professors should be open to it and encourage it. In fact, perhaps it should be the student's responsibility to establish such a relationship. I strongly suggest that every university student find at least one professor who knows the student's specific industry/profession, and with whom he feels connected. In this way, the student will have a person who knows the options available to people new to that field, and will have someone with whom to share thoughts, hopes, and dreams about his future in that field. Then the student and professor can see if there is common ground between them. Students who fail to take advantage of this are missing out on one of the greatest benefits of the student/professor relationship.

PROFESSOR PAUL WAPNER

One of my favorite techniques to enhance learning is to begin each class with a "tuning." Some students arrive in class having not spoken to anyone yet that day. Others arrive preoccupied with ongoing concerns or plans. Still others come to class ready to learn but shy or simply unsure how they will participate in the day's experience.

I try to bring students together by asking them to say a few words about what is most alive for them at this moment. The idea is to invite everyone to speak into the circle of the class as a way for students to get to know each other, create a comfortable learning environment, and help students transition to being in the classroom and turning their attention to the material at hand. I usually ask for a volunteer to begin the process and, after that person has spoken, to choose a direction. We then hear the answers of the entire class. I even participate in the exercise; I share what is alive for me when my turn arrives. For large classes, I ask simply for three words. For small seminars, I invite longer but still brief comments.

I teach seminars on politics and justify the exercise by reminding students that decision makers often arrive at the "situation room" or other venues with baggage from their personal lives or simply preoccupations that, if left unacknowledged, can potentially get in the way of sound, cooperative decision making. I also remind them that the exercise teaches us how to listen to others without reacting. As students share, no one interrupts or even responds. We let both difficult and joyful sharings stand and experience the challenge of listening and caring about each other without trying to fix our fellow classmates.

At the beginning of each semester, sharings are pretty bland. "I'm changing roommates." "My mom's birthday is today." "I'm trying to change majors." As the semester unfolds, however, sharings grow deeper. Students talk about reactions to course readings, feelings of despair about the world, or personal challenges. The idea is not to conduct a therapeutic sharing session but rather to hear from everyone and to allow students to understand the broader context within which our class conversation is taking place.

By asking students, "What is most alive in you?" the exercise also provides a practice for coming into the present moment. Having to reflect on what is going on with ourselves—intellectually, emotionally, bodily, or even spiritually—is a way to ground our present experience. It encourages us to drop the chatter going on in our heads and develop a capacity to zero in on our immediate sensations, thoughts, and feelings.

I refer to the exercise as "tuning" since, by collectively reflecting on where we are each coming from and what is going on at the moment, it brings us all to class. It helps us arrive mindfully and thus open to the topic of the day.

PHIL WARBURG, AUTHOR, LAWYER, ENVIRONMENTAL ACTIVIST

My best experience in college lay outside the bounds of traditional classroom learning. I was fascinated by communitarian movements of the nineteenth and twentieth centuries—an admittedly obscure topic but one that fit my interest in exploring radical alternatives to the high-consumption lifestyles that were pervasive in the 1970s, when I was in college, and are even more pervasive today. Not surprisingly, Harvard offered nothing remotely close to that subject. I therefore arranged an independent study with a lecturer in social studies, itself a highly flexible major. We crafted a syllabus and met weekly to discuss readings that ranged from social theory to ethnography. Later, in advising my undergraduate thesis, my tutor schooled me in survey research and interview methodology. He was more truly a mentor than any of the big-name professors who taught my other classes, and he is a close friend to this day.

The message I'd want to communicate is that one shouldn't feel constrained by formal course offerings. Use creativity and initiative to arrange a learning environment that matches one's interests and passions. This initiative-taking does more than satisfy a particular intellectual or normative concern; it is good preparation for crafting a worthy career path and a meaningful life.

PROFESSOR JOHN WATSON

Tests are assumed only to be tools for evaluating student learning, but they can do much more. Used strategically, they are effective teaching tools because I have found students are most receptive to learning immediately before and immediately after a test.

With that in mind, I conduct an intense review at the last class session before the test. Students show up laser-focused. The review consists primarily of having them work as a group through the last two iterations of the test from the immediately preceding semesters. They see it as a hack. Kids of this generation love hacks. It gives them the sense of outwitting the system.

They notice some questions pop up in both prior tests. They "figure out" that I consider these points of knowledge to be especially important for them to know, and I probably will ask about them on the new test as well. Hack!

And that's unavoidably true. Upon completing any course, there are some things every student must know. This tactic ensures the students learn them.

Of course, this requires me to create a new exam every semester. That's a good thing because it forces me to rethink and invent fresh approaches to the material. But, as you will see later, the students unwittingly help with this.

Immediately after an exam, many students are desperate to know how they did—though others just want to flee the stress. I have found that at this point they are wide open to seeing their errors and remembering them. This is a rich learning/teaching opportunity. Students deeply remember what they got wrong, more than what they got right. These are mistakes they will not likely repeat. That's learning.

When I grade the exams, I note the questions that were most often answered incorrectly. I see this as an indication of my failure to teach effectively. I redeem myself by letting the students know these badly taught concepts will return in altered form in the final exam. I ask them to formulate questions that will address the information in new ways and submit them to me. I actually use the best suggestions on the final and on the exam for the next semester's class. The students see the opportunity to create the questions as a hack because they will know the answers. As they figure out these new approaches, they are learning the material more deeply. I have just hacked them.

NICK ZACHAR, RECENT GRADUATE STUDENT

After four years of undergraduate schooling and an additional three years spent obtaining my master's degree, I would say I have had my fair share of professors. Especially in undergrad at a large state school, it seemed many were there just to satisfy their requirements as faculty.

It wasn't until graduate school that I first observed true passion for teaching, which I think is the key ingredient to teaching effectively. Passion for teaching includes passion for helping those willing to learn, and it is this passion that motivates those who may be less interested.

A few professors stand out in my experience as having this innate ability to blend instruction and motivation, and it was these professors who inspired me to act on my own dreams and aspirations. One of my aspirations is to teach, and I will most definitely refer to the positive experiences with these instructors, and learn from those who had the passion.

Appendix I

Teaching Workshop Handout

Inspiring Enthusiasm and Motivation in the Classroom

By Professor Chris Palmer, American University School of Communication

To develop a vibrant, productive, and memorable course, professors must continually work on inspiring students to become enthusiastic and motivated learners. Such students are engaged, active participants in their own learning.
  Below, you'll find suggestions in the following six categories:

I. Syllabus

II. First Classes

III. Classroom Atmosphere

IV. Classroom Specifics

V. Classroom Interactions

VI. Beyond the Classroom

Some of these suggestions may not work for you because of the size or content of your class. Classroom management strategies must be shaped around the maturity of the students, the expectations of the class, and the individual teaching style of the professor.
  By the end of this workshop, participants should have tangible ideas on how to engage their students. To evaluate this learning outcome, we will discuss these techniques as a group. All participants should be able to state a technique from this handout and explain how they will incorporate it into their courses next semester.

I. SYLLABUS

1. <u>Devise Specific Learning Outcomes</u>: In your syllabus, make the learning outcomes as specific and clear as possible, and relate these to the assignments and to your grading metrics. Professor Lyn Stallings recommends stating desired outcomes with a comment about how you propose to assess each outcome. In Stallings's math class, for example, one of her desired outcomes is, "By the end of this course, you should be able to communicate (written and spoken) mathematically using appropriate terminology and notation." Her methods of assessing this outcome are "corrections, test communication questions, board work, reading journals."

2. <u>Describe Class Format</u>: Describe in your syllabus the class format. For example: "We will strive for class sessions that are lively, engaging, fun, creative, and informative. Our format will combine discussion, presentations, guest speakers, case studies, in-class screenings, and analysis."

3. <u>Spell Out Expected Student Behavior</u>: Describe in your syllabus the behavior you expect from your students. For example: "Students are expected to come each week prepared to contribute their knowledge and share insights with their colleagues. We will all learn from each other. All reading and written assignments must be completed before coming to class, and written assignments must be free of spelling and grammatical errors. There will be extensive peer review and interaction. More than your physical presence is required in class. I am looking for attentiveness, vitality, and enthusiasm during class. Participation in class will raise your grades. The give-and-take of information, ideas, insights, and feelings is essential to the success of this class. Thoughtful, informed, balanced, and candid speech is most helpful, especially when critiquing each other's work."

4. <u>Describe Expected Professional Behavior</u>: You might even want to go a step further and add a paragraph to your syllabus describing the professional behavior you are looking for from your students. For example: "Students are expected to act in a professional manner, meeting deadlines, solving problems, cooperating with classmates, and generally contributing in a positive way to the class. Working in the real world often means searching for solutions in a group context. Teamwork, listening, empathy, enthusiasm, emotional maturity, and consideration of other people's concerns

are all essential to success. Please bring these qualities and values with you to class. It is as important to 'practice' these interpersonal skills as it is to learn new intellectual content. Students will be evaluated on their professional demeanor in class."

II. FIRST CLASSES

1. Learn Students' Names: Make a serious and obvious effort to learn your students' names within the first or second class. Learning students' names (and having students learn each other's names) creates a warm environment that encourages learning and participation. Address your students by name when speaking in class, and ask your students to address each other by name rather than "he" or "she." This practice helps students develop a connection with you and with each other. Some methods that can be used to learn names include creating "name tents" and placing them in front of each student, and having your TA take pictures of everyone and create a handout with names paired with photos.

2. Introduce Yourself: Many students will be interested in your background and experiences. Allow students to ask questions about you (McKeachie 23). Robert Magnan suggests that you play "Meet Your Teacher." Distribute the syllabus and relevant handouts and give students time to read everything. Then divide the class into groups and have them decide on questions to ask you (Magnan 5). Some professors include a brief bio in the syllabus to give students a way to talk to parents and friends about the instructor. (And of course faculty bios can be found in the department or division website.) Even after the first classes, look for opportunities to tell your students more about your professional experiences, relating these to the learning outcomes for the course. Students can learn from your success and especially from your mistakes. They should know that their professors are human.

3. Ask Students to Introduce Themselves: During the first class, have students introduce themselves and say something of substance about themselves. They might describe a goal they have, for example, or what they plan to do after completing their studies (Chicago Handbook 22). You could also have students interview one another and briefly present their partner to the class.

4. Fill Out Questionnaire: Have the students fill out a questionnaire about themselves, including contact information (name, phone number, school email address), goals, interests, and expectations for the course. Questions might include: "Why are you taking this class? What do you hope to learn? What are your career aspirations? Can you give me any hints about teaching/learning strategies that work well for you? What is your greatest hope for yourself in this class?" Discuss the students' answers when you meet with them one-on-one. A questionnaire like this helps you know more about your students and helps the students feel cared for.

5. Write a Letter to the Professor Dated the Last Day of the Semester: Ask each student as part of the first homework assignment to write you a letter, dated the day of the last class, describing how he performed outstandingly in your class and the kind of person he became because of it. This activity helps students begin the class with the end in mind. Return this letter to the students on the last day of class and discuss what they learned from the exercise. This exercise may not work for, say, a basic science course.

6. Meet One-on-One with Students: Tell your students that they have to meet with you within the first two weeks of the semester. In these meetings, learn more about each student, including background, interests, and life goals. Your goal is to treat every student as an individual. Make an effort to get to know individual students' interests and concerns, and to acknowledge each student's individuality. Learn about students' hopes and dreams. For large lectures where a professor cannot meet with everyone individually, invite students to meet with you in groups of three or four, or assign students to meet with a TA or another faculty mentor. Be aware of boundaries; there is a fine line between getting to know someone and prying. Be careful not to cross this line.

7. Learn from Your Students: Professor Ann Ferren recommends that during the first class you express to your students that you expect to learn from them, both during class discussions, and from their research and papers. Professor Darrell Hayes suggests also providing a short anecdote about something you just learned from a student.

8. Establish Standards of Grading: Professor John Douglass believes that it is important for students to understand what your standards of grading are. He recommends that you build assignments, quizzes, and/or other gradable events into your classes early in the semester, so that your students can judge your reaction to their work.

III. CLASSROOM ATMOSPHERE

1. Convey Your Passion: Convey your passion and enthusiasm for the subject and your willingness to provide individual help to students. Your body language and voice must convey the message, as Professor Patrick Allitt says, that there is nowhere else you'd rather be. Many professors like to walk among the students, being physically active and animated, and using their whole body and voice to reflect their great fascination with the subject matter. Classes can be much more engaging when professors move around rather than sit still or lecture from a lectern. When students see their professor's passion, they want to participate.

2. Create a Welcoming Environment: Effective professors create welcoming classroom environments that motivate students to thrive. They are committed to excellence in teaching. This commitment manifests itself as enthusiasm, responsiveness to students' email and office visits, and a willingness to go "beyond the call of duty."

3. Foster a Sense of Belonging and Respect: Students want to feel that they belong in the class and have friends there. They want to feel safe, respected, and cared for. The atmosphere must be inclusive and trusting, so that students feel that their views are heard and valued.

4. Encourage High Performance: It's important for students to take risks and leave their comfort zones. Professors should challenge students with more work than they think the students can handle, encouraging them to develop high-level critical and analytical thinking skills. Demand that your students push themselves further than they normally do.

5. Promote Active Engagement: Lecturing may work sometimes, but even dynamic lectures can be tedious for students. Most students learn best when they are actively engaged in their own learning, through reacting to lectures with questions and comments, participating in class discussions, and performing active learning exercises. (McGlynn 79, 86)

6. Sit in a Circle: For a small class, create a sense of community by sitting in a circle. The circle formation promotes dialogue and provides space for intentional and respectful engagement.

7. Make Every Class Writing-Intensive: Include a variety of writing assignments throughout the semester: informal and formal, in-class and

out-of-class, "thinking" pieces, interpretive essays, research papers, reports, and journals. Writing has a major role not only in student learning and engagement, but also in promoting critical thinking and intellectual curiosity. As Professor Chris Sten at George Washington University says, "students not only learn to write, but they also write to learn."

8. <u>Manage Large Lecture-based Classes</u>: If you have a large lecture-based class where many of the above ideas are irrelevant, you might try the following ideas. Chat informally with students before class and try to learn the names of some students. Set out a box by the door for feedback—questions, thoughts, suggestions, ideas, opinions, commentaries, critiques, and so forth. Begin or end your lectures with items from the box (Magnum 27). Announce at the beginning of the lecture that you will ask a student to summarize the lecture at the end of class. Or, less threateningly, have students spend three minutes at the end of class writing up the main points, or writing the most important thing that they learned (McKeachie 61). Have students stand up and stretch in the middle of class, no matter what the size. Make eye contact as you lecture and try to make eye contact with all students equally. Don't give the impression of teaching to the front of the room or only to a select group or population of students.

IV. CLASSROOM SPECIFICS

1. <u>Show up Early for Class</u>: Show up early for class so that you can connect with your students. Greet them warmly and engage them in conversation. Arrive meticulously prepared, including having backup plans and extra markers or chalk in your pocket.

2. <u>Take Roll</u>: Some professors believe it's the student's responsibility, as an adult, to attend class. There's merit to that argument, but I've found that students are more likely to attend class if they know I take roll. Most students feel that their professors more care about them when they keep track of attendance. Taking roll also helps both you and the students learn names.

3. <u>Start with Student Summary of Last Class</u>: Start class by asking a student to summarize the main points from the last class. This practice provides continuity, helps students who were absent to catch up, and allows students to become more comfortable with oral communication. During

the first class, let your students know about the oral summaries, so they can come to class prepared.

4. <u>Write the Plan for the Class on the Board</u>: Write the plan for the class on the board before students arrive. This practice helps students know what to expect and encourages participation. Mention where you are on this plan as the class unfolds. This practice gives you a chance to recap and answer questions. You don't have to cover everything in the plan. Remain flexible. The goal is to focus on student learning, not necessarily on covering every detail in the outline.

5. <u>Have the Students Stand up and Stretch</u>: Sitting for more than two hours (or even forty-five minutes) is too much for anyone. Once or twice during the class, ask all your students to stand up and stretch to break things up a bit, and to help keep them alert.

6. <u>Play Short Games</u>: For long classes, occasionally play a short game (sometimes called "ice-breakers"), especially early in the semester. Such games, which last no more than a few minutes, help the students get to know each other, remember each other's names, and bond. Games are a fun break from the intensity of class and can help build a sense of belonging and community. They can also increase students' motivation and desire to learn. If you e-mail me (christopher.n.palmer@gmail.com), I'll send you some games.

7. <u>Have Field Trips as Part of the Class</u>: Professor Kiho Kim recommends that professors take students on field trips and excursions whenever possible. He finds interacting with students in a non-classroom environment more engaging because the students tend to feel more relaxed.

8. <u>Invite Parents and Siblings</u>: As long as this conforms to school policy, tell your students that if their parents or siblings are ever in town, they are welcome to sit in on the class. This lets the guests see what a typical class is like.

9. <u>Complete the Class</u>: At the end of each class, summarize what was accomplished. Reinforce and underscore the two or three key messages or learning points you'd like the students to come away with. Go over the homework due at the start of the next class, providing a typed handout, so that there is no confusion about requirements and expectations. Another exercise for the end of class that can buttress learning is to ask your students to write a "minute paper" (see point 8 above). Ask your

students, "What is the most significant thing you learned today" and "What question is uppermost in your mind at the end of today's class" (Davis 56).

10. <u>End the Class on Time</u>: End the class on time to show basic consideration for the value of the students' time.

V. CLASSROOM INTERACTIONS

1. <u>Make the Class Interactive</u>: Make the class interactive and do everything possible to transform the students from passive observers to active players. Get the students out of their seats frequently to work on analyzing an issue in groups of two or three. Students learn more and retain more when they are actively involved, whether by taking notes, asking questions, or making comments. Professor Richard Linowes uses dyads (pairs) at the start of every class to "get all brains in the room operating at the same time," rather than just the brain of the person who happens to put her hand up. He uses dyads to comment on the news, report on developments in their investment portfolio, state their recommendations for the case study under discussion that day, and so forth. In this way, all students do their own thinking about an issue. The strategy also gives students a chance to practice what they want to say before Linowes calls on them. When students share their thoughts with another student first, the class discussion will be of a higher quality. This technique is sometimes called "Think/Pair/Share."

2. <u>Call on Students Constantly to Answer Questions</u>: Constantly call on individual students by name to answer questions without first asking for volunteers. This practice keeps the whole class awake and alert. Never go for more than three or four minutes without getting one of the students to speak. Never let your students get overly comfortable and lethargic. You want them to be on their toes and fully awake, knowing that you might call on them at any time to answer a question.

3. <u>Reassure Students You Will Come Back to Them</u>: If two or more students raise their hands at the same time, reassure those students not selected that you won't forget to come back to them for their questions in a moment.

4. <u>Find a Student's Strength</u>: Professor Amy Eisman says that if one student is particularly adept at a particular skill set, point it out and have

an expectation for the student to be the "expert." This raises the student in the esteem of classmates and encourages the student to stay abreast of the topic. Try to find a dozen students like this in your class for a variety of topics by being specific in your praise. Don't just say, "That was a well-written paper," but indicate exactly what about the ideas, or wording, or structure of the paper made it stand out. The idea is to help students learn.

5. Encourage Shy Students to Speak: Protect the soft-spoken and encourage shy students to speak. Don't allow long-winded or loud students to dominate the class conversation. For example, you might say, "Thank you, Susan. I want to hear more from you, but first I want to hear from others in the class." Call on those who don't speak much so that everyone is heard from. I had one student who was shy and hated to come to the front of the class to talk. At the same time, she was an excellent student and wanted to overcome her fear of public speaking. I worked out a plan with her to allow her, for the first few times, to present from her seat instead of coming to the front of the class. This technique helped, and she made great progress talking in class. Another idea is to pose a question and give a few moments for students to think. This can help shyer students participate because they will know what they want to say before the discussion begins (McKeachie 34). Professor Leena Jayaswal says that when a student writes a particularly good paper and is shy in class, she often mentions the student's name during class discussion, saying, "Well, Fred brought up a great point in his paper when he mentioned X. Fred, do you want to add more?" Jayaswal says this helps build confidence.

6. Listen Actively to Students during Discussions: During discussions, maintain strong eye contact with the student speaking so that she has your complete attention. Students want to be heard. By nodding, smiling, or otherwise acknowledging the student, you show that you are totally committed to listening and understanding what each student has to say. Give critical feedback, but look for ways to compliment the student for the observations she has made so that the student feels encouraged. Guide class discussions to prevent them from wandering too far off the mission (but don't stifle creative discussions, even if it's not exactly in your game plan for the topic).

7. Incorporate Peer Review: When students make presentations, which they should do frequently, encourage peer review. Get students to teach each other and to learn from each other. This engages them more than the professor performing a solo act.

8. Play "In the Spotlight": Occasionally play "In the Spotlight," in which a student comes to the front of the class and you interview him about his life, or the current assignment, or the in-class discussion topic, in a non-intimidating and friendly way for a few minutes. The purpose is for the student to practice oral communication and for the class to get to know the spotlighted student better. Tell your students, particularly grad students, that the class may well contain future creative or business partners, so that getting to know each other is important. Questions can be related to class material, or can be more general, such as, "Can you tell us about a turning point in your life?" or "What would you like to be doing in five or ten years?"

9. Do a Networking Exercise: In some of the early classes in the semester, give students a three-minute "networking" exercise. Before it starts, stress the importance to their careers of networking (making contacts and meeting key people). Then tell them to stand up, move around the room, and find a student they don't know or don't know well. Give them an exercise (such as a question relevant to the class or finding out something unique about the person) and then have them report back to the whole class on what they learned from each other.

10. Ask for Feedback from Students Early: One month into the class (about the fourth or fifth class), ask for feedback. Ferren recommends asking the students to answer three questions in writing: "What is helping you learn in this class? What is getting in the way of your learning? What are your suggestions for the rest of the semester?" Give them a leisurely ten minutes of silence to write their answers. Tell them to hand in the answers anonymously, so they can be brutally frank. Repeat this exercise about two months into the class. It will give you valuable information about what is and is not working, allowing you to change, modify, or tweak what you are doing. Always report back to the class on what you learned from the feedback, and the changes you intend to make as a result. Make it clear that you welcome candid and constructive feedback from students and make sure you implement the changes you promise to make. As Professor Angela McGlynn says, this exercise will empower your students, and send the message that you care about how they are doing in the course and are open to making changes for their benefit.

VI. BEYOND THE CLASSROOM

1. Manage Your Office Hours: Encourage students to drop by during office hours, even if they don't have specific questions. Leave your door open during office hours unless you are discussing a personal issue with a student. Have a sign-up sheet on your door so that students don't have to wait.

2. Reach Out to Students Who Miss a Class: Contact any students who don't show up to class to find out if they need help. Hayes says that if a student misses a class, he asks that student for a three to five-page analytic paper on a topic related to the missed class, showing that the student can apply the concepts covered in the class to a case or issue.

3. Be Responsive to Emails and Calls from Students: Respond promptly (within twenty-four hours) to all student emails and messages. Add your home, office, or cell phone number (wherever you prefer to be called) under your name at the end of the email so that students can call you if they wish. If you can't fully respond right away, write a brief response saying you will do so in a few days. Professor Rose Ann Robertson suggests keeping electronic copies of all emails with students (and faculty responses) for at least one semester after the class has ended to keep a record in case of any disagreements.

4. Give Students Feedback on Papers: Provide meaningful and meaty comments on homework assignments. Students want rigorous, critical, and detailed feedback that is presented in a constructive and encouraging manner. The more critically encouraging your comments, the better. Eisman remembers that renowned professor Ed Bliss used to say, "Criticize the product, not the person." A critical comment on a piece of homework might begin, "This paper missed the point" instead of, "You missed the point."

5. Permit Homework Counteroffers: Let your students take more control of their own learning by allowing them to counteroffer when you give a homework assignment. For many assignments, this won't be appropriate, but where it is appropriate, allow a student to say to you, "Professor, instead of homework assignment X, would it be possible for me to devote an equal amount of time, if not more, to assignment Y because this will be more helpful to me in my future career?" On the syllabus/assignment sheet, note with an asterisk the few assignments that are eligible for counteroffers.

6. Include Broader Career Questions: As the semester winds down, occasionally add into the homework some broader questions about future careers, such as, "What is the job you'd ideally like to be doing in five years, and what steps are you taking to achieve that goal?"

7. Request Early Submittal of Short Proposals: Ask students to submit short proposals about papers and projects well before the due date. Offer timely and extensive feedback on the proposals to make sure they are on the right track.

8. Call the Parents of Outstanding Students: Toward the end of the semester, select the top half dozen students in your class, and ask their permission (that's very important) to call their parents to tell them how well their son or daughter has done in your class. Once you receive permission, call the parents and tell them that they can be very proud of their son or daughter for the diligence, creativity, and tenacity the student has shown in your class. The parents will be delighted to receive this call from you and are likely to respond with how proud they are of their son or daughter. This message, in turn, is one that you can convey to the student. For a few of them, it may be the first time that they have heard their parents express such a message.

Thank you for participating in this workshop!

Appendix II

Finding a Great Mentor: Practical Tips

By Professor John Richardson

[*Note from Chris Palmer*: John Richardson is professor emeritus, School of International Service, American University (AU), Washington, DC, and, formerly, visiting professor, Lee Kuan Yew School of Public Policy and adjunct professor and resident fellow, Residential College 4, National University of Singapore. His essay below introduced an "after-dinner" discussion with about fifty American University students who were his neighbors in two adjoining residence halls where Richardson lived for nine years as AU's first faculty resident.]

Finding a faculty mentor is an opportunity that a relatively small undergraduate residential college such as American University offers. Classes often have no more than twenty or thirty students; sometimes they are even smaller. Faculty members are required to hold at least six "office hours" each week (though not all do so). Yet a surprisingly small number of students succeed in finding a mentor—an individual who (to use a common dictionary definition) "serves as a trusted friend, counselor and teacher" who will "help them advance their careers, enhance their careers and build their networks."

The experience shared by an AU senior with younger residents at a program I gave the other evening on the topic of finding a good mentor is typical. "I was sitting on a porch in Kenya," he told us, "and was facing the prospect of seeking faculty recommendations for graduate school applications. I realized there was not one faculty member who really knew me well. I finally picked two faculty members who taught classes in which I had done well. They did agree to write letters of recommendation for me. But I realized that in three years at AU I had not found a faculty member who was a real mentor."

Students may not be successful in finding mentors but, when asked, it is clear that they have a pretty good idea of what an ideal mentor might look like if they had one. When we brainstormed this topic, here are some the descriptive words that students participating in our discussion used: "patient," "knows how to get things done," "innovative," "approachable," "interested in you," "supportive," "well connected."

One problem students face in identifying potential mentors is that they lack a clear idea of which faculty members are likely to be the most promising candidates. Often they don't really grasp that the faculty members in front of their classes have very different career circumstances, relationships to the university, and discretionary resources of time and energy available for possible mentoring roles.

Students at AU will be taught by adjunct faculty, instructors on term-limited contracts (particularly language and college writing instructors), "temporary faculty" on term-limited contracts, faculty on "continuing contracts" but not eligible for tenure, "tenure-track" faculty, tenured associate professors, and tenured full professors. At AU, in contrast to many research universities, some undergraduate classes are taught by tenured full professors—I taught undergraduate classes in quantitative research methods for many years—but a goodly number are not.

Faculty members who are not tenured or on tenure track are less acceptable candidates than others to be mentors, because there is no assurance they will be around when a student needs them, especially during their critical senior year.

Tenure-track faculty are also less acceptable candidates than tenured faculty, though they are younger and often seem more approachable, because meeting the research requirements to gain tenure must be their priority. An open tenure-track position at AU is likely to have three hundred or more applicants. The position of "junior faculty" aspiring to tenure is very similar to the position of associates at a top Washington or New York law firm seeking to gain "partner" status. They should expect seventy-hour work weeks to be routine and ninety-hour work weeks to be fairly regular occurrences. Even after winning a tenure-track position, more than 30 percent will, for one reason or another, not make the grade or leave the university for other reasons. At some universities, attrition is much higher.

It is my view that tenured associate and full professors are the best candidates to be mentors for students. They will have more widely known professional reputations than will other professors. Their recommendation letters, if written well, will be the most credible.

But how are you, the student, to begin building that all-important relationship? You should not expect faculty members to take the initiative. You are most likely to be disappointed if you do. The most important principle to bear in mind is this: *to find a good mentor, one must be a good mentee.* A good mentee is a student whom a faculty member finds intrinsically interesting, most often because the student shares some of the faculty member's research interests and has something interesting to contribute to them.

The good news is that, when seeking a mentor, you need not, in fact should not, limit your search to faculty members from whom you are taking classes. Here is the process I recommend.

1. Devote a bit of thought to areas in which you might be interested. These can be quite broad. For example, as an undergraduate I was interested in medieval history and, later, in broad theories about the rise and fall of civilizations. As you take classes, and especially as you encounter new subjects, try to be self-conscious about what engages your interest and what does not.

2. Go to the websites of departments in areas you think might interest you and begin reading the biographies of faculty members. Pay particular attention to the biographies of more senior faculty, those holding the rank of associate and full professor. In addition to their biographies, pay particular attention to the areas they are researching and their recent publications. Identify one or more of these faculty members as possible mentors.

3. For the candidates you have identified, read one or more of their publications, especially their recent publications. This assumes their creative work is a publication, but applies to other areas as well. If a candidate mentor is a musician, listen to the professor's compositions or recordings. If a candidate mentor is a film-maker, watch one or more of that professor's recent productions, and so forth. You will note that the creative work of faculty members may not be related to the classes they are teaching.

4. Find out where the candidate-mentors' offices are located and what their office hours are. Stop by or, if necessary, make an appointment. Resisting any feelings of shyness or inadequacy, in the meeting initiate a conversation about the faculty member's research interest and see where it leads. Often the faculty member will be very receptive and responsive. Think about it. All of us like to talk about our own interests and share them with an individual who seems genuinely interested. Faculty members are no different.

5. If you seem to make a connection, engage further with the faculty member's research interests and arrange follow-up meetings. This is usually sufficient to create the momentum of a good relationship.

Here are four little-appreciated secrets about faculty members that may help you in your quest for a mentor.

1. A career experience that faculty members find most rewarding, that really turns them on, is when a student *learns something* in an area that the faculty member cares about. This observation comes from years of experience mentoring young faculty members at American University and from conversations with faculty members at many universities over the years.

2. A corollary is that faculty members are at least as interested in finding great mentees as students are in finding great mentors. A great mentee can be invaluable. Several have played pivotal roles in my book projects and other research. They have been the source of creative new ideas that have furthered my work. We have coauthored papers together, often with the mentee as lead author. I have found international travel opportunities and funding for mentees. In some cases, we have become lifelong friends and, yes, I have spent hours writing them great letters of recommendation. Other faculty members will recount similar experiences.

3. In many instances, faculty members are as shy and insecure about interacting with students, outside of a classroom setting, as students are about interacting with faculty members. Recognize that what you may interpret as arrogance, disinterest, or standoffishness may just be the same shyness and insecurity that you are feeling. Commit yourself to breaking down these barriers.

4. The faculty members you approach with expressions of interest and questions based on having familiarized yourself with their research will be amazed, since this almost never happens. Again, this is the voice of experience speaking. I consider myself to be among the more approachable AU faculty members. After all, I live in Anderson Hall. (I have also lived in a National University of Singapore residence hall mostly populated by seven hundred first- and second-year students.) Yet in years of teaching, probably no more than thirty students have sought me out for a conversation about my research.

I am not sure how the idea of reading about a faculty member's research interests first came to me but can remember when I first acted on it. My History of Civilization professor at Dartmouth College was John R. Williams. He was a quiet, reserved man and not a spellbinding lecturer, but in one of his lectures he spoke about his interest in Pope Gregory VII. I found an article he had written on the subject, read it, and went to his office, during office hours, for a discussion. I can still remember our first conversation, which I approached with considerable trepidation. I followed up with additional discussions and, in a more advanced class, wrote papers on the medieval papacy and the relationship between feudal and ecclesiastical institutions.

This process of engagement began a friendship that lasted until his death. Professor Williams became my honors program tutor in the philosophy of history, rereading works that he had not considered in years so we could talk about them together. In weekly meetings during my junior and senior years, we discussed the writings of Toynbee, Spengler, Hegel, Gibbon, and many other philosophers focusing on the question, "What explains the rise and fall of great civilizations?" He supervised my prize-winning thesis on the growth of central government institutions in twelfth-, thirteenth-, and fourteenth-century France. He insisted that I read original texts in Latin and French. I improved my proficiency in these languages partly to please him and live up to his expectations. (A mentoring relationship can be mutually reinforcing.) The thesis, along with his recommendation, were instrumental in my winning a full fellowship for doctoral study in political science at the University of Minnesota.

Over the years, I have been blessed with many mentors. Their photographic posters graced a wall of my faculty office at American University and in my "Resident Fellow" apartment at the National University of Singapore.

If you ask mentors, "How best can I express my thanks for all you have done?" they often will say, "Express your thanks by giving to others what I have given you." This brief reflection is one small way of expressing my thanks to the many mentors who have made a difference in my life.

Teaching as Performance Art

By Professor Thomas Kaufman
(filmmaker and author)

In 2015 I had the opportunity to teach film and video production at a university. I liked working with the students, but I also learned something: I could be a better teacher. Even though I tried my best—researched and prepared for the classes, had extensive PowerPoint presentations, brought in guest lecturers, and did lighting demonstrations—I felt, at the end and despite mostly favorable notices from my students, that I could do better.

I wanted to see other teachers at work. So I asked Professor Chris Palmer, who teaches at American University in Washington, DC, if I could sit in on his "Environmental Film Making" class. He agreed. I watched him teach and I noticed two things: First, the class had a definite rhythm. Second, it was teaching as performance art, in the sense that Chris was "on" for his class. What follows is a description of a class. I tried to catch the rhythms of the class by transcribing events as they happened. Take a look. Then after we'll ask Professor Palmer a few questions.

* * * * *

Chris Palmer enters the classroom well-dressed: suit, tie, suspenders. Enters enthusiastically, greets the class. Someone enters after him; Chris greets him by name. From the start Chris is positive, even about passing out a sign-up sheet and name cards. These cards are stiff cardboard, folded in half to make tents that sit on the students' desks. "Yes," he says, when he notices a student bringing in food, and "Oh, you brought a salad!" Once the students settle in, he introduces me to them.

Lucas takes a picture of the class. Chris picks it up and says he loves it, compliments Lucas on it.

Now Chris writes on whiteboard what they are covering today, tells them where to place homework. A student crosses the room to her seat. Chris tells her it was nice to hear from their mutual friend Sandy, and she agrees.

Another student brings in snacks, and Sabrina says she sent a snack email reminder. Chris says to her, "Aren't you efficient!"

He uses no PowerPoint.

A student arrives late with homework. Chris greets him warmly, says, "No problem," introduces me to him, then names out loud who's missing and says, "I'm sure they'll be here in just a minute."

He hands out graded homework to each student, saying the student's name, and that the students may call him Chris or Professor Palmer, whichever is more comfortable for them. Chris reminds them where this week's homework pile should go; then he collects the pile, telling them, "If you can't read my handwriting, call me."

All this time Chris has been in motion. Now he stops moving and tells the class that he enjoyed reading their half-page treatments, and that next week they need to hand in a five-page treatment. If they need more feedback than what he wrote on the papers he just handed back, they should contact him. If the students want to build on what they've done so far, he's delighted to talk with them about it, and they should call him up or see him in person. "Any questions?"

He says what he really liked was reading what the students are passionate about. Chris has arranged one-on-one meetings with each member of the class, and now he tells them to bring to their meeting the part of their home-work that describes what they are most passionate about, and to be careful not to lose that passion. Now his voice takes on an authoritative tone. For each student this statement will be a vital building block for their careers.

Some assignments are weekly, so there's always lots to talk about. Today's assignment was to write two paragraphs—one telling what they're passionate about, and the other about the biggest challenges they face in their profes-sional careers.

Chris calls on students to share their responses with the rest of class and tells them to be very conscientious about fulfilling their commitments. Emily asks how to share the responses. He says to use email through the Blackboard discussion board, then outlines the steps to do that.

He goes over the plan for tonight, which includes attending a screening upstairs in the Doyle/Forman Theater. Now Mohammed arrives. Chris asks him to sit, suggests various places where there's room (the seats are arranged in a U-shape), and the students chuckle at Chris's enthusiasm. He introduces me to Mohammed, who, though late, has brought snacks and drinks for everyone. We pass these around. Each week two students are assigned to bring snacks for the whole class to make the class more enjoyable. And, Chris says, it's easier for students to learn when they're not hungry.

Chris tells the class that tonight we have two guests, Stephanie and Brad, from the upcoming Environmental Film Festival in DC. They'll talk to the class, and that's a chance for the class to ask them questions about how they choose films for the festival, or how to find a job. It's a great opportunity, he tells them. Then they will screen previews of upcoming films in the theater upstairs.

Francesca arrives; he gives her a big hello, and she has the second part of the class snack. On a desk in the center of the room she piles up the snack containers.

Chris is very much on. It's a performance that would be impossible to capture as an online class. It's interactive. You need to be there.

He asks, "Has everyone signed up to see me? Every two to three weeks there's a one-on-one meeting. If you can't see me in person, call me," he says.

Now he asks Sam to pass out snacks, and he compliments Mohammed on what he brought. Chris is working hard to keep the class entertained. They pass the food around.

Now Jake walks in. Chris says, "Oh, it's so nice to see you. Where do you want to sit? So good to see you."

Okay, now for chapter 1 of *Shooting in the Wild*. So far ten students have left their comments on the online Blackboard discussion board, and he reminds the rest that they must do so before midnight tonight, "So the rest of you please add your comments." He names the ten students who left comments and thanks them. "Let me call on Emily to discuss her thoughts on chapter 1."

Chris proceeds to ask all ten students to elaborate on what the chapter sparked for them. Chris is engaged in the conversation through active listening, responding with "Yeah" and "Very good."

"Katie, any reaction to chapter 1? Daniel?"

Chris holds a cheat sheet with the ten students' names along with their comments. So he can ask them for their comments by going down the list. He's animated, claps his hands to start a new section of class, moves around classroom, telling them, "Good, well done!" Tells them in a quieter tone that he's missing assignments from a few students. "Now," he says, "let's discuss pitching an idea."

He asks Pat, "What does a good speaker do?" Pat gives an answer; then Chris asks Katie, and she responds, "Good, very good." Now hands go up, and the conversation takes in more students. He goes around the room and helps gets conversations flowing.

"Daniel, what is pitching?" Daniel answers. Chris helps him with the answer, adds detail. The students respond and Chris is appreciative. He says, "Very good, excellent."

Now Chris makes his first point: no one cares about your idea. The students laugh at this sudden reversal after all his positivity. "When you pitch it's like you're totally vulnerable. It is nerve-wracking and your heart is thumping." He beats his chest. "It's an awful situation, so you have to be enthusiastic and passionate. A pitch can be an hour long, but I will focus on a first pitch that's a few minutes long." While he's telling them to be enthusiastic and passionate, he himself shows those traits.

"To start, tell the listener about the genre of the project, then try to gain their interest—ask them a question relevant to the pitch and listen to the answer," just as Chris asks questions and listens in class. In a way, Chris is pitching his ideas to the class right now.

"You can't pitch your whole project, so a good thing is to say how you came up with the story, what's unique about it. Give a fresh angle to the program.

"Then, if you can, pull out a prop—a newspaper editorial, or a lump of coal from a mine disaster, or a photo of something relevant—a prop of some sort to illustrate your idea. You're also giving the listener something they can hold. By the way," he says, "this shows you have verve and panache," which makes the students chuckle.

"Then tell the listener thanks, and may I make an appointment to talk about this with you?"

He passes out what he wrote before class. It gives more detail on what he just outlined to the class. He gives them a minute to scan it, tells them they can read in detail later, then claps his hands and asks if anyone has a question.

Emily asks how one listens more than one talks. Chris responds by making it clear that he listened to the question and he stresses that pitching is not just you talking.

He calls names and asks them to stand up. He assigns the class to four groups and directs them to congregate in the four corners of the room. Students will take turns making a pitch to the others. Chris goes to each group in turn, coaching and encouraging them. After about five minutes, Chris calls on each of the students who pitched to explain what they learned from the exercise.

"Nella?" She replies, and he says, "Very good, but you need more enthusiasm and passion to come through." Then he asks Nella's group for their critiques. Now it's Mohammed's turn. Chris says he needs to get to the point more quickly, to use more energy when he talks. Chris asks Pat about Mohammed's presentation. Chris listens, saying, "Yes, right, very good point."

The guest lecturers, Stephanie Flack and Brad Forder, enter the classroom. Chris asks them to relax for a second while he finishes up.

Chris hands out a new homework sheet. He reminds the students that they will receive his weekly email to the whole class later tonight.

Chris passes out blank sheets of paper and asks the students to write on one side what they like about the class so far and what they want to continue doing, and on the other side what they think is missing from the class, what Chris could improve on, and if anything impedes their learning. He gives them two minutes to do this. He says, "It's anonymous, so be brutally frank. Your feedback will help me be a better teacher and improve the class. When you're finished look up at me."

When the first student looks up, he asks her to pick up the sheets from the rest of the class. Now he introduces Brad and Stephanie, the guest lecturers. He asks Brad how he got his job as a film programmer at a film festival. Chris sits with the students while Brad answers, then asks the students to ask Brad questions. They do. Stephanie joins in, and the two of them talk about what kinds of films they're looking for.

* * * * *

After class, I had questions for Chris, so I emailed him.

Q: Are you like this all the time? Are you ever in the "off" position?
I'm always like this when I'm with students. They are paying a lot of money to learn, and I feel a strong responsibility to give them their money's worth and give teaching everything I've got.

Q: Do you have a warm-up routine before class?
Yes, I work the muscles in my face strenuously, do an hour of exercise, exercise my voice, go over the essential behaviors I am seeking from myself: professional, dynamic, funny, caring, high standards, encouraging students to excel, pushing them to be outstanding, good eye contact, warmth, being passionate, being high energy, physically active, getting students to talk and be active, listening carefully, listening actively, being firm, inspiring, smiling, relaxed, engaging, enthusiastic, calm, not hurrying, standing up and stretching, highly competent, totally in charge, self-confident, dignified, authoritative, benevolent dictator, conversational, including no busy work.

Q: What have you got against PowerPoint? Isn't writing on a whiteboard old-fashioned?
I avoid PowerPoint slides because they are impersonal, tired, and often mind-numbing. They deflect me from my goal of painting a picture

with passion and language. Technology does not make someone a great teacher. Too often PowerPoint slides are an electronic crutch to help a professor avoid the hard work of practice. You are giving the presentation to provide leadership and inspiration to students and to help them learn. For this, the professor is the best visual. PowerPoint slides distract attention from the professor as the focal point of the room—and, therefore, dilute the impact of the professor's teaching and the students' learning.

Q: Do you always wear a suit and tie in class? If so, why?
Yes. To send a message to the students that I attach a lot of importance to the class, and that therefore they should, too. It's also a way of telling the students that I think they are special and deserving of my respect.

Q: What kind of mood or feeling do you want the class to have?
Vibrant, coruscating, effervescent, exuberant, optimistic, agreement that we are all here to learn.

Q: What kind of environment do you want in the classroom?
Safe, so students feel they can take risks, make mistakes, and come out stronger at the other end.

Q: There's an undeniable entertainment factor in your teaching. Is that important?
Yes, students won't learn if they are bored.

Q: It drives me crazy when students show up late. I've heard of professors locking their doors when class begins, yet you seem delighted with each late arrival.
I stress that I want students to arrive on time, but sometimes students are simply unable to arrive on time because of bad traffic or whatever. It's important that every student feel warmly welcomed into the community of the class. I want them to know that they have entered a place where they are valued, respected, and safe, and that they can take risks knowing that I will be a nurturing, caring presence—a benevolent dictator.

* * * * *

I came to this class to watch another teacher work. Right away I saw things I want to change when I teach a class the next time. I will:

- Use name cards to help me learn their names

- Bring passion, energy, and enthusiasm so the students feel it and try to respond in kind

- Fashion the lesson time as a performance

- Make the students feel they are in a safe and welcoming place

- Never act upset or disapproving

- Be polite and appreciative

- Help the students to relax and enjoy themselves, so it's easier for them to learn

Appendix IV

Rethinking Tenure

By Chris Palmer

It is difficult to get a man to understand something when his salary depends upon his not understanding it.

—Upton Sinclair

I arrived at Harvard's John F. Kennedy School of Government in the fall of 1972 knowing nothing about how American universities worked. As a Kennedy Scholar from Britain, I selected classes for my master's degree based on the issues I wanted to study, paying scant attention to which professors taught the courses. This was Harvard, after all, and I assumed all the teachers were competent.

I decided to take an economics course. The topic was highly germane to what I imagined at the time was my future career in the British government. Unfortunately, the course was taught by a professor who I quickly realized was past his prime.

The professor, who I shall, out of respect, call by the pseudonym Professor Smith, was doddery, unproductive, and uninterested in student learning. Yet, because he had tenure, he was guaranteed his job for the rest of his life, despite his shortcomings. He continued to receive a substantial salary and occupy a position that should have been held by someone with much higher pedagogical standards and with much more to offer students.

Forty years have passed since I arrived at Harvard, but in the world of tenured professors, little has changed. While tenure still has some benefits, it also has flaws that are hurting the quality of education that students receive. I believe it is time for a frank discussion about whether universities can afford to maintain the status quo. In my opinion, we cannot. It is time to rethink tenure.

THE PROBLEMS OF TENURE

The main problem with the tenure system is that lifelong job security removes the incentive for high performance. As University of Illinois professor and economist Jeffrey Brown explained in *Forbes*, tenure is essentially a form of job insurance. Insurance, while providing some benefits, also leads to moral hazard: the "well-established phenomenon that people behave differently when they have insurance than when they do not."[1] Tenure is not an effective incentive system to breed high performance.

Because of moral hazard, professors are unlikely to work as diligently with tenure as they would without it. Teaching effectiveness and research productivity will inevitably decline, although evidence (beyond anecdotes) to prove or refute this point is elusive.

Of course, many tenured professors continue to undertake groundbreaking research motivated by genuine interest in the field and by a desire to be recognized among their colleagues. Many tenured professors are also excellent teachers who take the time to nurture and develop their students, again motivated by forces outside the tenure system. However, tenure removes an essential feature of the competitive labor market: firing. Tenured professors are required only to meet basic expectations (showing up, teaching their assigned courses) to maintain their salary and status. The natural result is that some professors will work just a little bit less, and some (like Professor Smith) will stay at their jobs even after inadequacy, and even incompetence, set in.

The tenured professor in the academic world has job security unlike any employee in the corporate or public sectors. Columbia University professor and religion department chair Mark Taylor asked, "If you were the CEO of a company . . . would you offer anybody a contract with these terms: lifetime employment, no possibility of dismissal, regardless of performance? If you did, your company would fail and you would be looking for a new job. Why should academia be any different from every other profession?"[2] (In the past, perhaps faculty did need special protection to protect their intellectual freedom in the case of controversial ideological views. However, in my view, this unusual protection is no longer necessary in today's era, with the various federal laws prohibiting discriminatory firing practices.)

THE TENURE SYSTEM HAS ITS BENEFITS

To be fair, some argue that the tenure system provides important benefits. The original intent of tenure was to create an environment of intellectual freedom where professors could pursue their research and studies without fear of censure or of losing their jobs if they butted heads with entrenched powerful forces (or faced persecution from hostile faculty colleagues). With complete job security, the thought was, professors would be immune to pressure from school administrators and would be better able to focus their efforts on teaching and scholarship. Students would benefit from teachers who felt free and empowered.

Many professors, including Cary Nelson, an English professor at the University of Illinois and past president of the American Association of University Professors, still argue that the tenure system serves this important purpose. Nelson argues that long-term job security is the only system that encourages professors "to stay intellectually curious and take chances with unconventional work."[3]

Moreover, supporters of tenure argue that there is no widespread problem with incompetent or even inadequate professors. Nelson suggests that, because of the large supply of qualified PhDs relative to the number of teaching jobs available, bad professors do not receive tenure in the first place. Moreover, because the tenure committees know that paying the salary of a tenured professor is a long-term commitment, only "excellent," not just good, candidates receive tenure. In this way, the argument goes, the tenure system keeps professor quality high.[4]

Other persuasive arguments for tenure include attracting talented young people into academic life (in some cases over more lucrative career possibilities) and freeing professors from the obsession of making a living (so they can focus on some esoteric field and make erudite contributions).

WHERE DO WE GO FROM HERE?

There are powerful arguments on both sides of the debate. Unfortunately, it is difficult to have an honest and balanced conversation about tenure in the university setting because tenured professors—those who tend to have the most influence—have every incentive to maintain the system from which they benefit. No rational person would want to change a system that guarantees him job security for life, even though it creates incentives that tend to undermine the pursuit of excellence and encourage laxity.

I call on my fellow professors to set aside their self-interest and have an honest discussion about the merits of tenure going forward. From my perspective, it is clear that universities must reform the current system of tenure if they are serious about improving the standards of teaching and ensuring that students receive the education they paid for. But reforming the tenure system does not mean removing all job security for high-quality professors. There are middle ground solutions that are worth discussing.

For example, professors could receive five- to ten-year contracts and then come under review for contract renewal. This would allow professors a greater degree of security than many professions offer, while still giving incentive to keep up performance. By giving professors multiyear contracts instead of tenure for life, universities could hold on to valuable faculty and encourage their involvement in the school while maintaining the ability to fire underperforming or unproductive faculty. Mark Taylor has suggested a variation in which, after a period of three to five years, deserving faculty members should be given seven-year renewable contracts. To ease the transition to this type of new system, existing tenured faculty could be grandfathered in.[5]

CONCLUDING THOUGHTS

Our country's future depends on effective teaching and learning. By de-incentivizing professors to perform at the highest levels, tenure undermines the fulfillment of our core mission—student learning. We have institutionalized a system that is intrinsically inimical to excellence, and students suffer for it. At a time when America's total student loan debt has reached more than one trillion dollars and an increasingly louder chorus of voices questions the cost of higher education, we cannot afford inaction.

My colleague Professor Bill Gentile puts it bluntly: "As competition for students and their dollars becomes increasingly fierce, institutions still mired in a system that impedes excellence may lag behind universities with better incentives in place. Failure to modernize the system may threaten all of our jobs."[6]

There are countless tenured professors who are outstanding people, and I have many beloved friends who are tenured professors. These professors work as hard as ever, and I am impressed by their innate commitment to excellence. At the same time, I now ask them to take a step back and ask themselves if the current system is truly the best we can do. I believe that we can do better. For the sake of our students, we must.

WORKS CONSULTED

Brown, Jeffrey. "Professor Tenure as Insurance: What the Wall Street Journal Debate Missed." *Forbes*, June 25, 2012. www.forbes.com/sites/jeffreybrown/2012/06/25/professor-tenure-as-insurance-what-the-wall-street-journal-debate-missed.

Franz, Frank. "Keep Tenure: Fix the Problems." *American Physical Society*, June 1998. www.aps.org/publications/apsnews/199806/backpage.cfm. Based on an invited paper presentation at the 150th AAAS meeting.

Nelson, Cary. "At Stake: Freedom and Learning." *New York Times*, July 20, 2010. www.nytimes.com/roomfordebate/2010/07/19/what-if-college-tenure-dies/tenure-protects-freedom-and-students-learning.

Riley, Naomi Schaefer. "The Economic Upside to Ending Tenure." *Chronicle of Higher Education*, June 19, 2012. http://chronicle.com/article/Smart-Ways-to-End-Tenure/127940.

Riley, Naomi Schaefer, and Cary Nelson. "Should Tenure for College Professors Be Abolished?" *Wall Street Journal*, June 24, 2012. http://online.wsj.com/article/SB10001424052702303610504577418293114042070.html?mod=googlenews_wsj.

Rotherham, Andrew J. "Should Tenure Be Abolished?" *TIME Magazine*, June 30, 2011. www.time.com/time/nation/article/0,8599,2080601,00.html.

Ruffins, Paul. "The Fall of the House of Tenure." *Black Issues in Higher Education* 14 (October 16, 1997): 19–26.

Taylor, Mark. "Why Tenure Is Unsustainable and Indefensible." *New York Times*, July 19, 2010. www.nytimes.com/roomfordebate/2010/7/19/what-if-college-tenure-dies/why-tenure-is-unsustainable-and-indefensible.

Vedder, Richard. "Reducing Intellectual Diversity." *New York Times*, July 20, 2010. www.nytimes.com/roomfordebate/2010/07/19/what-if-college-tenure-dies/tenure-reduces-intellectual-diversity.

Notes

INTRODUCTION

1. Elizabeth Alsop, "Who's Teaching the Teachers?" *Chronicle of Higher Education*, February 11, 2018.

2. Patrick Allitt, *I'm the Teacher, You're the Student: A Semester in the University Classroom* (Philadelphia: University of Pennsylvania Press, 2005), ix.

3. Ken Bain, *What the Best College Teachers Do* (Cambridge, MA: Harvard University Press, 2004), 178.

4. Parts of this preface were inspired by chapter 14 in my book *Confessions of a Wildlife Filmmaker* (2015), as well as by several essays I authored that were published in *Faculty Focus* on March 21, 2013, and March 22, 2013. Thanks to Mary Bart for publishing the latter two essays. I also published six other essays on teaching in *Faculty Focus* in 2009 on January 21, January 22, January 27, January 29, February 3, and February 4.

CHAPTER 1

1. Michael Ross, "How Four Years Can (and Should) Transform You," *New York Times*, August 21, 2013.

2. See also "Higher Education's Public Purpose" by Bethany Zecher Sutton, chief of staff at AAC&U, June 20, 2016.

3. Ken Bain, *What the Best College Professors Do* (Cambridge, MA: Harvard University Press, 2004), 89.

4. Bain, *What the Best College Professors Do*, 92.

5. "The Case for College," a speech given by Drew Faust on October 24, 2014, at the Booker T. Washington High School for the Performing and Visual Arts in Dallas, Texas.

6. Dr. Leonard Sax has written eloquently on this topic in his book *The Collapse of Parenting* (New York: Basic Books, 2016), 187–99.

7. Stephen Brookfield, *The Skillful Teacher: On Technique, Trust, and Responsiveness in the Classroom* (San Francisco: Jossey-Bass, 2015), 246.

8. Alan Brinkley et al., *The Chicago Handbook for Teachers: A Practical Guide to the College Classroom* (Chicago: University of Chicago Press, 1999), 170.

9. Patrick Allitt, *I'm the Teacher, You're the Student* (Philadelphia: University of Pennsylvania Press, 2005), x.

10. Bain, *What the Best College Professors Do*, 40.

11. Allitt, *I'm the Teacher, You're the Student*, 74.

12. Peter Brown, Henry Roediger, and Mark McDaniel, *Make It Stick: The Science of Successful Learning* (Cambridge, MA: The Belknap Press of Harvard University Press, 2014).

13. Thomas L. Friedman, "Owning Your Own Future," *New York Times* op-ed, May 10, 2017.

14. Carol Dweck, *Mindset: The New Psychology of Success* (New York: Ballantine Books, 2016).

15. Salman Khan, "Let's Use Video to Reinvent Education," TED talk, March 2011, www.ted.com/talks/salman_khan_let_s_use_video_to_reinvent_education.

16. Angela Duckworth, *Grit: The Power of Passion and Perseverance* (New York: Scribner, 2016).

17. Dweck, *Mindset: The New Psychology of Success*, 196.

18. Dweck, *Mindset: The New Psychology of Success*, 196.

19. James Lang, *Small Teaching: Everyday Lessons from the Science of Learning* (San Francisco: Jossey-Bass, 2016), 213.

20. Brookfield, *The Skillful Teacher*, 213.

21. Maryellen Weimer, PhD, "Why We Teach," *Faculty Focus*, October 5, 2016.

CHAPTER 2

1. Parker J. Palmer, *The Courage to Teach: Exploring the Inner Landscape of a Teacher's Life* (San Francisco: Jossey-Bass, 1998), 10.

2. Palmer, *The Courage to Teach*, 11.

3. Palmer, *The Courage to Teach*, 12.

4. Palmer, *The Courage to Teach*, 2.

5. Personal interview with Professor Naomi Baron, May 2, 2017.

6. Neil Postman, *The End of Education: Redefining the Value of School* (New York: Knopf, 1995).

7. William Deresiewicz, *Excellent Sheep: The Miseducation of the American Elite and the Way to a Meaningful Life* (New York: Free Press, 2014).

8. Maryellen Weimer, PhD, "What about Teacher Entitlement?" *Faculty Focus*, November 8, 2017.

9. Wilbert J. McKeachie, *McKeachie's Teaching Tips: Strategies, Research, and Theory for College and University Teachers* (Boston: Houghton Mifflin, 2002), 302.

10. Mark Bauerlein, "What's the Point of a Professor?" *New York Times*, May 10, 2015.

11. James M. Lang, *Small Teaching: Everyday Lessons from the Science of Learning* (San Francisco: Jossey-Bass, 2016), 189.

12. Ken Bain, *What the Best College Teachers Do* (Cambridge, MA: Harvard University Press, 2004), 19.

13. Bain, *What the Best College Teachers Do*, 19.

14. Bain, *What the Best College Teachers Do*, 172.

15. Stephen D. Brookfield, *The Skillful Teacher: On Technique, Trust, and Responsiveness in the Classroom* (San Francisco: Jossey-Bass, 2015), 271.

16. James M. Lang, *Small Teaching: Everyday Lessons from the Science of Learning* (San Francisco: Jossey-Bass, 2016), 177.

17. Lang, *Small Teaching*, 176.

18. Lang, *Small Teaching*, 176.

19. Brookfield, *The Skillful Teacher*, 265.

20. Maryellen Weimer, PhD, "Taking Time to Refresh, Recharge, and Recommit," *Faculty Focus*, May 17, 2017.

CHAPTER 3

1. James M. Lang, *Small Teaching: Everyday Lessons from the Science of Learning* (San Francisco: Jossey-Bass, 2016), 175.

2. Lang, *Small Teaching*, 186.

3. Marilyn Goldhammer is associate director for pedagogy at American University's Center for Teaching, Research, and Learning.

4. For example, also see www.nwlink.com/~donclark/hrd/bloom.html.

5. Maryellen Weimer, PhD, "What Does Your Syllabus Say About You and Your Course?" *Faculty Focus*, August 24, 2011.

6. "Your Syllabus Doesn't Have to Look Like a Contract," by David Gooblar ("Pedagogy Unbound"), columnist at Chronicle Vitae, July 26, 2017.

CHAPTER 4

1. Carol Dweck, professor of psychology, Stanford University, quoted in the *New York Times* on June 23, 2016.

2. Carol Dweck, *Mindset: The New Psychology of Success* (New York: Ballantine Books, 2016).

3. Ken Bain, *What the Best College Teachers Do* (Cambridge, MA: Harvard University Press, 2004), 7.

4. Bain, *What the Best College Teachers Do*, 17.

5. Personal email from Professor Maggie Stogner to the author, July 25, 2018.

6. Maryellen Weimer, "Four Key Questions about Grading," *Faculty Focus*, August 6, 2014.

7. Ken Bain, *What the Best College Students Do* (Cambridge, MA: Harvard University Press, 2012).

8. Alfie Kohn, *Punished by Rewards: The Trouble with Gold Stars, Incentive Plans, A's, Praise and Other Bribes* (New York: Mariner Books, 1995).

9. Bain, *What the Best College Teachers Do*, 47.

10. David Brooks, *New York Times*, September 9, 2014.

11. Leonard Sax, *The Collapse of Parenting: How We Hurt Our Kids When We Treat Them Like Grown-Ups* (New York: Basic Books, 2016), 191.

12. Adam Grant, "Are You a Giver or a Taker?" TED talk, November 2016.

13. James Lang, *Small Teaching: Everyday Lessons from the Science of Learning* (San Francisco: Jossey-Bass, 2016), 206.

14. Weimer, "Four Key Questions about Grading."

15. Weimer, "Four Key Questions about Grading."

16. Kohn, *Punished by Rewards*.

17. Mary C. Clement, "Three Steps to Better Course Evaluations," *Faculty Focus*, July 30, 2012.

18. Weimer, "Four Key Questions about Grading."

19. Wilbert McKeachie, *McKeachie's Teaching Tips: Strategies, Research, and Theory for College and University Teachers* (Boston: Houghton Mifflin, 2002), 87.

20. Adam Grant, "Why We Should Stop Grading Students on a Curve," *New York Times*, September 10, 2016.

21. Patrick Allitt, *I'm the Teacher, You're the Student* (Philadelphia: University of Pennsylvania Press, 2005), 218–24.

22. Caroline Adams Miller, *Getting Grit: The Evidence-Based Approach to Cultivating Passion, Perseverance, and Purpose* (Boulder, CO: Sounds True, 2017), 36.

23. Miller, *Getting Grit*, 17.

24. Peter Brown, Henry Roediger, and Mark McDaniel, *Make It Stick: The Science of Successful Learning* (Cambridge, MA: The Belknap Press of Harvard University Press, 2014).

25. Brown, Roediger, and McDaniel, *Make It Stick*, 28.

26. Lang, *Small Teaching*, 20.

27. Lang, *Small Teaching*, 28.

28. Brown, Roediger, and McDaniel, *Make It Stick*, 30.

29. Rosamund Stone Zander and Benjamin Zander, *The Art of Possibility* (New York: Penguin Books, 2000).

30. Zander and Zander, *The Art of Possibility*, 26.

31. Zander and Zander, *The Art of Possibility*, 26.

32. Zander and Zander, *The Art of Possibility*, 31.

33. Zander and Zander, *The Art of Possibility*, 33.

34. Zander and Zander, *The Art of Possibility*, 36.

35. Zander and Zander, *The Art of Possibility*, 43.

36. Zander and Zander, *The Art of Possibility*, 46.

37. Private conversation on March 26, 2017.

38. Maryellen Weimer, "Five Ways to Get Students Thinking about Learning, Not Grades," *Faculty Focus*, April 12, 2017.

39. Weimer, "Five Ways to Get Students Thinking about Learning, Not Grades."

40. Weimer, "Five Ways to Get Students Thinking about Learning, Not Grades."

41. Sal Khan, "Let's Teach for Mastery—Not Test Scores," TED talk, November 2015.

42. Lang, *Small Teaching*, 207.

CHAPTER 5

1. Steven A. Meyers, "Do Your Students Care Whether You Care About Them?" *College Teaching* 57, no. 4 (2009): 205–10. Also available at http://blogs.roosevelt.edu/smeyers/files/2011/04/caring.pdf.

2. James M. Lang, *Small Teaching: Everyday Lessons from the Science of Learning* (San Francisco: Jossey-Bass, 2016), 193.

3. Maryellen Weimer, "Caring about Students Matters," *Faculty Focus*, November 11, 2015.

4. Ken Bain, *What the Best College Teachers Do* (Cambridge, MA: Harvard University Press, 2004), 26–32.

5. Lang, *Small Teaching*, 181.

6. Alexandra Svokas, "College Campuses Are Full of Subtle Racism and Sexism, Study Says," *Huffington Post*, January 12, 2015, www.huffingtonpost.com/2015/01/12/microaggressions-college-racism-sexism_n_6457106.html.

7. Derald Wing Sue, Christina M. Capodilupo, Gina C. Torino, Jennifer M. Bucceri, Aisha M. B. Holder, Kevin L. Nadal, and Marta Esquilin, "Racial Microaggressions in Everyday Life," *American Psychologist* (May–June 2007), https://world-trust.org/wp-content/uploads/2011/05/7-Racial-Microaggressions-in-Everyday-Life.pdf.

8. Stephen Brookfield, *The Skillful Teacher: On Technique, Trust, and Responsiveness in the Classroom* (San Francisco: Jossey-Bass, 2015), 120.

9. Sue, Capodilupo, Torino, Bucceri, Holder, Nadal, and Esquilin, "Racial Microaggressions in Everyday Life."

10. Brookfield, *The Skillful Teacher*, 10.

11. Brookfield, *The Skillful Teacher*, 111.

12. Brookfield, *The Skillful Teacher*, 113.

13. Brookfield, *The Skillful Teacher*, 122.

14. Daniel Chambliss and Christopher Takacs, *How College Works* (Cambridge, MA: Harvard University Press, 2014), 4.

15. Meyers, "Do Your Students Care Whether You Care About Them?" *College Teaching* 57, no. 4 (2009): 205–10.

16. Chambliss and Takacs, *How College Works*, ch. 6.

17. Chambliss and Takacs, *How College Works*, 47, italics in the original.

18. Tom Friedman, "It Takes a Mentor," *New York Times*, September 10, 2014.

19. Chambliss and Takacs, *How College Works*, 46.

20. Chambliss and Takacs, *How College Works*, 47.

21. Chambliss and Takacs, *How College Works*, 54.

22. Alan Brinkley et al., *The Chicago Handbook for Teachers: A Practical Guide to the College Classroom* (Chicago: University of Chicago Press, 1999), 22.

23. Wilbert McKeachie et al., *McKeachie's Teaching Tips: Strategies, Research, and Theory for College and University Teachers* (Boston: Houghton Mifflin, 2002), 23.

24. Robert Magnan, *147 Practical Tips for Teaching Professors* (Madison, WI: Atwood, 1990).

25. Lang, *Small Teaching*, 179.

26. *The Teaching Professor*, June–July 2017, summarizes this research.

27. K. M. Cooper, B. Haney, A. Krieg, and S. E. Brownell, "What's in a Name? The Importance of Students Perceiving That an Instructor Knows Their Names in a High-Enrollment Biology Classroom," *The Teaching Professor* (June–July 2017); Tamara Glenz, "The Importance of Learning Students' Names," *Journal on Best Teaching Practices* (April 2014); Maryellen Weimer, "The Importance of Learning Students' Names," *Faculty Focus*, August 2, 2017.

28. Chambliss and Takacs, *How College Works*, 162.

29. Lang, *Small Teaching*.

30. Chambliss and Takacs, *How College Works*, 162.

31. Rosamund Stone Zander and Benjamin Zander, *The Art of Possibility* (New York: Penguin Books, 2000).

32. Stephen R. Covey, *The Seven Habits of Highly Effective People: Restoring the Character Ethic* (New York: Simon & Schuster, 1989).

33. Bain, *What the Best College Teachers Do*, 136.

34. Bain, *What the Best College Teachers Do*, 139.

35. Bain, *What the Best College Teachers Do*, 141.

CHAPTER 6

1. Flower Darby, "Harness the Power of Emotions to Help Your Students Learn," *Faculty Focus*, January 3, 2018.

2. James M. Lang, *Small Teaching: Everyday Lessons from the Science of Learning* (San Francisco: Jossey-Bass, 2016), 174.

3. Lang, *Small Teaching*, 177.

4. Patrick Allitt, *I'm the Teacher, You're the Student: A Semester in the University Classroom* (Philadelphia: University of Pennsylvania Press, 2005), x.

5. Elena Aguilar, "Setting Intentions: A Powerful Tool to Help Us Learn," *Edutopia*, December 11, 2014.

6. Daniel Siegel, *The Mindful Brain: Reflections and Attunement in the Cultivation of Well-Being* (New York: W. W. Norton, 2007), 98.

7. Ken Bain, *What the Best College Teachers Do* (Cambridge, MA: Harvard University Press, 2004), 122.

8. Maryellen Weimer, "An Effective Learning Environment is a Shared Responsibility," *Faculty Focus*, June 18, 2014.

9. L. M. Lesser, "Opening Intentions," *The Teaching Professor* 24, no. 9 (2010): 4.

10. Lang, *Small Teaching*, 174–75.

11. Karin Kirk, "Motivating Students," *Teach the Earth*, http://serc.carleton.edu/NAGTWorkshops/affective/motivation.html.

12. Tierra M. Freeman, Lynley H. Anderman, and Jane M. Jensen, "Sense of Belonging in College Freshmen at the Classroom and Campus Levels," *The Journal of Experimental Education* 75, no. 3 (2010): 203–20, doi: 10.3200/JEXE.75.3.203-220.

13. Peter Brown, Henry Roediger, and Mark McDaniel, *Make It Stick: The Science of Successful Learning* (Cambridge, MA: The Belknap Press of Harvard University Press, 2014), 226.

14. Sarah Rose Cavanagh, "All the Classroom's a Stage," *The Chronicle of Higher Education*, June 27, 2017.

15. Micah Sadigh, "A Simple Invitation: Please See Me!" *Faculty Focus*, October 10, 2016.

16. Allitt, *I'm the Teacher, You're the Student: A Semester in the University Classroom*, 174.

17. Barry Casey, PhD, "Where's the Curiosity?" *Faculty Focus*, October 16, 2017.

18. Adam Grant's blog, October 2017, www.adamgrant.net/adams-blog

CHAPTER 7

1. M. Stains et al., "Anatomy of STEM Teaching in North American Universities," *Science* 359, no. 6383 (March 30, 2018): 1468–70.

2. Also quoted by Brian Gallagher in "Facts So Romantic," *Nautilus* blog, April 11, 2018.

3. Rhett Allain, "The Traditional Lecture Is Dead. I Would Know—I'm a Professor," *Wired Magazine*, May 11, 2017.

4. David Gooblar, "Your Students Learn by Doing, Not by Listening," *The Chronicle of Higher Education*, May 1, 2018.

5. Annie Murphy Paul, "Are College Lectures Unfair?" *New York Times*, September 13, 2015.

6. Craig Lambert, "Twilight of the Lecture," *Harvard Magazine*, March–April 2012.

7. Lambert, "Twilight of the Lecture."

8. Peter Brown, Henry Roediger, and Mark McDaniel, *Make It Stick: The Science of Successful Learning* (Cambridge, MA: The Belknap Press of Harvard University Press, 2014), 119.

9. Eric Mazur, "Confessions of a Converted Lecturer," YouTube lecture, November 12, 2009, www.youtube.com/watch?v=WwslBPj8GgI (accessed May 23, 2018).

10. Eric Mazur, "Farewell, Lecture?" *Science* 323 (January 2, 2009), www.sciencemag.org.

11. Mazur, "Farewell, Lecture?"

12. Lambert, "Twilight of the Lecture."

13. Stephen R. Covey, *The Seven Habits of Highly Effective People* (New York: Simon & Schuster, 1989).

14. Mazur, "Farewell, Lecture?"

15. Ken Bain, *What the Best College Teachers Do* (Cambridge, MA: Harvard University Press, 2004), 26–28.

16. B. S. Bloom, "Reflections on the Development and Use of the Taxonomy," in Bloom's Taxonomy: A Forty-Year Retrospective, Yearbook of the National Society for the Study of Education, ed. Kenneth J. Rehage, Lorin W. Anderson, and Lauren A. Sosniak (Chicago: National Society for the Study of Education, 1994), 93.

17. Maryellen Weimer, "More Evidence That Active Learning Trumps Lecturing," *Faculty Focus*, June 3, 2015.

18. James M. Lang, *Small Teaching: Everyday Lessons from the Science of Learning* (San Francisco: Jossey-Bass, 2016), 87.

19. Weimer, "More Evidence That Active Learning Trumps Lecturing."

20. Maryellen Weimer, "Changing the Way We Teach: Making the Case for Learner-Centered Teaching," *Faculty Focus*, June 1, 2011.

21. Angela Provitera McGlynn, *Successful Beginnings for College Teaching: Engaging your Students from the First Day* (Madison, WI: Atwood, 2001), 79.

22. William Deresiewicz, *Excellent Sheep: The Miseducation of the American Elite and the Way to a Meaningful Life* (New York: Free Press, 2016).

23. This list is inspired by Dr. Maryellen Weimer, who wrote on this topic in *Faculty Focus* on February 14, 2018.

24. Stephen Brookfield, *The Skillful Teacher: On Technique, Trust, and Responsiveness in the Classroom* (San Francisco: Jossey-Bass, 2015), discusses these issues eloquently, especially in chapters 6 and 7.

25. Kevin Gannon, "Creating the Space for Engaged Discussions," *Faculty Focus*, January 8, 2018.

26. More examples can be found in many books. One of the best is Wilbert McKeachie, *McKeachie's Teaching Tips: Strategies, Research, and Theory for College and University Teachers* (Boston: Houghton Mifflin, 2002).

27. I am grateful to my colleagues at American University's Center for Teaching, Research, and Learning for many of these ideas: www.american.edu/ctrl.

28. Hillary Steiner and Stephanie Foote, "Using Metacognition to Reframe our Thinking about Learning Styles," *Faculty Focus*, May 15, 2017.

29. For example, see https://edspace.american.edu/ctrl/portfolioitem/active-learning.

30. Brookfield, *The Skillful Teacher*, 95.

31. Brookfield, *The Skillful Teacher*, 8.

32. For more on Dr. Stephen Brookfield's well-thought-out system for collecting information from students, see pp. 34–37 in his outstanding book *The Skillful Teacher*.

CHAPTER 8

1. Todd Zakrajsek, "Students Who Don't Participate in Class Discussions: They Are Not All Introverts," www.scholarlyteacher.com/blog/ students-who-dont-participate-in-class-discussions.

2. Karin Fischer, "Colleges Adapt to New Kinds of Students from Abroad," *Chronicle of Higher Education*, May 29, 2011.

3. Maryellen Weimer, "Seven Characteristics of Good Learners," *Faculty Focus*, January 22, 2014.

4. Nicki Monahan, "Keeping Introverts in Mind in Your Active Learning Classroom," *Faculty Focus*, October 28, 2013.

5. Susan Cain, *Quiet: The Power of Introverts in a World That Can't Stop Talking* (New York: Crown, 2012), 5.

6. Maryellen Weimer, "Five Reasons Getting Students to Talk Is Worth the Effort," *Faculty Focus*, June 20, 2012.

7. Daniel Chambliss and Christopher Takacs, *How College Works* (Cambridge, MA: Harvard University Press, 2014).

8. Kevin Gannon, "Creating the Space for Engaged Discussions," *Faculty Focus*, January 8, 2018.

9. Alan Brinkley et al., *The Chicago Handbook for Teachers: A Practical Guide to the College Classroom* (Chicago: University of Chicago Press, 1999), 26.

10. Stephen Brookfield, *The Skillful Teacher: On Technique, Trust, and Responsiveness in the Classroom* (San Francisco: Jossey-Bass, 2015), 33.

11. Brookfield, *The Skillful Teacher*, 33.

12. Brookfield, *The Skillful Teacher*, 33.

13. Beverley Myatt and Lynne Kennette, "Towards a 'Positive U,'" *Faculty Focus*, January 9, 2017.

CHAPTER 9

1. Katherine Mangan, "The Personal Lecture: How to Make Big Classes Feel Small," *Chronicle of Higher Education*, December 4, 2016.

2. Daniel Chambliss and Christopher Takacs, *How College Works* (Cambridge, MA: Harvard University Press, 2014).

3. Dr. Sallie Ives, UNC Charlotte, "A Survival Handbook for Teaching Large Classes," March 22, 2000.

4. Rosealie Lynch and Eric Pappas, "A Model for Teaching Large Classes: Facilitating a 'Small Class Feel,'" *International Journal of Higher Education* 2, no. 6 (2017).

5. Lynch and Pappas, "A Model for Teaching Large Classes."

6. Lynch and Pappas, "A Model for Teaching Large Classes."

7. Kevin Gannon, "Creating the Space for Engaged Discussions," *Faculty Focus*, January 8, 2018.

8. Gannon, "Creating the Space for Engaged Discussions."

9. Gannon, "Creating the Space for Engaged Discussions."

10. Adam Wilsman, "Teaching Large Classes," Vanderbilt University, https://cft. vanderbilt.edu/guides-sub-pages/teaching-large-classes/.

11. The following paper from the University of Central Florida covers some of this material in a highly effective way: www.fctl.ucf.edu/teachingandlearningresources/ learningenvironments/largeclass.php.

12. Stephen Brookfield, *The Skillful Teacher: On Technique, Trust, and Responsiveness in the Classroom* (San Francisco: Jossey-Bass, 2015), 30.

13. More good ideas can be found in Adam Wilsman, "Teaching Large Classes," Vanderbilt University, https://cft.vanderbilt.edu/guides-sub-pages/ teaching-large-classes.

14. Robert Magnan, *147 Practical Teaching Tips for Teaching Professors* (Madison, WI: Atwood, 1990), 27.

15. Stephen Brookfield, *Becoming a Critically Reflective Teacher* (San Francisco: Jossey-Bass, 1995), ch. 6.

CHAPTER 10

1. Stacey Beth-Mackowiak Ayotte, "Is There a Place for Games in the College Classroom?" *Faculty Focus*, www.facultyfocus.com. Ayotte's article is included in a special report from *Faculty Focus* titled "Tips for Encouraging Student Participation in Classroom Discussions," edited by Dr. Maryellen Weimer.

2. Ayotte, "Is There a Place for Games in the College Classroom?"

3. Angela Provitera McGlynn, *Successful Beginnings for College Teaching* (Madison, WI: Atwood, 2001), 39.

4. Richard H. Kenney Jr., "Three Ways to Engage Students In and Outside the Classroom," *Faculty Focus*, March 20, 2017.

5. Josh Banas, Norah Dunbar, Dariela Rodriguez, and Shr-Jie Liu, "A Review of Humor in Education Settings: Four Decades of Research," *Communication Education* 60, no. 1 (2011): 115–44.

6. Maryellen Weimer, "Humor in the Classroom," *Faculty Focus*, November 2, 2016.

7. Weimer, "Humor in the Classroom."

8. M. B. Wanzer, A. B. Frymier, A. M. Wojtaszczyk, and T. Smith, "Appropriate and Inappropriate Uses of Humor by Teachers," *Communication Education* 55, no. 2 (2006): 178–96.

9. Alissa Klein and Christian Moriarty, "You're Funnier Than You Think: Using Humor in the Classroom," *Faculty Focus*, November 13, 2017.

10. Klein and Moriarty, "You're Funnier Than You Think."

11. Beau Golwitzer, "Improv in the Classroom," *Faculty Focus*, August 29, 2016.

12. Julia Miller, Kate Wilson, Jennifer Miller, and Kayoko Enomoto, "Humorous Materials to Enhance Active Learning," *Higher Education Research & Development* 36, no. 4 (2017): 791–806.

13. Andrew Reiner, "Focus 101: Curing Distraction in College Classrooms, One Deep Breath at a Time," *Washington Post Magazine*, April 10, 2016.

14. Reiner, "Focus 101."

15. More information on this topic can be found in the syllabus for my class "Design Your Life for Success." Please write to me if you'd like to receive a copy: christopher.n.palmer@gmail.com. Also see my book *Now What, Grad? Your Path to Success after College*, 2nd ed. (Lanham, MD: Rowman & Littlefield, 2018).

16. James M. Lang, *Small Teaching: Everyday Lessons from the Science of Learning* (San Francisco: Jossey-Bass, 2016). Chapter 9 contains an especially useful discussion of what Lang calls "big teaching."

17. Lang, *Small Teaching*, 220.

18. Gillian Parrish, "Expanding Learning Experiences with Virtual Guest Experts," *Faculty Focus*, February 27, 2017.

19. Parrish, "Expanding Learning Experiences with Virtual Guest Experts."

20. Randy Laist, "Getting the Most out of Guest Experts Who Speak to Your Class," *Faculty Focus*, May 11, 2015.

21. Personal email from Professor Rick Stack to author on August 21, 2018.

22. Personal email from Professor Rick Stack to author on August 21, 2018.

23. Kenney, "Three Ways to Engage Students In and Outside the Classroom."

24. Chris Palmer, "How to Network Effectively," *Realscreen* magazine, November/December 2008.

25. Palmer, *Now What, Grad?*

26. Personal email from Professor Rick Stack to author on August 21, 2018.

CHAPTER 11

1. James M. Lang, *Small Teaching: Everyday Lessons from the Science of Learning* (San Francisco: Jossey-Bass, 2016), 65.

2. Maryellen Weimer, PhD, "Interleaving: An Evidence-Based Study Strategy," *Faculty Focus*, January 18, 2017.

3. Lang, *Small Teaching*, 84.

4. Lang, *Small Teaching*, 84.

5. B. Dietz-Uhler and J. R. Lanter, "Using the Four Question Technique to Enhance Learning," *Teaching of Psychology* 36, no. 1 (2009): 38–41.

6. Maryellen Weimer, "Prompts That Get Students to Analyze, Reflect, Relate, and Question," *Faculty Focus*, August 28, 2013.

7. Dietz-Uhler and Lanter, "Using the Four Question Technique to Enhance Learning."

8. Weimer, "Prompts That Get Students to Analyze, Reflect, Relate, and Question."

9. Paul Tough, *How Children Succeed: Grit, Curiosity, and the Hidden Power of Character* (Boston: Mariner Books, 2013).

10. Chris Palmer, *Now What, Grad? Your Path to Success after College*, 2nd ed. (Lanham, MD: Rowman & Littlefield, 2018).

11. Dawn McGuckin, "Teaching Students about Their Digital Footprints," Faculty Focus, December 5, 2016.

CHAPTER 12

1. Steven Corbett and Michelle LaFrance, "It's the Little Things That Count in Teaching," *Chronicle of Higher Education*, September 9, 2013.

2. James M. Lang, *Small Teaching: Everyday Lessons from the Science of Learning* (San Francisco: Jossey-Bass, 2016), 209.

3. Stephen Brookfield, *The Skillful Teacher: On Technique, Trust, and Responsiveness in the Classroom* (San Francisco: Jossey-Bass, 2015), 195.

4. Marc Tessier-Lavigne, president of Stanford University, "Ensuring Academic Breadth: A Narrow Focus Doesn't Serve Students, or Stanford, Well," *Stanford Magazine*, January/February 2017.

5. Charles Dorn, "What Is College Good For? (Hint: More Than Just a Job)," *Chronicle of Higher Education*, August 1, 2017.

6. Charles Dorn's most recent book is *For the Common Good: A New History of Higher Education in America* (Ithaca, NY: Cornell University Press, 2017).

7. Bethany Zecher Sutton, "Higher Education's Public Purpose," Association of American Colleges & Universities, January 20, 2016, www.aacu.org/leap.

8. Sutton, "Higher Education's Public Purpose."

9. The Dalai Lama, *Ethics for the New Millennium* (New York: Riverside Books, 2001).

APPENDIX IV

1. Jeffrey Brown, "Professor Tenure as Insurance: What the Wall Street Journal Debate Missed," *Forbes*, June 25, 2012, www.forbes.com/sites/jeffreybrown/2012/06/25/professor-tenure-as-insurance-what-the-wall-street-journal-debate-missed/#658efba75e21.

2. Mark C. Taylor, "Why Tenure Is Unsustainable and Indefensible," *New York Times*, September 3, 2010, www.nytimes.com/roomfordebate/2010/07/19/what-if-college-tenure-dies/why-tenure-is-unsustainable-and-indefensible.

3. Naomi Schaefer Riley and Cary Nelson, "Should Tenure for College Professors Be Abolished?" *Wall Street Journal*, June 24, 2010, http://online.wsj.com/article/SB10001424052702303610504577418293114042070.html?mod=googlenews_wsj.

4. Riley and Nelson, "Should Tenure for College Professors Be Abolished?"

5. Taylor, "Why Tenure Is Unsustainable and Indefensible."

6. Personal email to author from Professor Bill Gentile on March 10, 2013.

Index

active learning, 155–57; anonymous feedback for, 86–87; case for, 79–80; characteristics of, 80–81; class feedback for, 87–88; exercises for, 82–84, 181; flipped classes for, 78–79, 81; for large classes, 103–5; nontraditional lectures and, 82–84; for quiet students, 89; STEM and, 75–76; by teaching, 77–78; think-pair-share of, 81–82

Active Learning Handbook (Bell and Kahrhoff), 155

Adler, Alfred, 75

affirmations, for caring, 53

Aguilar, Elena, 65

Aig, Dennis, 139

Albom, Mitch, 133

Allain, Rhett, 76

Allitt, Patrick, 4, 10, 12, 64, 72

American Association of University Professors, 205

American University (AU), 152, 167; Center for Teaching, Research and Learning, 5; COMM-568 given at, 119–20; Environmental Film Making class, 195; professors, 2, 18, 36, 43, 60, 84–85, 96, 122, 136, 138, 189; School of Communication, 1, 150–51, 177; School of International Service, 84, 189

Amherst College, 1

"Anatomy of STEM Teaching in North American Universities," 75–76

Anderson, Mrs., 170

appreciative pause, 86

The Art of Possibility (Zander, R., and Zander, B.), 42–43, 59

Assumption College, 120

astronomy, 9, 169–70

attendance: as mandatory, 4–5; taking of, 6, 28–29, 133, 137, 182

AU. *See* American University

Ayotte, Stacey Beth-Mackowiak, 113

Babbie, Earl, 140

Bain, Ken, 11–12, 62, 78; on caring, 48; on extrinsic rewards, 37; on grades, 36; on hard work, 22; on intentions, 67; on student personal development, 8–9

Baron, Naomi, 18, 23, 141

Barrow, John, 9

Bauerlein, Mark, 21

Beal, Endia, 157

beholding, 117

Bell, Daniel, 155

About the Author

Chris Palmer is a professor, speaker, author, and wildlife film producer who gives speeches and workshops on a variety of topics, including how to motivate and engage students, how to teach effectively, and how to achieve success and productivity.

His earlier books include *Shooting in the Wild* (2010), *Confessions of a Wildlife Filmmaker* (2015), *Now What, Grad? Your Path to Success After College*, 2nd edition (2015), and *Raise Your Kids to Succeed: What Every Parent Should Know* (2017).

Chris served on American University's full-time faculty at the School of Communication in Washington, DC, as Distinguished Film Producer in Residence for fourteen years before retiring to write more books and make more films. In addition to teaching filmmaking, he taught a class called "Design Your Life for Success."

He received the 2014 University Faculty Award for Outstanding Teaching at AU and also the 2015 University Film and Video Association Teaching Award.

He founded and directed AU's Center for Environmental Filmmaking. He also serves as president of the MacGillivray Freeman Films Educational Foundation, which produces and funds IMAX films.

Born in Hong Kong, Chris grew up in England and immigrated to the United States in 1972. As a filmmaker, he has swum with dolphins and whales, come face-to-face with sharks and Kodiak bears, camped with wolf packs, and waded hip-deep through the Everglade swamps.

He has spearheaded the production of more than three hundred hours of original programming for primetime television and the IMAX film industry, and has worked with the likes of Robert Redford, Paul Newman, Jane Fonda, and Ted Turner. He and his colleagues have won many film awards, including two Emmys and an Oscar nomination.

Chris spent twenty-five years working for the National Audubon Society and the National Wildlife Federation in top executive positions. For five years, he was a stand-up comedian and performed regularly in DC comedy clubs. In his twenty years before becoming a film producer, he was a high school boxing champion, an officer in the Royal Navy, an engineer, a business consultant, an energy analyst, an environmental activist, chief energy advisor to a senior U.S. senator, and a political appointee in the Environmental Protection Agency under President Jimmy Carter.

Chris holds a bachelor of science degree with first class honors in mechanical engineering from University College London, a master of science degree in ocean engineering and naval architecture, also from University College London, and a master's degree in public administration from Harvard University, where he was a Kennedy Scholar and received a Harkness Fellowship.

Chris can be reached at christopher.n.palmer@gmail.com. His website is www.ChrisPalmerOnline.com.

All proceeds from the sale of this book will go to fund scholarships for students at the American University School of Communication.